A Manager's Guide to Leadership

An action learning approach

SECOND EDITION

Mike Pedler, John Burgoyne, Tom Boydell

London   Boston   Burr Ridge, IL   Dubuque, IA   Madison, WI   New York   San Francisco   St. Louis
Bangkok   Bogotá   Caracas   Kuala Lumpur   Lisbon   Madrid   Mexico City   Milan   Montreal
New Delhi   Santiago   Seoul   Singapore   Sydney   Taipei   Toronto

A Manager's Guide to Leadership
Second Edition

ISBN 13: 978-0-07-712884-5
ISBN 10: 0-07-712884-2

 **Professional**

Published by:
McGraw-Hill Publishing Company
Shoppenhangers Road, Maidenhead, Berkshire, England, SL6 2QL
Telephone: 44 (0) 1628 502500
Fax: 44 (0) 1628 770224
Website: www.mcgraw-hill.co.uk

British Library Cataloguing in Publication Data
A catalogue record of this book is available from the British Library.

McGraw-Hill books are great for training, as gifts, and for
promotions. Please contact our corporate sales executive to discuss special quantity
discounts or customisation to support your initiatives: b2b@mcgraw-hill.com.

Printed in Great Britain by Bell and Bain Ltd, Glasgow.

Mixed Sources
Product group from well-managed
forests and other controlled sources
www.fsc.org Cert no. TT-COC-002769
© 1996 Forest Stewardship Council

The McGraw·Hill Companies

Contents

Acknowledgements

There are many people who have contributed to this book. Thanks to all of these, including our reviewers, who freely gave of their ideas, helped us to get stories straight and gave permission to use them.

Two people merit special mention for their contributions to this extensively revised second edition:

■ Phil Radcliff for his championing of the importance of context in leadership.
■ Tony Roycroft for his pioneering work with the *7 leadership practices*.

Preface: how to use this book

This book is an active guide to leadership rather than a stock of knowledge. It has a simple message: if you wish to contribute to leadership …

> … *discover the most significant challenges facing your organisation, decide what needs to be done, and do something that leads to a useful outcome.*

If asked to think of times when we were proud of ourselves, most of us can give examples of when we took the lead. These stories may come from work, or family life or outside work activities, but they all tend to be about times when we did something useful in difficult or testing situations.

Leadership is a doing thing; a performance art. It is not defined by any set of personal qualities or competencies, but by what we actually *do* when faced with a challenge. Challenges come from life and work, from the wider world and from our own questions about ourselves. Leadership is what we do when we acknowledge and respond to these challenges.

Why is leadership so important now?

> *If your organisation has only one leader, then it is almost certainly short of leadership.*
> **Gerard Egan**

Leadership is likely to be playing a more important part in your life now because it has become a matter of pressing importance for organisations, communities and societies. Good leadership overlaps with, but is different from, good management. Management efficiency and effectiveness have long been the hallmarks of organisational success; but this is no longer enough. Something else is needed.

Whether you work in a hospital or a large company, in a school or a local business, you have probably noticed this new concern with leadership. Your boss is talking about it, the government says how important it is, the newspapers deplore the lack of it – and you may even be the receiving end of initiatives to improve it.

What people are saying is that:

- Organisations are massively challenged by change and need more leadership.
- Good managers are always important, but it is the ability to lead in the conditions of uncertainty, confusion and risk that makes the vital difference.
- In the past leadership has been seen as the preserve of the few; today leadership is needed "at all levels" and "on every part of the pitch".

Most organisations and communities are short on this sort of widely distributed leadership. Leadership development programmes have been established, but tend to focus on the next set of top people. The talents and potentials of the great majority of people remain neglected.

Taking part in leadership

Leadership is … the collective capacity to create something useful.
Peter Senge

The talents of the many are ignored because of a strongly entrenched view that leadership is the preserve of the few. The potential for leadership is widely distributed among people. Organisations and communities are full of talented individuals, but they do not always work well together.

The challenges we face demand the concerted efforts of everyone in the situation. Enabling talented people to work better together is a critical leadership task in itself. To achieve the collective capacity to create useful things, we need a different image of leadership: one that emphasises the individual as connected to others in a collective effort. The unit of analysis for leadership is not the heroic individual, nor the undifferentiated community: *it is the connected individual creating a better world in good company.*

An action learning approach

This book is based on the assumption that leadership is about acting on the challenges facing us in our organisations and communities and learning from that experience.

Our perspective on leadership is strongly influenced by Revans' idea of action learning (1982; 1998). As good leadership has become more important, the need for this approach has become clearer. Action learning encourages us to resolve our own problems, by cautioning against reliance on experts or saviours and stressing the importance of allies, colleagues and friends.

Leadership means moving towards difficult and challenging situations, and not avoiding them, even when we have no clear idea of how to proceed. Without action there is no leadership, and, without learning, leadership will soon falter. Action learning proceeds via "questioning insight" – fresh questions bring different understandings that can prompt new actions. This book will help you to prioritise your leadership challenges and help you to get started on them by providing tools and resources for action and learning.

Action learning ideas appear at various points in this book, most obviously in Chapter 2 and Chapter 9, and generally act as a guiding philosophy for this take on leadership.

How to use this book

This book aims to be a useful and friendly guide to leadership. It encourages you to take action and to learn from that experience to develop yourself, your colleagues and your organisation. The self-development and action learning philosophy of the book is apparent in the diagnostic activities and tools which carry the message: *"here is a challenge – appraise it, act on it and learn from it"*.

All the chapters in this book are designed as provocations and calls to action and learning, and not as comprehensive or exhaustive treatments of these major themes of twenty-first century organisational life. Whole books and even literatures are available on each of these themes and it is not our intention to replace or rival these offerings. Such encyclopaedic treatments rarely act as spurs to action. Our purpose is to encourage action as a means of generating learning in those leadership situations of uncertainty and confusion where no ready-made solution is to hand. In such situations it is action that creates the information, and learning that enables the next intelligent step. Each of these chapters will help you get started on the action and learning cycle of leadership.

While being friendly and accessible, the tone of this book is assertive. The message is that leadership is everyone's business and that we should all get on with it. We are impatient with patronising views about special people or special qualities of leadership. While each person should become the leader that only they can be, we encourage everyone to seek good advice and expertise from colleagues rather than relying on experts. There are no experts in leadership, and it is best to put your faith in those people who want to change things and who are able to learn in that process of change.

Outline of content

The book is in three parts. Part 1 introduces the *Challenges, Context and Characteristics* or the "3 Cs" model of leadership, the *14 challenges of leadership* and provides the argument around which the book is structured. Part 2 develops the *7 leadership practices* that enable any leadership challenge to be successfully tackled. Part 3 focuses on leadership development and with how best to enhance the leadership capacity of individuals and organisations.

Part 1 introduces the "3 Cs" of leadership: *Challenges, Context* and *Characteristics*. The first of these is the *14 key challenges of leadership*:

- *Challenge 1*: Finding direction and strategy
- *Challenge 2*: Creating a learning organisation
- *Challenge 3*: New organisational structures
- *Challenge 4*: Powerful teams
- *Challenge 5*: Crafting cultures of innovation
- *Challenge 6*: Fostering diversity and inclusion
- *Challenge 7*: Promoting partnerships
- *Challenge 8*: Improving work processes
- *Challenge 9*: Streamlining
- *Challenge 10*: Encouraging social responsibility
- *Challenge 11*: Mobilising knowledge
- *Challenge 12*: Leading in networks
- *Challenge 13*: Managing mergers
- *Challenge 14*: Making major change.

Part 1 also includes the "challenge check" – a diagnostic framework to help you to prioritise your most important leadership challenges, together with an action learning process to help you to address any challenge.

The chapters in Part 2 of the book cover the *7 practices of leadership*:

- *Practice 1*: Leading Yourself
- *Practice 2*: Being on Purpose
- *Practice 3*: Power
- *Practice 4*: Risk
- *Practice 5*: Challenging Questions
- *Practice 6*: Facilitation
- *Practice 7*: Networking.

Each of these chapters includes activities and further resources to help you develop these critical leadership practices in yourself and with your colleagues.

In Part 3, Chapter 12 addresses the important question of leadership development. This chapter provides ideas, models, frameworks and activities to help with the development of leadership in both individuals and organisations.

References

Revans, R.W. (1982) *The Origins & Growth of Action Learning*. Bromley: Chartwell-Bratt.

Revans, R.W. (1998) *ABC of Action Learning*. London: Lemos & Crane.

Part 1

The Challenges, Context and Characteristics of Leadership

1

Leadership: what is it and are you part of it?

Leadership is ... "the activity of a citizen from any walk of life mobilising people to do something".
Ronald Heifetz

This chapter outlines our ideas about leadership, but before reading on, what do you think ...

- ◼ ... leadership is? How does it differ from management?
- ◼ And what would you say is the best way to learn about leadership?

Hold your thoughts in mind as you read on.

Are you part of leadership?

If you are a professional or a technical expert, perhaps an engineer, a pharmacist or an accountant, you may find yourself handling a lot of people and projects in your work. Perhaps you grumble about this; after all it is not what you were trained for – but perhaps it means that you are becoming a leader. You probably had a long period of education, training and development to acquire your professional expertise – what help can you get with becoming a leader?

The BBC had a slogan: "Manage well; lead more". What's the difference? Many people have the word *manager* in their job title, only to find that *leadership* is talked about as something more desirable. Whilst leadership and management link and overlap, we can say that leading is more concerned with finding direction and purpose in the face of critical challenges, whilst managing is about organising to achieve desired purposes: efficiently, effectively and creatively. Leadership also has a more moral aspect because it involves making choices and judgements between what is right and what is wrong.

Managing is more about bringing order and control. It implies systems and procedures that define work in ways that can be both enabling and restrictive. Management can sometimes be a dirty word, and experienced more as hindrance than as help. This surfaces a puzzle: enterprises rely more and more on professionals and knowledge workers, but such people often resist being managed and prefer to manage themselves. For these talented folk to work well together, and not to work in isolation, calls less for control and more for engagement though leadership.

Leadership creeps up on you. It is less easy to spot than management. Its presence or absence in a situation is less obvious at first sight. Unlike the promotion to manager, leadership doesn't arrive with a big bang on a particular day, but emerges unheralded and almost unnoticed. Leadership creeps up on us because we may not notice the extent of the difference that it makes. More sensed or felt than made explicit, its presence shows up in response to such questions as:

- Do you feel part of this – project, organisation, network? Or not?
- Do you have a sense of collective purpose, a shared understanding and a commitment to what is being done? Or not?
- Do you feel proud of the work you are doing? Or not?

So, are you part of leadership or not? And, if you are not leading, then what are you doing?

Supporting?
Resisting?
Bystanding?
Undermining?
Cheerleading? …
… or what?

If leadership concerns everyone, everyone who is concerned is doing *something*.

A leadership model

There is no single accepted definition of leadership. It is a contested topic, much discussed and debated. It is commonly associated with positions of authority, but whilst some top people have good leadership qualities, many do not. There is no single, defining set of personal qualities or competencies that fits all leadership situations and yet most leadership development programmes are based on specified competency models.

Leadership is best understood not as a position or a set of competencies but as an *activity* that generates socially useful outcomes. As a social activity, leadership can be described by its *Domains, Challenges and Practices*; the where, what and how of leadership:

- Where? 3 Domains that mark out the territory of leadership.
- What?   14 Challenges that signify the focus and *raison d'etre* of leadership.
- How?   7 Practices that define how leadership happens.

The 3 domains of leadership

Figure 1.1 shows the three domains that make up the province of leadership:

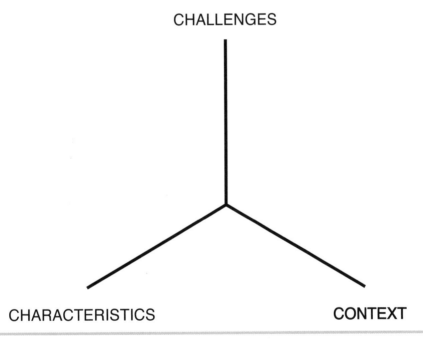

Figure 1.1 The 3 domains of leadership

- CHALLENGES are the critical tasks, problems and issues requiring leadership action.
- CONTEXT is the "on-site" conditions found in the challenge situation.
- CHARACTERISTICS are the qualities, competencies and skills of *all* the people in the situation that can contribute to leadership.

This is the territory of leadership. Without challenging tasks there is no call for leadership. All challenges are met in particular contexts or settings, and critical challenges require the talents, engagement and contribution of all those concerned.

■ The *Challenges* domain is principally concerned with recognising, mobilising and taking action in the face of critical problems and issues. Leadership is defined in action, by how we respond to challenges. It is thus a performance art; measured by what we *do* in this situation, here and now, and not what we are or what we know.

■ The *Context* domain means that leadership is always situated: always done *here*, in a specific location, with particular people. In this way, acts of leadership are always local and what works here and now, may not work in another place and time. It follows that there is no one right way to lead. The variety and complexity of contexts means that there is no one style or approach that fits all situations.

The *Context* domain is neglected in most leadership books and programmes. Thinking about the context heightens awareness of the need to work with all the other stakeholders and allies in the situation in a collective endeavour to create value.

■ The *Characteristics* domain is the primary focus of many leadership development programmes. This is partly due to the legacy of "Great Man" theories of leadership that make it the province of rare individuals with outstanding qualities. This still pervasive view allies itself to a training tradition that emphasises individual knowledge and skills. When this domain is overemphasised at the expense of *Challenges* and *Context* it encourages an individualistic and one-size-fits-all approach to leadership. Leadership development based on competency models lends itself to personal development, but does it produce leadership?

Our view is that the qualities, abilities, competencies and skills of all the people in the situation are important. Personal qualities are essential to leadership, but their value is shown as and when a particular person is able to make a contribution. Challenging situations frequently reveal hitherto hidden talents and call forth surprising qualities from unexpected quarters. What will be useful, when and from whom, is at best only partially predictable. Specifying certain fixed qualities in advance closes off possibilities and limits the "gene pool".

Realising the collective capacity to create value

Challenges define the need for leadership. In tough situations, we look for outstanding people to take the lead and carry the burden. We tend to think that we only make progress when we have a "leader with vision", and this tendency persists in many walks of life, from politics to business and, perhaps above all, in sport. Programmes of leadership development are consequently modelled on heroes with futuristic visions leading a mass of "followers". But, is this what is needed in your situation?

A critical view of this heroic tradition, where the leader stands out in front, apart and isolated, is that it infantilises the rest of us, and condemns us to dependency. Neither is it a very sustainable view of leadership, for heroes are often in short supply, partly because they are sacrificed as soon as they are seen to fail. It is obvious that, whilst some people are obviously better "players" than the rest of us, few organisational challenges are met by one person acting alone. A variety of talents abound in most situations, and the trick is to draw them together in a powerful collective force. Once a challenge is identified, the need is to mobilise everyone in the situation, enrolling colleagues, networks, communities and even whole organisations in the effort.

It is a puzzle of leadership that it is very personal, unique to each person, and yet to succeed it must become a collective endeavour. Culturally we have favoured the heroic and personal view and neglected the possibilities for shared and widely distributed leadership. Figure 1.1 can demonstrate some of these different possibilities.

A leadership thought experiment

Imagine yourself at the centre of Figure 1.1 as if you were in the centre of a garden with three radiating paths. Move out along one of the paths. Try each path in turn and then come back to the centre to try the others. Try to imagine the view from each perspective.

Notice that when you …

… approach the Characteristics pole, you move towards the individual and the personal qualities of leadership …

… but when you move towards either the Challenges or the Context poles, you get a more collective and situated view: what can we do about this challenge *here and now*?

How do you see leadership? Is it the province of heroes or more of a collective spirit, emerging from teams and committed groups? Perhaps both? We will be always grateful for heroic efforts in the service of the whole, and also for wise "positional leaders" who hold things together, but the truly demanding challenges facing us will not be met with just these scarce resources. In its fullest sense, leadership resides in the purposes of all the people in the situation and in the connections between them. We only realise that potential when we act as *connected individuals creating a better world in good company*.

This puts the responsibility for leadership on you as a person, but in company and relationship with other people. Yet there is a big snag here: when the heroic or positional leader fails, we know who to blame. To accept a part in leadership as the collective capacity to do better things, means to take credit when things go well, and to accept responsibility when they don't. That's why leadership is more about courage than competence; you have to be up for it in the first place and then when things don't work out you have to own up, stand up and learn to do better next time.

The 14 challenges of leadership

The *14 challenges of leadership* are those organisational problems and opportunities of the day requiring our best efforts at leadership (see Figure 1.2).

These challenges are representative, but not exhaustive, of the most important leadership challenges of the current era. They are chosen on the basis of our combined reading, research and consultancy experiences and from empirical research such as that conducted by the Council for Excellence in Management and Leadership (CEML), where one of the authors was Research Director.

Whilst the challengers are typical and representative of what we know, this does not mean that these are the right ones for you. You may be facing something different, and any challenge will certainly vary in specifics and context. What will hold is the principle on which this whole book is based: that leadership is defined by moving towards the challenges that face you and your colleagues, and not by moving away or trying to avoid them.

Chapter 2 details each of these *14 challenges of leadership* with cases, models and resources that will help you and your colleagues get started. This chapter also contains a "challenge check" to help you prioritise, and an action learning process to help you get started on any challenge. So, if your particular challenge of the moment is not listed here, you will still find materials that will help you move towards it. This is not a book to be read respectfully from front to back, but a guide to action. So use it to pick and choose, pick and mix, and to take from it whatever you want and can apply.

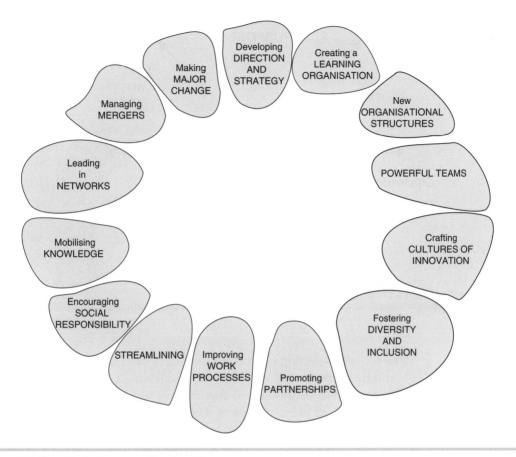

Figure 1.2 The 14 challenges of leadership

The 7 practices of leadership

> *… leadership is essentially a social activity and … may best be learned within a Community of Practice.*
>
> (Keith Grint)

The *7 practices of leadership* make up the "How" of leadership. Because leadership is an everyday social activity, we can see it as something we all do or *practise*. Just as builders apply their skills to the building of a house, or doctors practise medicine to promote health, the *7 practices of leadership* are the means for tackling the organisational challenges (see Figure 1.3).

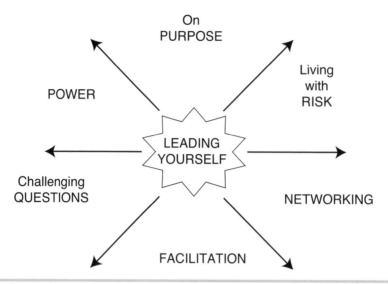

Figure 1.3 The 7 practices of leadership

The idea of leadership as a practice or set of practices opens up many new opportunities. Practice means doing, but also learning. It means that everyone can be involved in leadership and also improve with practice. Practice is also a more useful word than the more commonly used "competence". While competence implies ability, it does not necessarily imply action. Competence also puts the emphasis on past learning, whereas practice makes it plain that there is more to do. Thirdly, competence pretends at universal validity, while practice is always situated; it always takes place in a particular situation or context.

Practice as connecting people and challenges

One of the most important aspects of the idea of practice is that it provides a means of connecting with other people and with the challenges of leadership. If everyone is willing to contribute to leadership, this could become a leadership "community of practice", where all can learn with and from each other. Where leadership is widely distributed, it is not seen as just an individual activity but as a practice or practices that are embedded in the relationships of people at work.

The *7 core practices* link us to any organisational challenge through the actions we take; they are the means for approaching the *14 key challenges* in the outer ring of Figure 1.4.

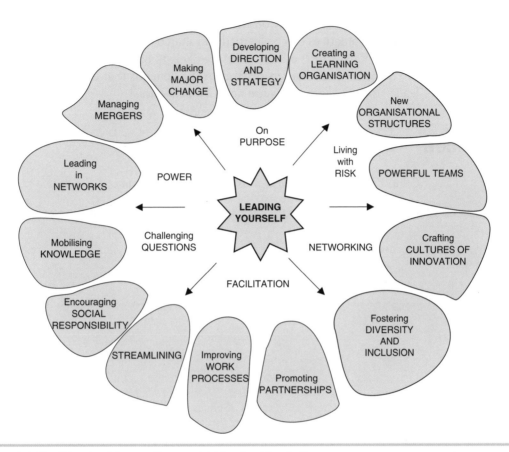

Figure 1.4 **The 7 leadership practices and 14 leadership challenges**

It is difficult to think of a significant leadership challenge that will not, for example, require you to ask challenging questions or to use your power wisely. In Part 2 of this book each of the *7 core practices* has its own chapter to help you develop and strengthen your leadership practices.

Conclusion

The leadership model presented in this chapter is based on the idea that leadership is what we do – or don't do – when faced by a challenge. Organisational challenges are in some ways predictable, but are always rendered unique by the specific contexts in which they occur. This puts a premium on learning in leadership. How well we are equipped for any challenge depends largely on the quality of our practices of leadership. These leadership practices can be learned and shared with colleagues, without whom our individual efforts at leadership are likely to be puny.

The next three chapters expand on the domains that define the territory of leadership: *Challenges*, *Context* and *Characteristics*.

References

Grint, K. (2005) *Leadership: Limits and Possibilities*. Basingstoke: Palgrave Macmillan (p. 115).

Heifetz, R. (1994) *Leadership without Easy Answers*. Boston: Belknap Press (p. 20).

The challenges of leadership

2

Leadership begins with a challenge. It happens when someone does something useful in a challenging situation.

This chapter is about taking stock of the challenges in your situation that require leadership. It will help you to answer these questions:

- What are your current challenges?
- How well do you understand them?
- And what can you do about them?

The chapter has two parts:

- Part A: Assessing your leadership challenges, describes 14 key leadership challenges and invites you to assess yourself and your situation: which challenges are you facing now or are likely to be in the near future?
- Part B: Getting started on your leadership challenges, asks you first to put your challenges in priority order and then provides an Action Learning Process that can be applied to any challenge to help you to get started.

Part A: Assessing your leadership challenges

Below are descriptions of *14 key leadership challenges* commonly found in organisational life. These are as follows:

- *Challenge 1*: Finding direction and strategy
- *Challenge 2*: Creating a learning organisation
- *Challenge 3*: New organisational structures
- *Challenge 4*: Powerful teams
- *Challenge 5*: Crafting cultures of innovation
- *Challenge 6*: Fostering diversity and inclusion
- *Challenge 7*: Promoting partnerships
- *Challenge 8*: Improving work processes
- *Challenge 9*: Streamlining

■ *Challenge 10*: Encouraging social responsibility
■ *Challenge 11*: Mobilising knowledge
■ *Challenge 12*: Leading in networks
■ *Challenge 13*: Managing mergers
■ *Challenge 14*: Making major change.

These 14 challenges are among the most important and critical of the present time. They turn up consistently in research findings and in the leadership literature. Perhaps most importantly, they also appear repeatedly in the action learning sessions that we have conducted with leaders from a wide range of organisations over many years. These are the questions and dilemmas most likely to keep people awake at night.

However, leadership challenges come in great variety, and if you are experiencing one not described here, we have left a blank section – "Challenge 15" – for you to write in your own. Part B of the chapter will work just as well with any challenge.

As you read through the *14 key leadership challenges* you can prioritise them in terms of the situation you are facing. At the end of each challenge is a challenge check that invites you to note:

■ the *importance* of this particular challenge for you and your organisation, and
■ your current collective *capability* in terms of this task.

The combination of importance and capability is what creates a priority for action and learning. The scores from each of the challenge checks can be summarised in Table 2.1 in Part B of the chapter to create a priority list. This can then be used to pick and choose those parts of this book to which you want to give most attention.

Challenge 1: Finding direction and strategy

The domain of leaders is the future.
Kouzes and Posner

Historically, management arises as an intermediate function between owners and workers. Managers were the organisers and the direct overseers of the production process, leaving owners free to direct their businesses. As businesses have grown in size and ownership has become more diffuse and institutional, leadership has emerged as a distinctive organisational role. Someone must offer a sense of direction and a vision of the future. Once a direction is clear, it is relatively straightforward to manage; that is, to plan, operate and oversee the process of achieving the objective.

Forward-looking, inspiring, strategic and innovative are all words used to describe those we call good leaders. Most definitions of leadership include this core requirement of finding direction and pointing the way to the future. This can be very difficult to do, but especially where events are moving rapidly, it is a requirement, not an option.

The ability to choose the right direction is sometimes called *vision*:

To choose a direction, a leader must first have developed a mental image of a possible and desirable future state for the organisation. This image, which we call a vision, may be as vague as a dream or as precise as a goal or mission statement. The critical point is that a vision articulates a view of a realistic, credible, attractive future for the organisation, a condition that is better in some important ways than what now exists.

(Bennis and Nanus, 1985, p. 89)

We have mixed feelings about this. Visions can blind as well as inspire. A future orientation is essential: but the vision thing is easily overdone, and can be hallucinatory. A sense of direction is more likely to come from knowing what you want, from understanding your purpose and from acting on this; what we term *being on purpose* (see Chapter 6). Being on purpose implies a future rooted in explicit values together with the will and energy needed to bring this about.

We are also unhappy with the implication that vision only comes from exceptional inspiration or from a single heroic leader. This social myth has all sorts of unfortunate consequences: it puts considerable pressure on positional leaders to have inspirational visions; it can give some people an overblown sense of their own perceptions, and, not least, it can result in the neglect of the contributions of everyone else. The terms leadership and management usually have status attached to them: to be "strategic" is to be important:

Our senior management used to be very hands on and involved in everything. Then we had an inspection in which they were told that they were not sufficiently strategic. Since then we haven't set eyes on any of them.
(Further Education College lecturer)

"They might call it strategy, but it feels like chaos to us.
(Prison Officer during a major reorganisation of the prison system)

Sound familiar? Here strategy is split from implementation, and those charged with operating the business are not involved. If leadership is a collective capacity to create value, then a singular focus on the "top of the shop" is unlikely to bring this about.

The starting point for a collective approach to developing direction and strategy is found in the actual work and the challenges faced there. What are we trying to do? What is stopping us? How can we move forward? These are the everyday questions in every working practice, in every workplace. Here is an example of a group of citizens trying to do just this:

A group of community midwives began meeting informally to talk about caring for women and babies with HIV/AIDS. It all started with two who met to have coffee and to catch up with each other. Their conversation led to HIV/AIDS, and this led to another meeting, this time involving some of the other midwives in the area. The meeting became a regular one open to all midwives in the city. Quite quickly it was apparent that the group had become an influential one. By creating a forum for a conversation that had not been happening before, they had fulfilled an unmet need. The Strategic Health Authority soon asked the group for advice on policy and also for help in implementation. Not all the group were keen on this idea. They came together voluntarily to resolve their own questions, but they are also potentially a valuable part of the public health system. Is this the sort of group we want to be?

In this example, direction comes from being clear about your purpose, from finding collective purpose and then by acting on this to bring about something useful. In Chapter 6, *Being on Purpose*, you will find several models and tools for helping you get started on this process. These include a model of a *learning approach to strategy* together with a questionnaire for using with your colleagues, and a tool for creating common direction in your organisation through *scenario thinking*.

Is *finding direction and strategy* a challenge for you and your colleagues? If so, how high a priority is it? Make a few notes in the challenge check below:

CHALLENGE CHECK: *Finding direction and strategy*

■ Is this a challenge you are currently facing?   YES [   ]   NO [   ]

■ Is it one you have faced in the past?   YES [   ]   NO [   ]

■ Do you expect to face this more in the future?   YES [   ]   NO [   ]

Taking these answers into account, make the following judgements:

1. CAPABILITY: How good are you at understanding and dealing with this challenge?

   Not good   4   3   2   1   Very good

2. IMPORTANCE: How important do you think this is going to be for your future?

   Not important   1   2   3   4   Very important

You can summarise the main points from this challenge check, along with all the others, in Part B of this chapter: *Getting started on your leadership challenges*.

Reference

Bennis, W. and Nanus, B. (1985) *The Strategies for Taking Charge*. New York: Harper & Row.

Further resources

A useful start might be made with Dilbert: http://www.youtube.com/watch?v=7lNQtweCoU0.

Henry Mintzberg, Bruce Ahlstrand and Joseph Lampel's *Strategy Safari: The Complete Guide Through the Wilds of Strategic Management* (Harlow: Pearson Education, 2nd edition, 2009) is a readable overview and critique of 10 major schools of strategic management thinking. Perhaps the best-known standard textbook in this area is Gerry Johnson, Kevan Scholes and Richard Whittington's *Exploring Corporate Strategy: Text and Cases* (Harlow: Pearson Education, 2007) now in its eighth edition. This is intended primarily for MBA programmes and its main purpose is to help students pass exams.

More simple and practical approaches can be found in abundance. These include Neville Lake's *The Strategic Planning Workbook* (London: Kogan Page, 2006) and Erica Olsen's *Strategic Planning for Dummies* (Hoboken: Wiley, 2007). As its title suggests, John Bryson and Farnum Alston's *Creating and Implementing Your Strategic Plan: A Workbook for Public and Nonprofit Organizations* (San Francisco: Wiley, 2004) focuses specifically on those sectors in the USA. You might wish to try Neil Russell-Jones and Phil Hailstone's *The Strategy Pocketbook* (Alresford: Management Pocketbooks 2007). People tend either to love or to loathe these "Bite size messages with a big impact" pocketbooks: http://www.pocketbook.co.uk. On the bite-sized front http://www.12manage.com/i_s.html gives excellent descriptions of well over 100 strategy methods, models and theories.

You can use business games and simulations to learn about strategy. Two relatively simple ones that can be used for self-learning are available at http://www.btplc.com/societyandenvironment/Businessgame. They are free of charge although users are invited to contribute to BT-sponsored charities. More complex simulations are provided online by Industry Masters at http://www.industrymasters.com/single_users.html for which there is a modest charge.

A whole new set of strategic challenges are likely to be coming your way as the "net generation is changing your world" according to Don Tapscott's *Grown Up Digital* (New York: McGraw-Hill, 2008) and Don Tapscott and Anthony Williams' *Wikinomics: How Mass Collaboration Changes Everything* (London: Atlantic Books, 2008). Other useful resources in this emerging area include Amy Shuen's *Web 2.0: A Strategy Guide: Business Thinking and Strategies Behind Successful Web 2.0 Implementation* (Sebastopol: O'Reilly Media 2008); Charlene Li and Josh Bernoff's *Groundswell: Winning in a World Transformed by Social Technologies* (Boston: Harvard Business Press, 2008); and Andrew McAfee's *Enterprise 2.0: New Collaborative Tools for Your Organization's Toughest Challenges* (Boston: Harvard Business Press, 2009).

Challenge 2: Creating a learning organisation

He not busy being born is busy dying.
Bob Dylan

Reg Revans' ecological formula:

$$L \geq C$$

holds that learning (L) in any organism, from simple cells to complex human organisations, must equal or exceed the rate of change (C), otherwise that organism will be in decline, falling behind the times.

Organisations start as ideas in the heads of people and, when young, are busy, active places, full of natural learning. As they get older, as original markets decline or the founders grow weary, that vital working and learning energy can get lost. Learning organisations make conscious efforts to retain this energy:

> *A learning company is an organisation that facilitates the learning of all its members and consciously transforms itself and its context.*
> (Pedler, Burgoyne and Boydell, 1997, p. 3)

Today there are huge pressures on leadership to deliver demanding performance goals, to deal with high levels of environmental change and to innovate – all at the same time. The Holy Grail is the performance culture that is also a learning culture, where people are encouraged to pursue results energetically and also to learn from their experience by continuous open and critical review.

Can these two be done together? This is a "big ask". The downsides of performance management are as well understood as the benefits. How can we manage performance without making people target-obsessed, risk-averse, closed and defensive? In this context, leadership must create the processes, structures, cultures and relationships that balance performance with development to protect the precious capacity for learning.

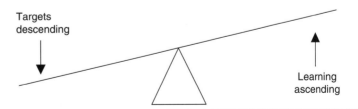

Figure C2.1 The see-saw of performance and learning

This balancing act is attempted in different ways; the philosophy of one organisation we know can be summed up as:

Meeting your targets gives you headroom for development.

What is the philosophy in your organisation? In our travels we have found different people and places interpreting the learning organisation idea in marvellously diverse ways. Here are four stories, all responses to the question "How is your business a learning organisation?":

In this company we have declared that we are going to be a learning organisation. Not only this but that we are going to be a world class learning organisation! We have a "learning table" at lunchtimes – where you can have a free lunch but you have to talk about learning in some way to the other people you find there.

I am the medical director in a university hospital. The hospital is full of different professional groups – doctors, nurses, therapists, researchers, technicians of many varieties – this can be bad for patients. We started a disease management programme and all the professionals learned to define this process together. This is a seed for a new learning culture.

To us being a learning organisation means sustainability. A manager I know wanted to develop his people but had little money. So he made his poor performers redundant and made a considerable investment in training the others. Customer satisfaction went from 60% to 90% – but how do you sustain this?

For 10 years I was the manager in a publishing company, I then left to become a wife and mother at home. After some time I got in touch with a local organisation that helps people to learn to deal with themselves and others in a development process. Now, with seven others whom I met, we are going back to work in profit and non-profit organisations. We always work in pairs to evaluate our work. We have four meetings a year to share and help each other.

Is this giving you any ideas? There are many paths, and on the principle that "the wisdom to fix this business resides within", it is important to work out what might work for you and your colleagues, and what might be sustained.

Leadership and learning are closely connected. Following new paths leads to exploration, discovery and learning. In the learning organisation, leadership can be defined as *learning on behalf of the organisation*.

Is Challenge 2: *creating a learning organisation* a challenge for you and your colleagues? If so, how high a priority is it?

CHALLENGE CHECK: *Creating a learning organisation*

■ Is this a challenge you are currently facing? YES [ ] NO [ ]

■ Is it one you have faced in the past? YES [ ] NO [ ]

■ Do you expect to face this more in the future? YES [ ] NO [ ]

Taking these answers into account, make the following judgements:

1. CAPABILITY: How good are you at understanding and dealing with this challenge?

   Not good   4   3   2   1   Very good

2. IMPORTANCE: How important do you think this is going to be for your future?

   Not important   1   2   3   4   Very important

Again you can add these scores from this challenge check to the summary in Part B of this chapter: *Getting started on your leadership challenges.*

Reference

Pedler, M., Burgoyne, J. and Boydell, T. (1996) *The Learning Company: A Strategy for Sustainable Development*. Maidenhead: McGraw-Hill.

Further resources

The learning organisation builds on ideas such as Donald Schon's "loss of the stable state", in which the experience of living with increasing change is linked with the need for learning (*Beyond the Stable State*, New York: Norton, 1973). Excellent accounts of this, and Schon's later work, often with Chris Argyris, can be found at http://www.12manage.com/methods_organizational_learning.html; another excellent on-line source is http://www.infed.org/thinkers/et-schon.htm, posted by *infed*, a not-for-profit "space for people to explore the theory and practice of informal education, social action and lifelong learning". Also posted by *infed* at http://www.infed.org/lifelonglearning/b-lrnsoc.htm is *The Theory and Rhetoric of the Learning Society*, which takes some of those ideas further. A specifically relational view of leadership is Sue Gilly's (1997) *A Different View of Organizational Learning*, which can be found at http://home.flash.net/~jteague/Sue/orglearn.html. For a more academic and critical treatment try: Wang and Ahmed's "Organizational Learning: a critical review", *The Learning Organization* 10(1), 2003, pp. 8–17.

    The works so far cited are largely conceptual. More practical guidelines can be found in Pedler, M., Burgoyne, J. and Boydell, T., *The Learning Company: A Strategy for Sustainable Development* (Maidenhead: McGraw-Hill, 2nd edition, 1997)) which offers 11 characteristics of a learning organisation, a questionnaire for assessing your organisation, many "glimpses" of practice, and other practical tools. *The Learning Company Toolkit* (Maidenhead: Peter Honey, 2000) by the same authors can be found at www.peterhoney.com. Practical tools and activities can also be found in Senge, P., Roberts, C., Ross R., Smith, B. and Kleiner, A., *The Fifth Discipline Fieldbook* (London: Nicholas Brealey, 1994). Other good sources of ideas, examples and activities include Dixon's *The Organizational Learning Cycle: How We Can Learn Collectively* (Aldershot: Gower, 1999) and Marquardt's *Building the Learning Organization* (Mountain View: Davies-Black, 2002).

Challenge 3: **New organisational structures**

Form follows function.
Alfred Chandler

For many new positional leaders there is a great pressure to change things; and this usually means changing the structure. There is no area of leadership where the satirical "Ready, Fire, Aim!" applies more aptly. Yet, since Alfred Chandler at least, we know that form should follow function: any new organisational structure should be based on the new strategy.

So, the first question is: What are the new business purposes, aims and objectives? The second is: what structures will best enable these purposes and goals?

In any large enterprise the form that delivers the function must somehow pull together complexes of product and service streams, market and user demands and lots of specialised departments and units. Creating order via taxonomies of roles, responsibilities and relationships, is no easy matter to get right, or to get right for long.

From hierarchies to networks?

Perhaps the shortest way of describing the history of organisation development is as a progression from hierarchies to networks. As the oldest form of organisation, hierarchy can be traced back in military and church practices for thousands of years. In the late nineteenth century, Max Weber described the structure of bureaucratic roles as the most efficient way of achieving the command and control of business and even warned of some its dangers.

Yet, it was not until the second half of the twentieth century that this classical model began to be seriously challenged. By this time, the limitations of bureaucratic structures were becoming obvious, especially because of their inability to adapt and learn in the face of changing and turbulent markets. A new science of organisational design sought to loosen up the bureaucracy and produce more flexible alternatives. One promising example is the matrix organisation, which sets out to balance the vertical and the horizontal; offsetting the powerful functional silos of finance, operations, R&D, etc., with cross-cutting project teams and task forces focused on value chains. Yet this dual focus proves hard to manage; the "pay and rations" silos tending to win the power struggles with the projects and business teams.

A current design favourite is the managed network. This aims to combine a flattish hierarchy with free-ranging capacity for peer networking. The ideal is a cluster or system of interacting units rather than a single, bounded entity. Yet, however "loosely coupled", the managed network retains a core which sets strategic direction and manages performance against targets and contracts.

The dilemmas in this type of structure are what to let go and what to hold tight on to; how to devolve, sub-contract and maximise local freedom while retaining collective direction and control.

Rabobank

The Netherland's Rabobank has built on its cooperative history to transform itself with three levels of internal networks. The chief executive explains: "The hierarchical, pyramidal structure, with its tendency to uniformity, belongs to the past. The present era demands differentiation and specification, and with that, units with a large degree of autonomy."

This new organising model aims to serve market and client needs by the better use of the knowledge and expertise of all employees, especially front line service staff. This knowledge is so widely distributed that

> *it has become impossible and unnecessary to manage organisations from the top. Hence it is better to think in terms of the network concept. ... Central to [this] is that all cells, call them expertise centres, in the network have their own responsibility. One cannot speak of subordination, but of mutual service rendering based on equivalence. It is a living organism, in which every cell performs its own function, without getting formalised instructions. The core notions of a network are* working together *and* environmental awareness. *Only by realising that your behaviour affects other cells in the system, will you make good choices.*

> (Pettigrew and Fenton, 2000, p. 160)

Is there any one right structure for an organisation?

We have learned that organisational design is no science. There are too many variables and dilemmas for any rational solution. A strong design brings clarity and can make organisational life simpler and less stressful, but the stronger the design, the more resistant it is to change. Designers may say that their structures last for five or six years, but do they allow for the emergence of the unanticipated and for incremental restructuring on the basis of learning?

There are technical issues here and sources for further study are given below. One way of approaching this challenge is not to rely too much on any one structure, and to acknowledge that organisations generally contain many possible structures. To test this hypothesis, take your own organisational chart with its formal lines of communication and accountability. Use coloured pens to draw the other, more informal, links that make things happen. Who actually does business with whom? Which people have close connections and relationships? Who really talks to whom? Who has the ear of whom? Who do you know who can get things done for you?

Is Challenge 3: *new organisational structures* preoccupying you and your colleagues? Is it a priority?

CHALLENGE CHECK: *New organisational structures*

■ Is this a challenge you are currently facing?   YES [ ]   NO [ ]

■ Is it one you have faced in the past?   YES [ ]   NO [ ]

■ Do you expect to face this more in the future?   YES [ ]   NO [ ]

Taking these answers into account, make the following judgements:

1. CAPABILITY: How good are you at understanding and dealing with this challenge?

   Not good   4   3   2   1   Very good

2. IMPORTANCE: How important do you think this is going to be for your future?

   Not important   1   2   3   4   Very important

Add the scores from this challenge check to the summary in Part B.

Reference

Pettigrew, A. and Fenton, E. (2000) *The Innovating Organisation*. London: Sage.

Further resources

Henry Mintzberg (*Mintzberg on Management* New York: iBooks, 2007) describes seven basic "organizational configurations" which are summarised at: http://www.12manage.com/methods_mintzberg_configurations.html. Another exploration of different organisational forms is Iyer's *Fueling Innovation Through New Organisational Forms* (Real Innovation, 2006–2009) which is posted at http://www.realinnovation.com/content/c090209a.asp.

Mintzberg doesn't give much consideration as to *why* different configurations or forms emerge. In contrast, Fritz Glasl's *The Enterprise of the Future: Moral Intuition in Leadership and Organisational Development* (Stroud: Hawthorne Press, 1997) offers an evolutionary perspective and model – as organisations grow and mature they find it necessary to take on a different form. A similar US model by Greiner and Schein is well summarised at http://www.12manage.com/methodsgreiner.html and http://www.walterhottinga.com/?p=207.

Other works on new forms stress dialogue and collaboration. Skyrme, D.J. *Knowledge Networking* (Oxford: Butterworth-Heinemann, 1999) contains much information, points to ponder and checklists. His website at http://www.skyrme.com/ is engaging and informative. Other useful resources are Beverlein *et al.*'s *The Collaborative Work Systems Fieldbook: Strategies, Tools and Techniques* (San Francisco: Jossey Bass/Pfeiffer, 2003) and Beverlein and Harris' *Guiding the Journey to Collaborative Work Systems: A Strategic Design Workbook* (San Francisco: Pfeiffer, 2003).

Business process re-engineering is another strategy that has significant implications for organisational design and structure, as is lean thinking. Further resources for these can be found under Challenge 8: *improving work processes* later in this chapter. Chapter 11 of this book on *networking* will also help you to think more deeply and creatively about organisational structure. If this challenge is a high priority for you and your colleagues, then this seventh leadership practice might be the best place to go next.

On the other hand if you are a fan of Dilbert try: http://www.youtube.com/watch?v=YTDWL9OBtLI.

Challenge 4: Powerful teams

How can a team of committed individuals with individual IQs above 120, have a collective IQ of 63?
Peter Senge

The organisation of golden dreams is made up of cohesive teams in which people pool their skills, talents and knowledge to tackle complex problems and come up with groundbreaking solutions. Suffused with spirit, these teams have no barriers, no factions and produce consistently high quality. Dream on. In reality, teams can be stuck, stodgy, unambitious or riven by internal conflicts and expending their energies in "turf wars". Some teams look good, full of talented individuals, but they are unsupportive to one another and come apart at the seams under pressure.

Despite this, the stock of the team concept remains very high. Teams are the basic unit of organisation for people and tasks, and good teamworking ability is a prize asset. As competition has increased and standards have risen, clients and customers demand more. Teams now have to meet the needs of complex sets of stakeholders rather than just keeping a single sponsor happy.

The best teams are largely self-managing, taking responsibility and making local decisions. Creating these autonomous and self-managing teams and project groups has become a key business capability. Today's teams are often made up of people who belong to several other groups and projects at the same time; they may be led "remotely" and meet virtually and electronically as well as face to face.

Team building?

How do we get powerful and creative teams? Much "team building" seems to assume that this is a just a matter of putting all the blocks in place. But whilst it is relatively easy to set up a new team with good working habits, it is very much harder to rescue an old and dysfunctional team. It's a bigger job still to develop a teamworking culture, but, whilst you may occasionally find a dream team in a poor culture, powerful teams are at home in an organisational culture of trust, support, interdependence and collaboration.

Getting into box 4

Many teams stick to tried and tested methods because they don't feel safe or confident enough to venture further. Such teams do not go into unknown territory; they stay in box 1 in Figure C4.1 – what the former US Defence Secretary, Donald Rumsfeld, famously described as the "known knowns":

… there are known knowns; there are things we know we know. We also know there are known unknowns; that is to say we know there are some things we do

not know. But there are also unknown unknowns – the ones we don't know we don't know.

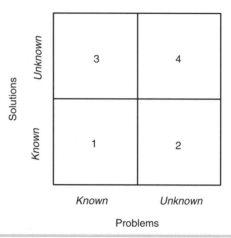

Figure C4.1 Getting into box 4

Powerful teams will also attempt boxes 2, 3 and especially box 4 – getting among the known unknowns and even the unknown unknowns to discover tomorrow's problems (and their solutions).

Support and *challenge for high power*

The ability to face challenges on the outside, comes from inner strength. Powerful teams have highly developed levels of challenge and support. These apparently opposed qualities are actually found together: the ability to push and challenge each other depends on feeling a high level of security and support and vice versa. This is the engine for innovation and risk taking.

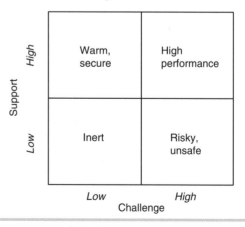

Figure C4.2 Building support and challenge

Some teams are high on support but low on challenge. They play safe. These are not powerful teams. Some teams don't feel safe at all. These aren't powerful teams either.

Is Challenge 4: *powerful teams* a priority for you?

CHALLENGE CHECK: *Powerful teams*

■ Is this a challenge you are currently facing?   YES [   ]   NO [   ]

■ Is it one you have faced in the past?   YES [   ]   NO [   ]

■ Do you expect to face this more in the future?   YES [   ]   NO [   ]

Taking these answers into account, make the following judgements:

1. CAPABILITY: How good are you at understanding and dealing with this challenge?

   Not good   4   3   2   1   Very good

2. IMPORTANCE: How important do you think this is going to be for your future?

   Not important   1   2   3   4   Very important

Add the scores from this challenge check to the summary in Part B.

Further resources

There are many books and resources for teams and team development. Among the best known is Katzenbach and Smith's *The Wisdom of Teams – Creating the High Performance Organisation* (Maidenhead: McGraw-Hill, 2005) and its complement by the same authors, *The Discipline of Teams* (New York: Wiley, 2001). These provide comprehensive models, cases, tools and techniques for developing teams. Another good pair of books are P. Lencioni's *The Five Dysfunctions of a Team: A Leadership Fable* (San Francisco: Jossey-Bass, 2002) and his *Overcoming The Five Dysfunctions of a Team: A Field Guide for Leaders, Managers, and Facilitators* (San Francisco: Jossey-Bass, 2005). One of an excellent series on working together in health and social care is Jelphs and Dickinson's *Working in Teams* (Bristol: Policy Press, 2008).

A different approach is taken by Rickards and Moger in *Handbook for Creative Team Leaders* (Aldershot: Gower, 1999). They studied a large number of teams and classified them as either dream teams, standard teams or teams from hell (an example of which is the final Thatcher cabinet).

More simply written and down-to-earth works include M. Maginn's *Making Teams Work: 24 Lessons for Working Together Successfully* (Columbus: McGraw-Hill, 2004); and I. Fleming's *The Teamworking Pocketbook* (Alresford: Management Pocketbooks, 2004). From the same publisher is Fleming's *The*

Virtual Teams Pocketbook and Tizzard and Hailstone's *Teambuilding Activities Pocketbook* (both 2006).

Perhaps the best-known development model for groups is the "Forming, Storming, Norming and Performing" of Tuckman *et al.* The original reference is hard to obtain but good online summaries are: http://en.wikipedia.org/wiki/Forming,_storming,_norming_and_performing and http://www.12manage.com/methods_tuckman_stages_team_development.html.

There are many ways to build support and challenge. Power in a team can be built by practising action learning – as in the challenge process at the end of this chapter. You will also find lots of ideas for developing these qualities in Chapters 9 and 10 – on the leadership practices of *challenging questions* and *facilitation*.

Challenge 5: Crafting cultures of innovation

I kissed a lot of frogs until I got a prince.
Attributed to Art Fry, the developer of Post-it notes

Innovation is achieved not through better managing but through leadership. Innovative cultures nurture creativity in everyone, and not just in their "stars". Such cultures have the knack of turning creative ideas into innovative actions. They need space and freedom to develop, and this is the leadership task.

As applied to organisations, culture means the prevailing pattern of values, knowledge and behaviour – "how we do things around here"; and with how these habits have developed and been passed on. The metaphor is borrowed from biology, where it refers to the careful nurture and growth of living systems – cells, plants and whole ecologies. With the limitations of structural change now widely understood, leaders seeking more innovative cultures must follow a deeper and more enduring change effort.

Actually, we all understand what an innovative culture looks and feels like.

Innovative financiers

In answer to the question "What would make this company more innovative?", a group of financial services managers quickly produced a long list of suggestions, including the following:

- taking more risks
- support from managers for taking risks
- support from colleagues for trying new things
- talking about the job and your practice
- challenges from colleagues about your practice
- much more experimenting, trying new things out
- being less critical, more appreciative of other people's efforts
- encourage people to freewheel, run with their ideas
- combine ideas, build on suggestions
- benchmark what others are doing
- trying out things that work in other companies
- learning from our mistakes
- sharing the knowledge of what works across this company
- set up processes for gathering new ideas
- invite outsiders in and send insiders out
- put idea generation on the meetings agenda
- set up little experiments
- encourage people to move round and change teams

■ encourage job shadowing
■ make sure that teams are made up of different sorts of people
■ high diversity of people in the company
■ build networks and networking opportunities.

And this is only part of their list. These managers understood the question immediately and knew exactly how they would recognise and experience an innovative culture.

Culture change is hard

So, this challenge is not about understanding but about action. A big mistake here is of thinking that talking about something makes it happen. When a new leader announces that the culture around here must change, they generally know what they want, and will commend most of the things on the financiers' list. The problem is that they don't know how to make it happen.

Almost everyone knows that culture does not change by command, and that patterns of thinking and acting are remarkably persistent. In fact, the effort involved in re-shaping or re-framing the culture is so considerable, that only certain circumstances can justify it. For example, when:

■ the environment is changing quickly and the market is very competitive or the current values are likely to threaten our future
■ the organisation is in generally very bad shape, with low output, quality and morale
■ the company is growing very rapidly and needs to make a step-jump in how it operates (Deal and Kennedy, 1982, pp. 159–161).

Businesses recognise this difficulty and often try to deal with it by getting rid of senior people and bringing in new ones. The new ones bring with them their own trusted people and articulate a different view of how life should be. Whilst this can be part of the effort, a cultural change only happens when lots of people start doing things differently all over the organisation. When this gets underway the new way can become contagious, like a rolling wave. This does not happen just because of a few new people at the top – however inspirational they are.

Getting started

Deal and Kennedy's words "re-shape" and "re-frame" are important here. It is more sensible to think in terms of influencing or adding to cultures rather than changing them. Culture is what we do, a living thing, and constantly evolving. Becoming more innovative means building on what exists now, with all the informal webs of people and relationships that are involved. So, the first step on the road is to find out what exists already and "scan the culture": What is it like here? How do you get things done? Who shares knowledge and learns from who?

Ground rules

While you are getting a good picture of your existing culture, you can still get started on doing it. Start close to home: call up your team, agree some new rules and apply these to all your tasks from now on. For example, do the following:

■ ask people for help on tasks
■ put three options for action in every business case
■ build "experiments at the margin" into all programmes
■ say what risks you are taking and why this is worthwhile
■ ensure that task groups have at least one person from outside the team
■ hold "after-action reviews" to capture the learning
■ say "Please" and "Thank you" and "Well done" a lot more.

But don't:

■ criticise without offering new options
■ discourage people from trying new things
■ re-invent things when you can borrow them from what works elsewhere
■ innovate on other people's turf without checking
■ run other people down.

Is Challenge 5: *crafting cultures of innovation* on your priority list?

CHALLENGE CHECK: *Crafting cultures of innovation*

■ Is this a challenge you are currently facing?   YES [ ]   NO [ ]

■ Is it one you have faced in the past?   YES [ ]   NO [ ]

■ Do you expect to face this more in the future?   YES [ ]   NO [ ]

Taking these answers into account, make the following judgements:

1. CAPABILITY: How good are you at understanding and dealing with this challenge?

   Not good   4   3   2   1   Very good

2. IMPORTANCE: How important do you think this is going to be for your future?

   Not important   1   2   3   4   Very important

Add the scores from this challenge check to the summary in Part B.

Reference

Deal, T.W. and Kennedy, A. (1982) *Corporate Cultures: The Rites and Rituals of Organisational Life*. Reading, MA: Addison Wesley.

Further resources

The grandfather book in this field is perhaps Everett Rogers' *Diffusion of Innovations* (New York: Simon & Schuster, 5th edition, 2003) which makes it clear that organisational networks are central to efforts at innovation. For this reason see the further resources for Challenge 12: *leading in networks* and Chapter 11: *Practice 7: networking*.

Frans Trompenars' *Riding the Whirlwind: Connecting People and Organizations in a Culture of Innovation* (Oxford: Infinite Ideas, 2007) cites a number of barriers to innovation, including what he refers to as the "commoditization of education – a prime killer of innovation" – and offers alternatives to well-established frameworks such as the Myers–Brigg Indicator and other "linear models that cannot fully capture a person's creativity"; he emphasises the "functional use of humour". Although focusing mainly on issues around design, Neumeier's *The Designful Company: How to Build a Culture of Nonstop Innovation* (Berkeley: Pearson/New Riders, 2009) has much of interest about innovation in general, including an overview of the nature of "wicked problems". Perhaps more practical is Kelley and Littman's *The Ten Faces of Innovation: Strategies for Heightening Creativity* (London: Profile Books, 2008). And as so often there is a Management Pocketbook: D. Miller, *Nurturing Innovation Pocketbook* (Alresford: Management Pocketbooks, 2009).

If you are looking for case examples: http://individual.utoronto.ca/markfederman/CultureOfInnovation.pdf includes a short but enlightening case story of the invention of Adobe Acrobat, and another case of India's Tata Group can be found in J. Scanlon's (2009) "How to build a culture of innovation" on the *Business Week* site at http://www.businessweek.com/innovate/content/aug2009/id20090819_070601.htm?chan=innovation_innovation+%2B+design_top+stories. YouTube has a number of short but relevant videos including "Creating a culture of innovation" by Harvard Business Publishing at http://www.youtube.com/watch?v=KyqHGdIMcas) and http://www.youtube.com/watch?v=UWgLOfExBqw. Also try http://www.youtube.com/watch?v=JrlSHZ0anAM&feature=PlayList&p=3327073C4983A302&index=0&playnext=1. For an exciting if sometimes confusing site about creating conditions in which innovation can flourish, try http://www.1000ventures.com/business_guide/innovation_aweorg.html.

To measure the quality of your climate for innovation, a survey tool – the Dolphin Index Indicator – can be found at http://www.innovationclimatequestionnaire.com/.

Challenge 6: Fostering diversity and inclusion

> *Only variety can absorb variety.*
> **W. Ross Ashby**

The English cybernetician Ross Ashby explored the notion of organisations as self-organising or self-regulating systems. His *Law of Requisite Variety* holds that, in order to deal with the challenges coming from that environment, the internal diversity of any system must match the variety and complexity of that environment.

Questions of diversity and inclusion are a growing focus of concern in organisational life. The defensive reason for attending to these questions is to avoid human resourcing and industrial relations problems. Organisations lacking good equal opportunities practices will eventually suffer such problems as labour shortages in key posts.

The strategic argument for fostering diversity and inclusion is to ensure future survival and success through engaging the energies and ideas of the widest possible variety of people. Anthropologist Gregory Bateson pointed out the learning potential of personal and cultural differences many years ago. He noted that all learning proceeds from difference, and the more open we are to difference, the greater the ability to learn and to embrace change and development. Difference and diversity therefore hold the key to many of the aspirations of leadership.

Fostering diversity means being able to attract, engage and inspire all the different kinds of people from any population or society. Gender, race, age, ability and sexual orientation are some of the kinds of difference most often discussed, but the myriad dimensions of diversity in people are far more complex and multiple.

Dialogue and the politics of inclusion

Inclusion is the related notion that those affected by decisions should also participate in those decisions. Including local voices is not just a matter of listening to people. Senior people often fear a loss of control and lack the skills and courage to handle the ensuring dialogue:

> *The politics of inclusion are not faint-hearted efforts at making everybody happy enough. Inclusion means more than taking people's views into account in defining the problem. Inclusion may mean challenging people, hard and steadily, to face new perspectives on familiar problems, to let go of old ideas and ways of life long held sacred. Thus, inclusion does not mean that each party will get its way. Even the most well-crafted efforts at inclusion can rarely prevent the experience of loss by some … Furthermore, from a strategic*

standpoint, some parties often must be excluded from the problem-solving process.

(Heifetz, 1994, p. 240)

Stakeholders in the whole system

Leadership groups who have held their nerve and travelled the dialogue route, are usually surprised by the goodwill, responsiveness and sheer volume of ideas when different groups of people are properly invited to take part. The idea of stakeholders to a system means that we all have a share, a stake in the success or failure of the enterprise. A simple stakeholder analysis is a way of harnessing diverse interests and energies in the face of a challenging situation for any organisation or community:

Stakeholders	What is their view of the problem or issue?	What is their desired picture of the future?
Internal groupings		
1.		
2.		
3.		
4.		
Etc.		
External stakeholders		
1.		
2.		
3.		
4.		
Etc.		

Figure C6.1 A stakeholder analysis

Whole systems development involves working with all the stakeholders in a situation to meet a challenge. In part, this is a response to the growing complexity of business issues and of partnership and network relationships. This is inclusive "big tent politics" where all the people who might be part of the problem are also part of the solution: actions generated are taken on the basis of "nothing about us without us".

Getting the whole organisation into the room

This is part of a historical trend, away from a reliance on experts and towards people taking more control over their working lives:

- 1900 – experts solve problems
- 1950 – "everybody" solves problems
- 1965 – experts improve whole systems
- 2000 – "everybody" improves whole systems (Weisbord and Janoff, 1995, p. 2).

Getting everybody engaged in improving things means bringing in all groups, especially those who are not usually heard. In seeking uniformity of performance and behaviour, organisational systems may often suppress diversity. Unlocking the potential of the whole organisation means being clear about what is held tight and what can be loosened to release the potential of diversity and inclusion.

Is this Challenge 6: *fostering diversity and inclusion* important to you and your organisation?

CHALLENGE CHECK: *Fostering diversity and inclusion*

- Is this a challenge you are currently facing?   YES [ ]   NO [ ]

- Is it one you have faced in the past?   YES [ ]   NO [ ]

- Do you expect to face this more in the future?   YES [ ]   NO [ ]

Taking these answers into account, make the following judgements:

1. CAPABILITY: How good are you at understanding and dealing with this challenge?

   Not good   4   3   2   1   Very good

2. IMPORTANCE: How important do you think this is going to be for your future?

   Not important   1   2   3   4   Very important

You can add the scores from this challenge check to the summary in Part B.

References

Heifetz, R. (1994) *Leadership without Easy Answers*. Cambridge, MA: Belknap Press.

Weisbord, M. and Janoff, S. (1995) *Future Search: An Action Guide to Finding Common Ground in Organizations and Communities*. San Francisco: Berrett-Koehler.

Further resources

This is another field where lots of resources are to be found. These tend to divide into two camps: those that deal with compliance and risk management and those that emphasise the positive benefits of diversity.

The Chartered Institute of Personnel & Development (CIPD) is a rich source of information and guidance on diversity issues. Useful starting points might be *Managing Diversity in Practice* by Ahu Tatli, Gary Mulholland, Mustafa Ozbilgin and Dianah Worman (London: CIPD, 2007) and *Diversity: An Overview* (London: CIPD, 2008) which is a good basic guide to some of the issues involved and can be found at http://www.cipd.co.uk/subjects/dvsequl/general/divover.htm. There are a number of CIPD factsheets on all aspects of diversity including disability, age, race, religion, sex discrimination and gender reassignment, harassment and bullying and employing people with criminal records. From the European Union, http://www.diversityatwork.net/EN/en_about.htm contains links to a number of product sheets, e-learning courses and case studies, with helpful guidance aimed specifically at local government at http://www.idea.gov.uk/idk/core/page.do?pageId=7345916.

Most of these sources given above tend to look at legal and moral issues around diversity. Other books stress the value of diversity and the practical business benefits of encouraging it, such as Jackson and Taylor's *The Power of Difference: Exploring the Value and Brilliance of Diversity in Teams* (Kemble: Management Books, 2000, 2008). S.E. Page's *The Difference: How the Power of Diversity Creates Better Groups, Firms, Schools, and Societies* (New Jersey: Princeton University Press, 2007) is more academic and contains a number of relevant stories. Clements and Jones' *The Diversity Training Handbook: A Practical Guide to Understanding and Changing Attitudes* (London: Kogan Page, 3rd edition, 2008) is very practical and includes exercises, models, checklists and guidelines.

Another more academic text emphasising the positive is Thomas' *Diversity Resistance in Organizations* (New York: Psychology Press/Taylor & Francis, 2008) which notes the practices and behaviours in organisations that interfere with the use of diversity as an opportunity for learning and effectiveness. B. Kandola in *The Value of Difference: Eliminating Bias in Organizations* (Oxford: Pearn Kandola, 2009) differentiates between diversity and inclusion. Using actual cases, this book queries the "good for business" case in favour of the argument for social justice.

Challenge 7: Promoting partnerships

No company can go it alone.
Doz and Hamel

Introduction

Rosabeth Moss Kanter (1994) coined the term "collaborative advantage" for the benefits accruing to those with a well-developed capacity to collaborate with others. Good partners add value by bringing in new skills, resources or customers. Small firms can extend their range by linking with others, larger companies can achieve global reach via strategic alliances, and in the UK's public services, a duty to partnership is intended to provide more joined-up and better quality services. In a networked world the ability to partner and to find good partners is a vital core competence for the corporation.

Iridium

In the early 1990s Motorola initiated a global alliance to build a mobile communications network. Based on 62 orbiting satellites, this would have significant advantages over ground-based technologies, but to do this Motorola needed a wide range of partners to supply the funds, ownership rights and capabilities which it did not itself possess. A coalition of no less than 17 equity holding partners was assembled, including for example, Nippon Iridium, which was in itself an alliance of 18 partners. These partners provided all sorts of expertise from ground communications to space-based technologies, and also held ownership and traffic rights which were crucial to success in a situation where Iridium was competing in a race with other similarly assembled partnerships. This $3.4 billion investment is intended to boost Motorola's (and its partners') position in global cellular communication. (Doz and Hamel, 1998, pp. 3–4)

In the current era, few organisations go it alone. While most partnerships are more modest in scope than Iridium, and more locally based, firms increasingly look to concentrate on core business, looking for niche markets, and locating themselves within larger supply-chain networks. In health and social care where services are faced with too much demand, local area partnerships allow different agencies to pool resources, share knowledge and increase the effectiveness of service delivery.

How to develop a partnership

The downside is that good partnerships take time and resources to develop; they don't just happen. Sometimes the costs of partnering outweigh the benefits. Success depends on getting two things right: starting off well and then maintaining the relationship. Time spent on establishing the right initial conditions and then on creating a high quality joint development process is vital to both small local collaborations and large strategic alliances. The first step is to look at the match between the parties and to do what accountants call the "due diligence" process:

- *The strategic match* – do the partners complement each other in terms of competencies, assets, markets, etc.?
- *The organisational match* – are the parties compatible in terms of organisational structures, cultures and ways of doing things?
- *The expectations match* – are the partners similar in motives and intentions? Do they want the same thing? Is this a defensive or a developmental initiative?

After a sound start, the success of any partnership depends on how it matures. Good ones can create opportunities not seen at the outset, but poor ones can drain energies and take years to untangle. The quality of the relationship can be judged by asking:

- *Sharing*: how open is this partnership? Does the agreement allow for sharing of knowledge about technology, information systems and markets?
- *Review and evaluation*: how do we review and evaluate the way this partnership is working?
- *Learning opportunities*: what processes exist to learn from each other around work methods, systems, skills and so on?

The evolution of partnership

A key test is how the partners work with the differences that inevitably emerge over time. Successful partnerships evolve in their ways of thinking and responding to differences within the relationship – see Figure C7.1.

Stage 1 = Separate and isolated

"They're different from us" (and we don't really want to have anything to do with them).

Where the contractual terms are tightly set, and the parties protect their knowledge assets from each other.

Stage 2 = Curious and exploratory

"They're different from us" (and that's interesting).

Here the partners start to notice each other and ask questions about how each does things. To question and to wonder is to create the conditions for learning.

Stage 3 = Joint enquiry and co-creation

"We are different ..." (and through understanding and using these differences we're working together to generate something new and exciting).

One plus one equals three and more. The key in stage 3 is how diversity leads to learning and innovation; unlike stage 1 where difference is not noticed or is suppressed.

Figure C7.1 The evolution of partnership

It is the quality of the learning conversations between the partners that allows them both to share knowledge, skills and understandings and can also enable the adjustment of expectations over time. These skills in partnering are widely applicable; once you have had a good experience of partnership, you will be keen to repeat it. Who else could we link up? What else could we do with the right partner?

How important is Challenge 7: *promoting partnerships* for you and your colleagues?

CHALLENGE CHECK: *Promoting partnerships*

■ Is this a challenge you are currently facing?   YES [   ]   NO [   ]

■ Is it one you have faced in the past?   YES [   ]   NO [   ]

■ Do you expect to face this more in the future?   YES [   ]   NO [   ]

Taking these answers into account, make the following judgements:

1. CAPABILITY: How good are you at understanding and dealing with this challenge?

   Not good   4   3   2   1   Very good

2. IMPORTANCE: How important do you think this is going to be for your future?

   Not important   1   2   3   4   Very important

You can add the scores from Challenge 7: *promoting partnerships* to the summary in Part B at the end of this chapter.

References

Doz, Y. and Hamel, G. (1998) *Alliance Advantage: The Art of Creating Value through Partnering*. Boston: Harvard Business School Press.

Kanter, R.M. Collaborative advantage: the art of alliances. *Harvard Business Review* **72**, no. 4 (July–August 1994): 96–108.

Further resources

The resources in this field tend to be either very practical and specific to a business area, for example, health care or construction, or more academic and wide ranging. Examples of the former are John Bennett and Sarah Peace's *Partnering in the Construction Industry: A Code of Practice for Strategic Collaborative Working* (Oxford: Butterworth Heinemann, 2006) and Glasby and Dickinson's *Partnership Working in Health and Social Care* (Bristol: Policy Press, 2008). More theoretical is Chris Huxham and Suzanne Vangen's excellent *Managing to Collaborate: The Theory and Practice of Collaborative Advantage* (Abingdon: Routledge, 2005).

More practical general works include E. Lank's *Collaborative Advantage: How Organizations Win by Working Together* (Basingstoke: Palgrave Macmillan, 2006); A. Darby's *Alliance Brand: Fulfilling the Promise of Partnering* (Chichester: Wiley, 2006); T. Lendrum's *The Strategic Partnering Pocketbook: Building Strategic Partnerships and Alliances* (Maidenhead: McGraw-Hill, 2004) and the Harvard Business Review's *Harvard Business Review on Strategic Alliances* (Boston: Harvard Business School, 2002).

Many of the wicked problems of leadership crop up in the public services and there are good resources in this area concerned with the issues of cross-boundary, inter-agency and whole systems working. Julian Pratt, Pat Gordon, Diane Pampling and Margaret Wheatley's slim volume *Working Whole Systems: Putting Theory into Practice in Organisations* (Oxford: Radcliffe Publishing, 2nd edition, 2005) is well worth attention.

Other resources in this area include Dickinson and Peck's *Managing and Leading in Inter-Agency Settings* (Bristol: Policy Press, 2008) and Sullivan and Skelcher's *Working Across Boundaries: Collaboration in Public Services* (Basingstoke: Palgrave Macmillan, 2002).

A. Deering and A. Murphy in *The Partnering Imperative* (Chichester: Wiley, 2003) use a framework based on the three stances of leadership outlined in Chapter 4 to create a partnering grid for locating partnering ventures. Another approach to "scoring" your partnership based on a partnership growth model is L. Segil's *Measuring the Value of Partnering* (New York: AMACOM, 2004). Finally, Maclean and Moffatt offer an interesting account of a "Stance 3" leadership approach to partnering in "Culture change as a conversation" (*Converse*, Issue 6, pp. 17–19, 2009) which can be found at: http://www.ashridge.org.uk/Website/IC.nsf/wFARATT/Culture %20Change%20as%20a%20conversation/$file/CultureChangeAsA Conversation.pdf.

Challenge 8: Improving work processes

Targets can seriously damage your health.
Simon Caulkin

This is the Cinderella of challenges. Given many apparently more pressing matters, it is easy to take your eye off the ball here. Yet the continuous improvement of service quality and efficiency is no longer an option but a requirement. The danger for those in leadership positions is of becoming detached and distant from the core value creating processes of their organisations.

The challenge of *improving work processes* involves mapping the value chain across the boundaries of organisational functions and units, spotting the bottlenecks and then "re-engineering" processes and resources to speed up the flow.

Improvement – not targets ...

Improving work processes is *not* about setting targets. The great quality guru, W. Edwards Deming (1986), saw that targets cause us to focus on what is easily measured, and not on what really matters. Targets lead to cheating, because they are nearly always associated with rewards or punishments and we put energy and creativity into meeting, or appearing to meet, them rather than focusing on systematic work improvement. Targets also cause "sub-optimisation" where the performance of the whole suffers because particular individuals or groups are too focused on their own targets. Shiftworkers, for example, can look good by hammering their machines, depleting supplies or messing up the environment; leaving the next shift to pick up the pieces.

To make sustainable improvements in work performance you have to be serious about it. Many methods for the systematic improvement of work processes have been devised, including perhaps the best known PDSA (Plan–Do–Study–Act) cycle. The DMAIC process is a more recent version:

- **D**efine the opportunity for improvement; select a process to be worked on, identify its customers and what they require of it.
- **M**easure the performance of the chosen process – how well is it doing, compared with what its customers would like?
- **A**nalyse the data and causes of shortfalls in actual performance compared with desired performance.
- **I**mprove the process – remove the causes of the problems.
- **C**ontrol the process – that is, make sure that the new performance is maintained and that faults and problems to not creep back in.

Start with what your customers say

The starting point for reviewing any process is what our customers think about us.

Whitegoods plc

Whitegoods manufactures kitchen appliances. The board wanted to know how the company compared with leading competitors in the eyes of their retailers. A survey on customers' experiences of Whitegoods' service was conducted using telephone interviews. The aim was to highlight "moments of truth" – where people experience the service quality and form a judgement of it. The analysis of the data showed up 10 "moments of truth": when the customer …

1. … obtains information on products and prices
2. … decides which products to stock
3. … negotiates prices and discounts
4. … places an order
5. … receives staff training, e.g. on new products or new Whitegoods' systems
6. … receives delivery of goods
7. … receives an invoice
8. … sends items under warranty for repair
9. … seeks information on delivery dates and back orders
10. … wishes to return unsold stock.

For each moment of truth, customers were asked to rate Whitegoods as poor, moderate or good against their best performing competitor.

After discussing the ratings and their importance, Whitegoods decided to concentrate on three of these moments: numbers 1, 3 and 8. Three project groups were then set up and each proceeded with the next steps in the DMAIC process.

Whitegoods have made a useful start on their service improvement journey. How well they get on will depend on what changes they manage to make in the way they do things.

How important is Challenge 8: *improving work processes* for you and your colleagues?

CHALLENGE CHECK: *Improving work processes*

■ Is this a challenge you are currently facing?   YES [ ]   NO [ ]

■ Is it one you have faced in the past?   YES [ ]   NO [ ]

■ Do you expect to face this more in the future?   YES [ ]   NO [ ]

Taking these answers into account, make the following judgements:

1. CAPABILITY: How good are you at understanding and dealing with this challenge?

   Not good   4   3   2   1   Very good

2. IMPORTANCE: How important do you think this is going to be for your future?

   Not important   1   2   3   4   Very important

Add the scores from the challenge of *improving work processes* to the summary in Part B of this chapter.

Reference

Edwards Deming, W. (1986) *Out of the Crisis*. Cambridge: Cambridge University Press.

Further resources

W. Edwards Deming remains a source of great wisdom and advice on work improvement. Among other insights he described rewards for individual or group targets as being dysfunctional and as worsening overall performance due to what he termed "sub-optimisation": see H. Neave, *The Deming Dimension* (Knoxville: SPC Press, 1990). More recently Simon Caulkin has noted the disastrous impact that targets can have on health services ("Targets can seriously damage your health", *The Observer*, 4 November 2007). Another strong critique of targets and rewards is A. Cohn's *Punished by Rewards* (Boston: Houghton Mifflin, 2000).

Interesting comments on each of Deming's 14 points and seven deadly diseases can be found at http://www.endsoftheearth.com/Deming14Pts.htm. The Deming forum website at http://www.deming.org.uk/ offers conferences, seminars, booklets and an excellent free downloadable paper – *Managing Transformation Means Transforming Management* at: http://www.deming.org.uk/downloads/managing_transformation_means_transforming_management_sopk2.pdf.

Deming's profound insights into the nature of management and leadership seem to have been largely lost in the continuous improvement tools and techniques that now hold sway. There are many sources on six sigma and DMAIC (Describe, Measure, Analyse, Improve, Control) which allegedly help you to get things right almost all the time. A very thorough and rather expensive one is Pyzdeck and Keller's *The Six Sigma Handbook* (New York: McGraw-Hill, 3rd edition, 2010). Not as comprehensive but still good is Brue's very short *Six Sigma for Managers: 24 Lessons to Understand and Apply Six Sigma Principles in Any Organization* (New York: McGraw-Hill, 2005). Others include George *et al.*'s *The Lean Six Sigma Pocket Toolbox: A Quick Reference Guide to Nearly 100 Tools for Improving Process Quality, Speed and Complexity* (New York: McGraw-Hill, 2005); P. Keller's *Six Sigma Demystified: A Self-Teaching Guide* (New York: McGraw-Hill, 2005); Pande and Holpp's *What is Six Sigma?* (New York: McGraw-Hill, 2002) and Pande, Neuman and Cavanagh's *The Six Sigma Way Team Fieldbook* (New York: McGraw-Hill, 2002).

The roots of six sigma are very much in manufacturing. Works that look at it specifically in a service context include G. Taylor's *Lean Six Sigma Service: A Guide to Greenbelt Certification and Bottom Line Improvement* (Fort Lauderdale: J. Ross, 2009) and M. George's *Lean Six Sigma for Service: How to Use Lean Speed and Six Sigma Quality to Improve Services and Transactions* (New York: McGraw-Hill, 2003).

For sceptical views of six sigma see Dilbert at http://www.rokblog.com/wp-content/uploads/2007/02/dilbert.jpg and a fascinating YouTube video at http://www.youtube.com/watch?v=GXVgsPxQR54&feature=related where "Dr Deming" played by an actor is critical of the way six sigma and lean are implemented: "There will be no true improvement or sustained improvement or change without change in leadership and its ways."

Challenge 9: **Streamlining**

> *Muda – the Japanese term for any activity that*
> *consumes resources but creates no value.*
> **Jim Womack and Dan Jones**

Introduction

Outsourcing, downsizing, right-sizing, restructuring, delayering, re-engineering and lean thinking have succeeded each other in the management vocabulary over the past 25 years. Streamlining focuses on re-aligning business activities to meet customer or client definitions of value, and aims to be more of a continuous process. Like lean thinking, streamlining involves cutting back here in order to develop over there, moving people and resources to where they are most needed *now*.

Streamlining is the business equivalent of gym work. It is about toning up, slimming down, building muscles around the key areas. When Unilever slimmed down from 700 to 200 brands over five years, the message was simple: stick to the core businesses and look at all aspects of service delivery to cut waste and improve flow. This mindset is marked by constant challenging and questioning:

- ■ Can we do this more simply?
- ■ How can we get rid of activity?
- ■ Where can we take stuff out of the back office and put it in the front line?
- ■ How can we get more for less?
- ■ What do we need to invest in? … and especially …
- ■ Which are the areas for development *and* where shall we make cuts?

Several of these questions were haunting George, the owner of an electronics company employing 47 people:

TechStar

TechStar manufactures communications technologies for much larger companies looking for sophisticated solutions to service delivery processes. It has invested heavily in R&D and like many small, entrepreneurial companies, its fortunes are strongly affected by the economic cycle. After several quarters of recession, TechStar has cash flow problems and its bankers are asking for economies now in exchange for further injections of funds.

TechStar's management team agrees that something should be done. A temporary, across-the-board, 15% wage cut is one of the options; another is to reduce the staff by 10%. No-one much likes either option. What should George do?

Is it fair?

George's motivation is less about cost-cutting and more with how to weather the crisis by slimming down while preparing for future growth. Streamlining involves pain, and this pain is made worse by the dishonest rationalisations and justifications that are common in such exercises. Simple rules of thumb such as "last in; first out" are tempting in these difficult situations, but are they fair? Any decision can be rationalised – one list of justifications runs to more than a dozen, from rights to ability, from seniority to need, without exhausting the possibilities (Solomon, 1993, pp. 238–239) – but the question is: does it *feel* fair?

Streamlining in a learning company

Elizabeth Michel-Alder, a Swiss consultant, believes that the principles of participation and learning for all can be applied to these tough situations. She worked with a hospital obstetrics clinic, which had high levels of staff and a reputation for excellent service. The new hospital CEO demanded that the clinic lower their overall costs, while allowing for some small investments to increase efficiency. Elizabeth is engaged to help "re-engineer" the clinic and proposes two operating principles:

- Staff involvement in the planning and implementation of the restructuring.
- Implementing solutions that increase options and open up new possibilities.

An initiative group of some 30 people representing all types of staff – doctors, nurses, midwives, physiotherapists, secretaries, bookkeepers, housekeepers and technicians – is established in an interesting way: half are *selected* as "must be there's", and half are *elected* as delegates by these various groups. Using agreed ground rules, especially including a "no compulsory redundancies" rule, the group accepts the responsibility for leading the reshaping of the clinic. Over the next three months, together with lots of coaching from the consultant, the group works through an agenda beginning with the questions:

- What kind of results are we looking for? What should be the strong points of our clinic in the future?
- What opportunities can we imagine for the future?
- What is good and excellent about what we do now and what should be retained and maintained? What has to be left behind or changed?
- What are our fears about restructuring? What are the possible losses and gains?
- How will we cope with the difficult challenges and feelings?

Everyone works on solutions to these questions, in small task groups, and in the whole group for making decisions. Feelings are strong and open – despair, hope, fear, loss, sadness, optimism. Groups or named individuals are commissioned to research priority areas for change and timetables are agreed for action. After eight months the results are impressive:

- Three nurses have found new jobs elsewhere, and about half of the staff are working to different, sometimes shorter, hours; no-one was let go.
- A woman gynaecologist has been employed (they were all men before).
- New services such as birth preparation and health maintenance have been developed and are generating new income.
- The hierarchy is flatter, there is more team work and the atmosphere has become more enthusiastic and creative.
- Costs are lowered by 17% (the CEO asked for 20%).

Developments and cuts run together in business. Leadership textbooks are better at the former than the latter, but both make up the business cycle. Smoothing and streamlining growth and contraction is a critical and neglected leadership challenge. Minimising pain and waste, helping people to cope with change, and seeking creative ways to reallocate people and resources, make up this important role.

Is Challenge 9: *streamlining* a current priority for you and your colleagues?

CHALLENGE CHECK: *Streamlining*

- Is this a challenge you are currently facing?　　　　　　　　YES [ ]　　NO [ ]

- Is it one you have faced in the past?　　　　　　　　　　　YES [ ]　　NO [ ]

- Do you expect to face this more in the future?　　　　　　YES [ ]　　NO [ ]

Taking these answers into account, make the following judgements:

1. CAPABILITY: How good are you at understanding and dealing with this challenge?

   Not good　　　　　　　　　　4　　3　　2　　1　　　　　Very good

2. IMPORTANCE: How important do you think this is going to be for your future?

   Not important　　　　　　　　　1　　2　　3　　4　　　　　Very important

You can add the scores from this challenge to the summary in Part B of this chapter.

Reference

Solomon, R.C. (1993) *Ethics and Excellence: Cooperation and Integrity In Business.* Oxford: Oxford University Press.

Further resources

James Womack and Dan Jones provide a good basis for this philosophy of management with *Lean Thinking: Banish Waste and Create Wealth in Your Corporation* (London: Simon & Schuster, 2003) and *Lean Solutions: How Companies and Customers can Create Value and Wealth Together* (London: Simon & Schuster, 2007). Jim Collins' *Good to Great* (London: Random House, 2001) provides a different and convincing slant. His focus is on the wider disciplines that give companies enduring strength, and on the dedication, perseverance and personal humility needed by leadership to bring this about.

A number of the resources already given for the previous challenge – improving work processes – combine lean thinking with six sigma (see Taylor, G. 2009, George, M. *et al.* 2005 and George, M. 2003 under Challenge 8: *improving work processes*). Other useful titles include NJ. Sayer and B. Williams, *Lean for Dummies* (Hoboken: Wiley, 2007) and T. Devane, *Integrating Lean Six Sigma and High Performance Organizations: Leading the Charge Toward Dramatic, Rapid, and Sustainable Improvement* (San-Francisco: Jossey-Bass, 2004).

In a public service context, Radnor, Walley, Stephens and Bucci report on an *Evaluation of the Lean Approach to Business Management and its Use in the Public Sector* (Edinburgh: Scottish Executive Social Research, 2006) available at http://www.scotland.gov.uk/Resource/Doc/129627/0030899.pdf. For anyone looking for a concise guide to streamlining, Maxine Conner, Sandra Knott and Brenda Bulman's *Excellence in the Public Sector: Re-designing The Patient/User Experience* (Chichester: Kingsham Press, 2003) is a short but well-written and illustrated guide to applying the principles of process thinking to healthcare. Considerable work has been done on applying lean principles in the NHS; an overview – Jones and Mitchell, A *Lean thinking for the NHS,* (London: NHS Confederation, 2006) – is posted at http://www.leanuk.org/downloads/health/lean_thinking_for_the_nhs_leaflet.pdf. The NHS Institute has published a number of lean case studies, downloadable from http://www.institute.nhs.uk/quality_and_value/lean_thinking/leean_case_studies.html and there is also an NHS Lean Discussion Forum that appears to be openly accessible at http://www.networks.nhs.uk/forums/forumdisplay.php?f=84.

Challenge 10: Encouraging social responsibility

Think global; act local.
Environmentalists' slogan

It is said that managers do things right, but that leaders do the right things. But, what is right? And, with whose rights are we concerned? The impact of corporations on society is increasingly subject to scrutiny and critique. The traditional directors' "trust us" is giving way to a new, stakeholder-led "show me". The concern with social responsibility or CSR (corporate social responsibility) signals a growing awareness of the social, environmental and ethical implications of business activities.

However, this is a topic to be approached with some caution. CSR tends to be prominent in public statements made by senior figures, and is increasingly part of branding and corporate positioning. When companies make great play of their environmental awareness, a healthy scepticism may be in order. CSR is only loosely connected with the notion of ethical management, which is still largely seen as a personal responsibility.

Although private sector organisations provide many of the most developed examples of CSR policies and practices, the questions of responsible behaviour apply to everyone. Public service, higher education and voluntary sector organisations are also now considering their impacts and undertaking CSR assessments based on the list of 65 criteria from the Institute for Business Ethics (IBE).

The Co-operative Bank

Under the auspices of its ethical policy launched in 1992, the Co-operative Bank has turned away over £1 billion in businesses that operate in areas of concern to customers. The bank will not deal with companies involved in arms dealing, animal testing, exploitative labour practices and nuclear power. As part of the Co-operative Group, its Sustainability Report for 2007/8 includes sections on international development and human rights, on diet and health, on climate change and toxic chemicals.

The performance of the Co-operative Bank demonstrates strong evidence for its value-based stance. With business growing at 14% and scoring highly for customer satisfaction, the bank is looking good in an era where many other bankers have been disgraced. The bank believes that about one third of all new customers open accounts because of its policies, and it puts a value on its ethical stance of about a quarter of overall profits.

And the Co-operative Bank is not alone. CSR is perhaps best seen as enlightened self-interest; virtue pays, according to the IBE, which argues that

UK companies with codes of business ethics perform better in financial terms. While the existence of a code is hardly a guarantee of virtue – Enron had a good one apparently – they do tend to be associated with other desired qualities. The IBE again found a strong correlation between having an ethical code, addressing "non-financial risks" effectively and being an "admired company" (Caulkin, 2003).

Leading responsibly

First you need a good policy. There are four steps to take here, starting with the question:

Q1: Why do we need an ethical or CSR system?

- What are the drivers?
- What is the business case?
- What are our peers doing?

Once you have a positive case, the second set of questions is:

Q2: What should our ethical or CSR system look like?

- What areas should it cover, e.g. ethical, environmental, etc. (and what do these mean to your business?)?
- What corporate systems are needed to deliver it?

As an example the framework in Figure C10.1 is from Cadbury Schweppes plc.

Four CSR areas	Four CSR system levels
Ethical trading	Commitment
Employees	Policy and strategy
Community	Implementation and verification
Environment	Communication

Figure C10.1 **A 4 × 4 CSR framework**

A third set of questions concerns the commitments you intend to make:

Q3: What are the specific areas in which we wish to make commitments?

- For example, ethical trading, employees, environment, communities, human rights, etc.

The fourth and final step is to conduct a gap analysis and establish some baselines:

Q4: Where are the gaps and what actions will we take to fill them?

■ How well are we doing now against our social responsibility framework?

Figure C10.2 expands on Figure C10.1 to create the basis for an implementation plan.

CSR system / CSR areas	Leadership commitment (board-level values and principles)	Policies and strategies (policies, codes, strategies in all areas)	Implementation and verification (systems, business processes, work programmes, steering groups)	Communication and reporting (audits, surveys, evaluations and reports, meetings and forums)
Ethical trading. For example, on procurement, supplier policy, supplier assessment, etc.				
Employees. For example, on rewards, health, safety, quality of working life, training, etc.				
Environment. For example, on environmental impact and management, waste and recycling, green issues, etc.				
Communities. For example, social impact and creating value in communities, donations, volunteering, etc.				

Figure C10.2 A CSR gap analysis

Now all you have to do is to get on with the job. Is Challenge 10: *encouraging social responsibility* a priority for your organisation?

CHALLENGE CHECK: *Encouraging social responsibility*

■ Is this a challenge you are currently facing?　　　　　YES [　]　　NO [　]

■ Is it one you have faced in the past?　　　　　　　　YES [　]　　NO [　]

■ Do you expect to face this more in the future?　　　　YES [　]　　NO [　]

Taking these answers into account, make the following judgements:

1. CAPABILITY: How good are you at understanding and dealing with this challenge?

   Not good　　　　　　　　　4　3　2　1　　　　　Very good

2. IMPORTANCE: How important do you think this is going to be for your future?

   Not important　　　　　　　1　2　3　4　　　　　Very important

Add the scores from this challenge to the summary in Part B of this chapter.

References

The Cooperative Group (2008) *The Cooperative Group Sustainability Report for 2007/8* http://www.goodwithmoney.co.uk/assets/Uploads/Documents/Co-opSustfull.pdf.

Caulkin, S. (2003) Ethics and profits do mix. *The Observer*, 20 April.

Further resources

For thorough and substantial views on the current state of CSR, see A. Crane and D. Matten, *Business Ethics* (Oxford: Oxford University Press, 3rd edition, 2009); and B. Blowfield and A. Murray, *Corporate Responsibility: a Critical Introduction* (Oxford: Oxford University Press, 2008). Asongu's "The history of corporate social responsibility" (*Journal of Business and Public Policy* 1, (2), 2007) http://www.jbpponline.com/article/viewFile/1104/842 provides a thoughtful overview. It looks at the different motives for espousing CSR, including moral and ethical responsibility perspectives, avoiding the greater evil of statutory regulation and seeing it as a route to further profits.

Mallen Baker is a commentator and advisor on CSR who has lively websites at http://www.mallenbaker.net/csr/about.php, and http://www.businessrespect.net/. These are full of up-to-date news and stories from round the world. Tricky issues and paradoxical questions such as "is McDonalds a responsible firm because it uses environmentally friendly packaging or an irresponsible one because it contributes to mass agricultural production?" are explored by D. Vogel in *The Market for Virtue: the Potential and Limits of Corporate Social Responsibility* (Washington: Brookings Institute, 2005).

Wikipedia's page http://en.wikipedia.org/wiki/Corporate_social_responsibility includes a large number of links to other sources. Another potential starting point is the CIPD's *Corporate Social Responsibility Factsheet* at http://www.cipd.co.uk/subjects/corpstrtgy/corpsocres/csrfact.htm. They also publish I. Redington's *Making CSR Happen: The Contribution of People Management Research Report* (London: CIPD, 2005), a summary of which is available free of charge at http://www.cipd.co.uk/subjects/corpstrtgy/corpsocres/_mkngcsrhpn.htm. Ashridge Business School publish L. Olsen's *Catalogue of CSR Activities: a Broad Overview* (2005) which is also freely downloadable at http://www.ashridge.org.uk/Website/IC.nsf/wFARPUB/Catalogue%20of%20CSR%20Activities:%20A%20broad%20overview?OpenDocument.

Challenge 11: Mobilising knowledge

> *The single greatest challenge … is to raise the productivity of knowledge and service workers. This challenge … will determine the very fabric of society and quality of life in every industrialised nation.*
> **Peter Drucker**

The three traditional economic resources of land, labour and capital have now become four. The knowledge era puts a premium on learning and knowledge development, while information technologies provide the tools for knowledge sharing and deployment. This is a dazzling and somewhat overexcited world, governed by dramatic laws:

- *Moore's law* – the power of computing doubles every 18 months.
- *The law of storage* – for a given cost, storage capacity doubles every 12 months.
- *The law of fibre* – bandwidth capacity doubles every nine months.

Consequent to this excitement, "knowledge management" (KM) is replete with large and sophisticated management information systems, which lead the unwary into expensive purchases that often fail to deliver. A fourth law offers a useful directional clue:

- *Metcalfe's law* – network power increases by the square of the people interacting.

It is people who generate and share knowledge, and, as corporate success increasingly depends on this ability, it is organising with knowledge that is the focus. Customers need the best advice and information, but do they get it? Leaders need feedback and intelligence to inform good decisions, but information in organisations does not easily flow uphill. Just collecting and storing "knowledge" is of little use.

Knowledge keeps no better than wet fish

The British mathematician A.N. Whitehead pointed this out in 1932. More recently Nancy Dixon (2000, pp. 148–160) suggests three fundamental shifts in how we see knowledge:

- From expert to distributed.
- From being seen as an individual possession to knowledge as embedded in group or community.
- From knowledge as a stable commodity to knowledge as dynamic and ever changing.

Knowledge is a living process, used when people put it into action, in practice. It is distributed all over the organisation, and the core KM task is to enhance and maximise the flow of knowledge rather than seek to capture and store it.

A strategy for mobilising knowledge

Knowledge needs to be managed as part of business processes and work practices and not as an abstract entity. KM systems are the foreground but what lie behind them are the business practices and processes which are essential to organising with knowledge. Behind all this are the cultural norms and practices that influence people's actions (see Figure C11.1).

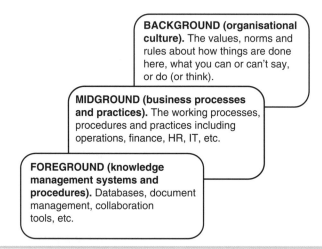

Figure C11.1 Organisational knowledge mobilisation. (Adapted with permission from the original by Inter-Logics.net Ltd.)

Unless the culture develops to support and encourage these knowledge management and deployment processes, then they will not happen.

The key to this is to make the KM strategy the servant and not the driver in these essentially human exchanges. Building a knowledge strategy from the bottom-up means working with the energy of the people with the know-how to help them develop their knowledge and to share it with whoever might find it useful.

To develop an effective knowledge strategy you have to do as much work on the culture at one end and on the linkage to business performance at the other, as you do on the actual KM paraphernalia (see Figure C11.2).

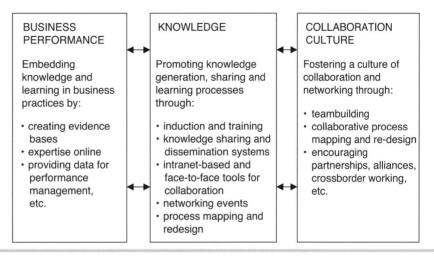

Figure C11.2 **A knowledge strategy**

Should you take the lead on a knowledge strategy for your organisation? Some companies have already institutionalised this work and appointed CKOs – chief knowledge officers – but if you can take a lead, then:

■ Hold in your mind that KM strategy is not a document but a living process practised by people, work groups, project teams and multiple communities of interest, knowledge and practice.
■ Build on what already exists rather than investing heavily in new kit before you know how it will work.
■ Start with something simple that you can actually implement.

Is Challenge 11: *mobilising knowledge* a priority for your organisation?

CHALLENGE CHECK: *Mobilising knowledge*

■ Is this a challenge you are currently facing?   YES [ ]   NO [ ]

■ Is it one you have faced in the past?   YES [ ]   NO [ ]

■ Do you expect to face this more in the future?   YES [ ]   NO [ ]

Taking these answers into account, make the following judgements:

1. CAPABILITY: How good are you at understanding and dealing with this challenge?

   Not good   4   3   2   1   Very good

2. IMPORTANCE: How important do you think this is going to be for your future?

   Not important   1   2   3   4   Very important

Add the scores from the challenge of *mobilising knowledge* to the summary in Part B.

References

Drucker, P. (1991) The new productivity challenge. *Harvard Business Review*, Nov.–Dec. p. 69.
Dixon, N. (2000) *Common Knowledge: How Companies Thrive by Sharing What They Know*. Boston: Harvard Business School Press.

Further resources

There are a number of different views as to what "knowledge management" is about.

An excellent general overview is D. Hislop's *Knowledge Management in Organizations* (Oxford: Oxford University Press, 2nd edition, 2009). This is basically a standard text with a website, organised by the book's chapters, at www.oxfordtextbooks.co.uk/orc/hislop2e/. This in turn links to further rich sources of information, case studies, papers and blogs, although some of these are only available to lecturers who have adopted the book for students. Other good sources include A. Jashapara, *Knowledge Management: An Integrated Approach* (Harlow: Pearson Education, 2004); T.H. Davenport and L. Prusak, *Working Knowledge: How Organizations Manage What They Know* (Boston: Harvard Business School Press, 2000) and K. Dalkir, *Knowledge Management in Theory and Practice* (Oxford: Butterworth-Heinemann, 2005).

Simplifying a complex picture, there seem to be four main perspectives on KM:

- As knowledge databases with an emphasis on IT systems. See, for example: H. Benbya, *Knowledge Management: Systems Implementation: Lessons from the Silicon Valley* (Oxford: Chandos, 2008) and I. Hawryszkiewycz, *Knowledge Management* (New York: Palgrave Macmillan, 2009).
- As intellectual capital. See, for example: D. Andriessen, *Making Sense of Intellectual Capital: Designing a Method for the Valuation of Intangibles* (Oxford: Elsevier Butterworth-Heinemann, 2004); G. Roos, S. Pike and L. Fernstrom, *Managing Intellectual Capital in Practice* (Oxford: Elsevier Butterworth-Heinemann, 2005); and R. Baker's *Mind Over Matter: Why Intellectual Capital is the Chief Source of Wealth* (Hoboken: Wiley, 2008).
- As social processes for knowledge creation and sharing. Classics here are Nonaka and Takeuchi's *The Knowledge-creating Company* (New York: Oxford University Press, 1995) and on communities of practice, Wenger's *Communities of Practice: Learning, Meaning, and Identity* (Cambridge: Cambridge University Press, 1998) and the subsequent Wenger,

McDermott and Snyder's *Cultivating Communities of Practice: A Guide to Managing Knowledge* (Boston: Harvard Business School Press, 2002).

■ As a business strategy. See, for example: D. Skyrme, *Capitalizing on Knowledge: From E-business to K-business* (Oxford: Butterworth-Heinemann, 2001). Many of the useful resources in this emerging area are already listed under Challenge 1: *Finding direction and strategy*, see Shuen, (2008); Li and Bernoff (2008); and McAfee (2009).

Finally, various KM definitions can be found at http://www.knowledge-management-online.com/Definition-of-Knowledge-Management.html#VisitorPages. Although this is basically part of a consultancy's website, "Knowledge Management Online – Open Source KM", it contains many useful documents and other sources.

Challenge 12: Leading in networks

*Networks are the basic principle of organisation
for all forms of life – cellular, animal and human.*
Fritjof Capra

Manuel Castells (2000) argues that we live in a networked society, where the Internet provides both the conceptual model and the practical enablers of inter-connection. Networking is a personal activity of making, keeping and using contacts, and also an organisational task to achieve productive working with different groups and agencies. For businesses, the seminal notion is the value chain that extends beyond the boundaries of the single organisation. The contemporary language of contracting, alliances, partnerships and interlocking ownership emphasises the importance of collaboration and connectedness.

Networks place a premium on collaboration, negotiation, brokering and diplomacy; they call for leadership skills in reading and influencing complex patterns of power and relationships.

Living systems

From a networks perspective, organisations are living systems like flocks of birds or shoals of fish, as:

> *a system of independent agents that can act in parallel, develop models as to how things work in their environment, and, most importantly, refine those models through learning and adaptation.*

(Pascale, Millemann and Goija, p. 5)

The key idea here is that living systems are highly adaptive and deal much better with complexity than those that are centrally controlled. This is because of the *self-organisation* principle, found in many natural systems. Living systems adapt via simple rules such as "watch what your neighbour does and follow". While a machine can be controlled, a living system can only be disturbed or influenced. Members respond to impulses not instructions, and attempts to command will naturally lead to resistance to change. This perspective highlights the informal relationships of communication, friendship, networks and alliances that exist in and around formal organisations. These invisible and shifting patterns hold the key to greater flexibility, learning capability and creative potential.

How do they work?

Networks are groups of:

> *... individuals, organisations and agencies organised on a non-hierarchical basis around common issues or concerns ...*
>
> (WHO, 1998)

Networks connect people through:

- common goals
- personal relationships of reciprocity and trust
- self-initiated action and exchange
- nodes (e.g. individuals, teams or organisations); ties (links and relationships) and spaces for emergence and new activities
- the value of their knowledge, usefulness, sharing and innovativeness and not because of any formal position or rank.

In practice, networks in and around organisations are always managed to some degree. This is a paradox; and constitutes the central challenge for leadership: *how can we maximise the advantages of self-organisation while achieving overall alignment and control?*

Cyborg leadership

A clue is that despite being full of networks, organisations also have many machine-like qualities. As well as wanting to be self-organising, we are also willing to behave in remarkably orderly ways, conforming to all sorts of rules, processes and procedures. This dual "cyborg" nature of human organising, part-machine, part-living system, means that the leadership task is to specify the minimum "machine" that allows space and headroom for the living system to emerge and self-organise.

As networks come in many varieties, how they may be led, facilitated and developed depends on their purposes. Here are three different examples:

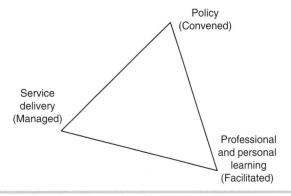

Figure C12.1 **Three types of network**

■ *Learning networks* attract members around common development needs. They exist to share ideas, good practice and the solving of technical problems. They need relatively few resources or rules and are *facilitated*.

■ *Policy networks* are a mainstay of government and international bodies. They produce ideas, models and potential agreements, and are *convened* and *chaired*.

■ *Service delivery networks* have agreed procedures, clear "bottom lines" such as service improvement, cost reductions or other synergies, and elements of hierarchy. These networks are *managed* from various distributed points.

Network organisations need both to be designed and allowed to emerge. The leadership task is to specify the minimum "machine" that allows for this emergence and self-organisation.

Is Challenge 12: *leading in networks* a priority for your organisation?

CHALLENGE CHECK: *Leading in networks*

■ Is this a challenge you are currently facing?   YES [ ]   NO [ ]

■ Is it one you have faced in the past?   YES [ ]   NO [ ]

■ Do you expect to face this more in the future?   YES [ ]   NO [ ]

Taking these answers into account, make the following judgements:

1. CAPABILITY: How good are you at understanding and dealing with this challenge?

   Not good   4   3   2   1   Very good

2. IMPORTANCE: How important do you think this is going to be for your future?

   Not important   1   2   3   4   Very important

Add the scores from Challenge 12: *leading in networks* to the summary in Part B.

References

Capra, F. (2002) *The Hidden Connections – A Science for Sustainable Living*. London: HarperCollins.
Castells, M. (2000) *End of the Millennium*. Oxford: Blackwell.
WHO (1998) *Health Promotion Glossary*. Geneva: WHO/HPR/HEP/98.1.

Further resources

Networks are omnipresent and ubiquitous in human life and because of this, are hard to pin down as a field. Wikipedia has a good page on social networks and social network analysis at: http://en.wikipedia.org/wiki/Social_network and although there is not much here that is directly relevant to leadership, it does demonstrate the width and depth of that field.

Network ideas have been applied to organisational life for many years; see, for example, *Networks and Organizations: Structure, Form and Action*, edited by R. Eccles and N. Nohria (Boston: Harvard Univerity Press, 1994). But they are still in their early days in terms of successful implementation and application. A major problem is reconciling the essential autonomy of network actors with central alignment and control.

Many of the resources for this challenge are shared with those for Practice 7: *Networking* (see Chapter 11). A general introduction to network ideas is provided by Fritjof Capra in his *The Hidden Connections: A Science for Sustainable Living* (London: HarperCollins, 2003), which makes a commonly asserted point that network principles underlie all life forms including those in organisations. Several authors have attempted to capture network ideas and apply them to organisations. Goold and Campbell have applied these ideas in more detail in *Designing Effective Organisations: How to Create Structured Networks* (San Francisco: Jossey Bass, 2002); as have J. Child, D. Faulkner and S. Tallman in *Cooperative Strategy: Managing Alliances, Networks, and Joint Ventures* (Oxford: Oxford University Press, 2005); while Considine, Lewis and Alexander focus specifically on organisational change in public service in *Networks, Innovation and Public Policy: Politicians, Bureaucrats and the Pathways to Change Inside Government* (Basingstoke: Palgrave Macmillan, 2009).

Neil Farmer's *The Invisible Organisation: How Informal Networks can Lead Organisational Change* (Aldershot: Gower, 2008) is a more managerial attempt that emphasises the importance of informal networks to organisational performance. This book is strong on approaches to organisational network analysis, but naive on power dynamics, and tends to assume that networks can be commanded. D. Skyrme's *Knowledge Networking: Creating the Collaborative Enterprise* (Oxford: Butterworth-Heinemann, 1999) is another account from a knowledge management perspective, again avoiding many of the difficult questions.

The NHS has pioneered the use of organisational networks to deliver services to patients, notably the use of cancer networks to improve patient care. NHS Networks sets out to promote and connect the many networks which exist in the NHS. Their website includes a network directory, news stories and discussion forums: www.networks.nhs.uk. An interesting story of applying network principles to community organising is William Traynor and Jessica Andors' *Network Organizing: A Strategy for Building Community Engagement* (NHI Shelterforce Online: Issue 140, March/April, 2005) which can be found at: http://www.nhi.org/online/issues/140/LCW.html.

Finally, and in conjunction with Lancaster University, we are continuing our interest in leading in networks with a collaborative project. For information see http://stringbag.net.

Challenge 13: **Managing mergers**

It is not the strongest of the species who survive or even the most intelligent,
but the most responsive to change.
Charles Darwin

Mergers and acquisitions are forms of change management, but they have a distinctive flavour that calls for special leadership. The difference can be summed up by the word "synergy"; for a merger to be worthwhile, 2 + 2 must = 5 (or more).

But, despite their popularity as a quick way of growing businesses, according to KPMG (2001), perhaps 70% of mergers and acquisitions fail to add value. Why is this so? Aside from the CEO's ego (which can be a considerable factor), most attention in merger situations is concerned with questions of strategic "fit" and the financial and legal aspects of due diligence. Yet the failure to harvest synergies is more likely to be found in *how* the merger is done. How things are integrated is as important as what is merged. As ever in change management, it is the people issues that make it easier to say than to do:

> *People-based assets are difficult to manage – it is not a simple task to harness people's intellects, emotions and imaginations. Nor is it easy to persuade employees to behave in certain ways or to endorse cherished corporate values.*
> (Devine, 2002, p. 9)

First lesson: don't hand it over to the planners! Pulling off the value-adding merger requires a remarkable effort at the involvement and integration of the people who will power the new business. Take the risk and uncertainty out of the merger process and you also remove the opportunities for local ownership that can generate new solutions and ways to "beat the plan". This is a particular leadership challenge that includes project planning and logistics, but crucially requires an affinity for handling personal relationships and for working with cultural differences and sensitivities.

Working with energy

At their best mergers have been described as controlled explosions of energy; but in all cases they constitute major upheavals. There are many forms of energy around at these times, negative and positive, including the following:

- emotional energy from risk, vulnerability and uncertainty
- conflict potential of "tribal battles"
- loss and bereavement of past, place, meaning and personal identity
- new personal development possibilities and opportunities
- energies from new purposes of improved products or services.

If you are leading a merger, you need to recognise and be able to work with, these energies. While they can look frightening, they are also the sources of new power.

An integration structure

During the upheaval some sort of scaffolding is useful to support the building of the new organisation. This temporary organisation provides a bridge between the existing organisations, so that both may carry on functioning. This framework usually includes:

- A visible leadership group which sets the targets and timetables, describes the new culture and is on hand to resolve any conflicts.
- An integration team drawn from different specialisms that designs, plans, co-ordinates and oversees the integration. This group coordinates the task teams, coaches on local action and facilitates organisational learning between the leadership and the task teams.
- Task teams – project groups responsible for local action and learning, and for working out how best to integrate in particular sites or situations.

The art of integration

The middle position of the integration team gives them unique access to the system, and their facilitation skills are crucial in circulating intelligence and learning throughout. The art of integration requires the facilitation of many tricky tasks including:

- helping develop new meanings and purposes
- avoiding the project management trap
- creating a holding framework to give people time to experiment and adjust
- being inclusive and empowering
- maximising learning opportunities
- working with the energies and synergies.

Is Challenge 13: *managing mergers* a priority for you at this time?

CHALLENGE CHECK: *Managing mergers*

■ Is this a challenge you are currently facing? YES [ ]   NO [ ]

■ Is it one you have faced in the past? YES [ ]   NO [ ]

■ Do you expect to face this more in the future? YES [ ]   NO [ ]

Taking these answers into account, make the following judgements:

1. CAPABILITY: How good are you at understanding and dealing with this challenge?

   Not good   4   3   2   1   Very good

2. IMPORTANCE: How important do you think this is going to be for your future?

   Not important   1   2   3   4   Very important

Add the scores from Challenge 13: *managing mergers* to the summary in Part B.

References

Devine, M. (2002) *Successful Mergers: Getting The People Issues Right*. London: Profile Books.
KPMG (2001) *Creating Shareholder Value through Mergers and Acquisitions*. London.

Further resources

C. Cooper and S. Cartwright's *Managing Mergers, Acquisitions and Strategic Alliances: Integrating People and Cultures* (Oxford: Butterworth-Heinemann, 2nd edition, 1996) is a good introduction to the process and the pitfalls. Very comprehensive and replete with tools is Galpin and Herndon's *The Complete Guide to Mergers and Acquisitions: Process Tools to Support M&A Integration at Every Level* (San Francisco: Wiley, 2nd edition, 2007). For a scholarly survey of the research evidence on mergers and acquisitions (M&A), see Cartwright and Schoenberg's "Thirty years of mergers and acquisitions research: recent advances and future opportunities" (*British Journal of Management*, 17 (S1): S1–S5, 2006).

No sensible leadership will enter a merger without extensive *due diligence* of the legal and financial sort; however, the less tangible areas such as those involved with people are often neglected. A recent survey indicates that poor post-merger performance is either very often or always attributable to management issues: see Harding and Rouse's "Human due diligence" (*Harvard Business Review*, 85(4) 2007, April). Marion Devine's *Successful Mergers: Tackling the people issues* (London: Economist Books, 2004) is a good guide with examples and lessons from many organisations for dealing with the human aspects.

There are many resources warning of the dangers inherent in the merger process, many of them from consultants who want to demonstrate the right way forward. Worth a read is A. Mitchell and S. Hill's "The great mergers and acquisition gamble" (360°: *The Ashridge Journal*, Autumn, 2004, pp. 23–31) at http://www.ashridge.org.uk/Website/IC.nsf/wFARATT/The%20Great%20 Mergers%20and%20Acquisitions%20Gamble/$file/TheGreatMergersand AcquisitionsGamble.pdf. *Executive Insights* has a recent paper: D. Astorino, "Five roadblocks to successful acquisition integration" (*Executive Insights*, 24(2), 2009) at http://www.rhrinternational.com/Abstracts/V24N2-Successful-Acquisition-Integration.aspx, while a short video featuring "The top 5 mistakes to avoid" by Steven Ramirez, M&A Integration Consultant, can be found at http://www.bnet.com/2422-13722_23-186403.html.

Mergers nearly always trigger off numerous emotional reactions. A rather expensive book that focuses specifically on these – what causes them, their effects, how to manage them – including four in-depth case studies, is V. Kusstatscher and C. Cooper's *Managing Emotions in Mergers and Acquisitions* (Cheltenham: Edward Elgar, 2005).

The CIPD provides a good, freely available overview at http:// www.cipd.co.uk/subjects/corpstrtgy/mergers together with a useful factsheet on TUPE – the transfer of undertakings – at http://www.cipd.co.uk/ subjects/emplaw/tupe/tupe.htm?IsSrchRes=1. Wikipedia has a page that leads you off into many different aspects of M&A at http://en.wikipedia.org/wiki/ Mergers_and_acquisitions. And another no-charge resource giving down-to-earth guidance on M&A issues is provided by Business Link at http://www.businesslink.gov.uk/bdotg/action/detail?r.s=sc&r.l1=1074404796 &r.lc=en&r.l3=1074407579&r.l2=1074404799&type=RESOURCES &itemId=1074409301.

Challenge 14: Making major change

Change is required. There is a process of change
just as there is a process of manufacturing or for growing wheat.
How to change is the problem.
W. Edwards Deming

Overseeing change and helping people through it is a hallmark of leadership. This quality is the most common differentiator between managing and leading but the evidence for success is poor. Most leaders seem to rely on large-scale, top-down, rolled-out change programmes, yet all the evidence is that these are ineffective and tend quickly to run into the sands.

Ideas about how to change are changing. Kurt Lewin bequeathed us a durable three-stage model over 50 years ago:

$$\text{Present state} \longrightarrow \text{Transition} \longrightarrow \text{Desired state}$$

This depiction of a smooth linear passage from one state to another has long been disputed; Lewin's model assumes that we can bring about the desired future as a new state, *and* hold other things steady while we do this. In unpredictable conditions, where the ground shifts under our feet even as we start on the changes, such control is illusory. The insights of systems thinking and complexity theories suggest a different approach:

> *The only way to lead when you don't have control is you lead through the power of your relationships. You can deal with the unknown only if you have enormous levels of trust, and if you are working together and bringing out the best in people.* (Margaret Wheatley, 2002)

"Relational leadership" entails letting go and keeping faith in others. In the face of complexities, the best response may be openness about the uncertainties and trust in others to share the responsibility for choosing the next step. This is not about abdication – leaders always take responsibility for purpose and direction – but about a new leadership priority of engaging others in the decisions, planning and implementation of change.

Life cannot be directed

The old view of change assumes a mechanical universe operating to causal laws, where organisations are seen as machines with people who act rationally, in units that mesh together – all of which can be "re-engineered". Complexity science starts from a critique of this deterministic view. Organisations are viewed as living systems, that are both complex and adaptive:

- multiple connectedness between diverse parts (complex)

- the capacity to change and to learn from experience (adaptive)
- a whole set of people or agents (system).

Life cannot be directed because it organises itself, in patterns of relationships that we are able to learn. From this perspective, there are three useful principles to guide change:

1. *Minimum critical specification* – what is the minimum (not the maximum) that can be specified in advance for this change situation?
2. *Equifinality* means that there are different, but equally useful, paths to the same place. This is hard to grasp for many people because it contradicts so much expert one-best-way advice.
3. *Simple rules* to be used by everyone to guide their actions to enable widespread adaptive change. In a densely connected web of agents acting on their own local knowledge and sense of how things work, individual moves are not controlled by any centre but are influenced and co-ordinated on the basis of general rules, e.g.:

Five simple rules for modernising the UK's NHS:

- see things through patients' eyes
- find a better way of doing things
- look at the whole picture
- give frontline staff the time and the tools to tackle the problems
- take small steps as well as big leaps.
  (Fillingham in Attwood *et al.*, 2003, p. 24).

Simple rules can enable rapid learning, through stories of problems, mistakes and solutions transmitted from person to person and communicated organisation-wide.

A change architecture

A complex systems approach to major change will still include a detailed and well-planned programme, incorporating for example:

- *Diagnosis*: what kind of change – incremental, radical, crisis or transformational?
- *The business case for the change.*
- *Engaging sponsors and stakeholders.*
- *Mobilising and involving people* – as change agents in design and project teams, etc.
- Project management – *what are the targets, milestones and metrics, etc.?*
- Communications – *visions, benefits, targets, progress, etc.*
- Visible tangible leadership *from the top throughout.*
- Evaluation.

But it will do these things very differently – not top-down but in response to dialogue.

The aim of a change architecture is to create spaces for action and learning at local levels, and then for the sharing of this learning in a system-wide process of creating meaning and direction. It aims to allow for the emergence of good ideas and important learning on the way to implementing any change:

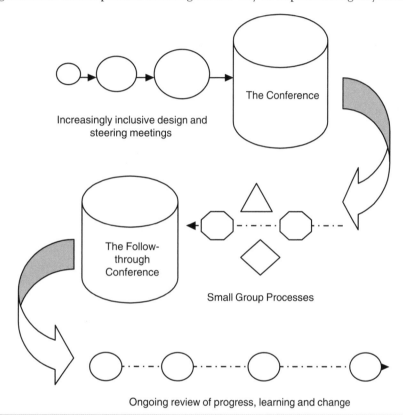

Figure C14.1 A change architecture. (Source: Attwood *et al.*, 2003.)

This sort of whole systems design requires the facilitation of leadership in three arenas, as shown in Figure C14.2.

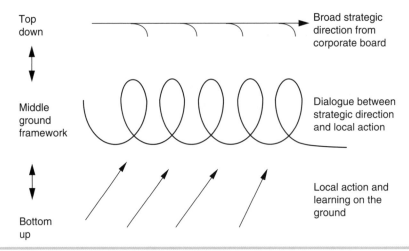

Figure C14.2 Three leadership arenas. (Source; Attwood *et al.*, 2003.)

Visible, committed leadership is needed at the strategic level. This first leadership arena provides a sense of purpose and direction and avoids interfering in the details of who does what and when. The second focus is on encouraging local leadership in all individuals, groups and project teams who can contribute to the desired change. All action and learning starts locally: people in different situations will have different views of how to proceed and what will work locally (the equifinality principle). "Middle ground frameworks" can then connect top-down and bottom-up at forums and meetings where all have a chance to give their views and tell their stories. Here, through listening, questioning and dialogue, people make sense of the big picture and plan their future action and learning.

How important is Challenge 14: *making major change* for you and your colleagues?

CHALLENGE CHECK: *Making major change*

■ Is this a challenge you are currently facing?   YES [   ]   NO [   ]

■ Is it one you have faced in the past?   YES [   ]   NO [   ]

■ Do you expect to face this more in the future?   YES [   ]   NO [   ]

Taking these answers into account, make the following judgements:

1. CAPABILITY: How good are you at understanding and dealing with this challenge?

    Not good   4   3   2   1   Very good

2. IMPORTANCE: How important do you think this is going to be for your future?

    Not important   1   2   3   4   Very important

Add the scores from Challenge 14: *making major change* to the summary in Part B.

References

Attwood, M., Pedler, M., Pritchard, S. and Wilkinson, D, (2003) *Leading Change: A Guide to Whole Systems Working.* Bristol: Policy Press.

Wheatley, M. (2002) *The Servant Leader from Hero to Host – An Interview with Margaret Wheatley.* Sutton: The Greenleaf Centre for Servant Leadership.

Further resources

There are numerous works and resources on organisation change, some of which take very different perspectives. For example, Chris Grey's *A Very Short, Fairly Interesting and Reasonably Cheap Book about Studying Organisations* (London: Sage, 2005) takes a critical approach in questioning many taken-for-granted assumptions about change, including the idea that we live in a period of "unprecedented" change (and that therefore we must continue to change things faster and faster).

Returning to the mainstream, there are several good overviews on "change management" such as Colin Carnall's *Managing Change in Organizations* (Harlow: Pearson Education, 5th edition, 2007) which is a comprehensive and practical approach offering a step-by-step guide to diagnosis and change methods for all organisations. Other tested and tried resources are D. Anderson, *Organization Development: The Process of Leading Organizational Change* (Thousand Oaks: Sage, 2010); B. Burnes, *Managing Change* (Harlow: Pearson Education, 5th edition, 2009); and L. Holbeche, *Understanding Change: Theory, Implementation and Success* (Oxford: Butterworth-Heinemann, 2006).

More practical and tool-oriented works include E. Cameron and M. Green, *Making Sense of Change Management: A Complete Guide to the Models, Tools and Techniques of Organizational Change* (London: Kogan Page, 2nd edition, 2009), D. Cohen, *The Heart of Change Field Guide* (Boston: Harvard Business School Press, 2005), which is a sequel to J. Kotter and D. Cohen, *The Heart of Change: Real-Life Stories of How People Change Their Organizations* (Boston: Harvard Business School Press, 2002); and L. Anderson and D. Anderson, *The Change Leader's Roadmap: How to Navigate your Organization's Transformation* (San Francisco: Jossey-Bass/Pfeiffer, 2001).

For more dialogic and participative change strategies try Weisbord and Janoff's *Don't Just Do Something, Stand There!: Ten Principles for Leading Meetings That Matter* (San Francisco: Berret-Koehler, 2007); and also by Weisbord, *Productive Workplaces Revisited: Dignity, Meaning, and Community in the 21st Century* (San Francisco: Jossey-Bass, 2nd edition, 2004); and *Future Search: an Action Guide to Finding Common Ground in Organizations and Communities* (San Francisco: Berret-Koehler, 2nd edition, 2000). "Whole systems working" is the term used in Attwood, Pedler, Pritchard and Wilkinson in *Leading Change: A Guide to Whole Systems Working* (Bristol: Policy Press, 2003) and also by Michael Fullan in *All Systems Go: The Change Imperative for Whole System Reform* (London: Sage, 2010). Patricia Shaw takes a dialogical approach to complexity and change in *Changing Conversations in Organizations: A Complexity Approach to Change* (London: Routledge, 2002).

Challenge 15: _____

(Write in your own here)

Here are some questions to help you describe this challenge:

■ How would you describe this challenge?
■ What are its key aspects?
■ How does it impact on you?
■ Can you think of any sources of help and follow-up?

How important is this Challenge 15: _____ for you and your colleagues?

CHALLENGE CHECK: ____

■ Is this a challenge you are currently facing?   YES [ ]   NO [ ]

■ Is it one you have faced in the past?   YES [ ]   NO [ ]

■ Do you expect to face this more in the future?   YES [ ]   NO [ ]

Taking these answers into account, make the following judgements:

1. CAPABILITY: How good are you at understanding and dealing with this challenge?

   Not good   4   3   2   1   Very good

2. IMPORTANCE: How important do you think this is going to be for your future?

   Not important   1   2   3   4   Very important

Add the scores from your Challenge 15: _____ to the summary in Part B.

Part B: Getting started on your leadership challenges

The first step is to prioritise your leadership challenges. Then you can move on to the following section: *taking the lead on your challenge*.

Prioritising your leadership challenges

Now that you have worked through the *key challenges* of leadership, transfer your ratings from each challenge check into Table 2.1 below.

Put your ratings of capability and importance for each of the challenges into columns 1 and 2 of Table 2.1 and then multiply them together to give an overall priority ranking in column 3.

Table 2.1 Your priority leadership challenges

Challenges	Capability Your rating on how good you are with each one: from 4 to 1	Importance Your rating on how important each one will be: from 1 to 4	Priority Your priority for development: multiply columns 1 and 2
1. Finding direction and strategy			
2. Creating a learning organisation			
3. New organisational structures			
4. Powerful teams			
5. Crafting cultures of innovation			
6. Fostering diversity and inclusion			
7. Promoting partnerships			
8. Improving work processes			
9. Streamlining			
10. Encouraging social responsibility			
11. Mobilising knowledge			
12. Leading in networks			
13. Managing mergers			
14. Making major change			
15.			

A note on the scoring in Table 2.1

The numbers for capability and importance in the challenge checks run in opposite directions; that is, a "4" for capability means that you are *not* good at this, whereas a "4" for importance means that this challenge is *very* important.

The logic behind this is that it is the combination of your capability and the importance of the challenge that creates the priority; so, supposing you have a very important challenge, about which you have low capability, this would create the highest possible score, i.e. $4 \times 4 = 16$.

If, on the other hand, you rate a challenge as less important (say as 1 or 2), then however good you are at it, this combination will produce a lower score and priority.

Running the numbers in different directions creates a wider spread of scores than would otherwise be the case. Without this device, the scores for capability and importance might tend to cancel each other out.

Weighing up your priority rankings

Your high priority scores indicate the challenges to which you need to pay most attention. However, the scores in Table 2.1 are just indicators, and as with any metric, they should be tested against common sense. Ask yourself:

- Does this priority ranking make sense to me?
- Would my mentor or boss agree with it?
- Do my colleagues think like me on this?

If the answer to any of these questions is "no", then think again. Start by talking to other people to check their perceptions of the situation.

Depending on your priorities, there are clues and references in each of the challenge descriptions above to help you decide which chapters to dig into next. All seven of the chapters in the next part of this book offer ideas, activities and suggestions for developing your leadership practices to tackle such challenges. Choose your top priorities for development and follow the leads to useful action and learning.

Taking the lead on your challenge

This last part of the chapter offers an action learning process that can be applied to any challenge. However difficult and daunting your situation, action learning can help. This approach was devised by Reg Revans to help leaders and managers to resolve their tough challenges by working together. His very pragmatic philosophy stresses both action, as a means of learning, and learning, as the key to more effective action.

Tackling demanding challenges requires different qualities and skills from the rational tools of managing. These include asking questions and not rushing to solutions, taking considered and deliberate risks and learning from this. Beyond individual skills, this work requires resourceful people to engage together in processes of action, learning, exchange and collaboration.

You can tackle this process on your own, working through step-by-step on paper or in your head; but it is much better done in a small group, with the steps being done "live" in speech and action.

With your challenge in mind, follow steps 1–5 below:

- define the challenge
- explore the challenge
- create options for action
- take action
- reflect and learn from the experience.

Step 1: define the challenge

First, describe and write down the challenge or situation facing you and your colleagues, in two or three sentences. Don't go on too long – summarise it. Here's an example:

> *We are drifting. We seem to be a bit lost. For several years now we have been doing OK, but what we are doing no longer works. We should be doing something different but what?*

Perfect, we get the picture. This is a variety of Challenge 1, *Finding direction and strategy.*

Now, *rephrase* your description of the challenge to start with the words: "How can we …". For example:

> *How can we … do something different from what we have been doing? What we have been doing has served us well for the last few years, but is now beginning to fail. How can we start to do things differently?*

Can you see the differences in the two statements? The first is a bit helpless, even despairing; the second is more inquiring, and has a different tone. The plaintive wail of *We should be doing something different but what?* becomes a more hopeful and future-oriented *How can we start to do things differently?*

This question is more positive because it contains the seeds of action and learning. We may not know what to do about the situation as it stands, but instead of being left in a state of helplessness, this question suggests that there are possibilities and options for action.

Step 2: explore the challenge

Once you have an agreed description and definition of your challenge, you are ready to open it up and explore it. Revans proposes six fundamental questions for action learning (1998, pp. 33–41), three of them for the exploratory or *diagnostic* phase:

1. What are we (this group, or organisation that we are now helping) really trying to do?
2. What is stopping us from doing it?
3. What can we do about it?

These fundamental questions are to be pondered and discussed, elaborated and debated using all the sources of information and intelligence that can be found, until the challenge has been thoroughly explored and analysed to the satisfaction of the group. *(As noted above, although you can tackle this process on your own, the limits of one intelligence and one perspective become rather obvious in this questioning and searching process.)*

Revans' three diagnostic questions can be developed in many ways. Here are some additional questions for the diagnostic process:

- Can you tell us the story as it happened?
- What is the biggest difficulty or problem?
- Can you explain that further?
- What don't you know about the situation?
- How do you feel about what is going on?
- What questions does that raise?
- How do other people in the situation – colleagues, friends, partner, boss, etc. feel about this?
- What have you learned from that?
- What could you do differently?
- What do you want other people to do differently?
- What judgements are we making about the other person and/or the situation?
- How do you/we know this?

There are many such questions and this exploration may take more than one meeting and even weeks or months depending on the nature of the challenge. At the close of any session, people can agree actions to be taken to bring more learning and intelligence back to future meetings.

Step 3: create options for action

You can't resolve a challenge by talking about it, however seductive that may be (and it is!) Now create some options for action based on your current understanding of the challenge. What are the options for action now?

Of course, your understanding of the challenge is still incomplete, so there is some risk here. But you will not learn or progress more without action. What steps, as small as you like, could you take now? List all the possibilities.

Revans has three more fundamental questions that might help here; he called these the *therapeutic* questions:

4. Who *knows* (understands) about the problem being tackled?
5. Who *cares* (genuinely wants something done) about the problem?
6. Who *can* (has enough power to) get something useful done about it?

These questions are about finding the help that will be needed for the resolution of any tough challenge. If the challenge was easily resolved from our own resources, then we would have done it by now. For the real challenges we will need help from various allies, especially in terms of knowledge, commitment and power. Some allies will be found near at hand, perhaps among your co-leaders and in known networks, but others may take more courage and initiative to find.

At a management conference in a specialist equipment company, Jack spoke about his ambition to wean a big potential customer away from a rival group. The CEO, who had dropped in for lunch, said "Is there any way that I can help you with that?" but Jack looked embarrassed and a bit confused by this response. Would he take up the offer and go to see the CEO?

One thing is for certain: Jack would be more likely to take this step if he was in a group of colleagues who knew about his ambitions, who were set up to support (and to challenge) him, and who wanted to see him succeed. In this set of circumstances, a good group would make sure he made the appointment *and* brought back home the story of this encounter and its results. This is action learning at work.

Here are some more questions you can use in this preparing for action phase:

■ What would make the situation better?
■ What result do you/we want?
■ What is the best possible outcome from this situation?
■ How would someone you most admire deal with this situation?
■ What new knowledge or understanding do we need?
■ Where can we find it?
■ Who are our allies in this situation?
■ Who else wants to see this challenge dealt with?

■ What do we need from them?

■ What do you most need from us now?

■ How can we help you move forwards on this issue?

■ What is the most extreme measure you could take?

■ Can we think of three options for action?

■ What are the pros and cons of each of these options?

■ What first steps are you/we going to take before our next meeting?

Step 4: take action

Go and do this action, carefully observing yourself, others and the situation so that you can bring back the story of your experience to the next meeting.

Learning comes first from the action, second from the observation of the experience of action (what actually happened?), and thirdly from reflection on the experience. In the telling of these accounts, and in the reflection and the discussion that follow, are the clues to learning about the challenge and how it might be better tackled.

So take courage and act. It helps to know that an action does not have to be "successful" for it to result in learning; any action you take will produce experience that can be learned from.

Step 5: reflect and learn from the experience

In the cycle of action learning, the penny often drops in the process of hearing someone talk about what they have done, what happened and what sense they made of it.

Sometimes this comes in the form of a slow dawning, perhaps in the realisation that this group knows more about this situation than anyone else in the business; sometimes it suddenly becomes clear that there are other people who are also concerned about this issue; sometimes perceptions can alter radically, as when a meeting with an important person reveals them not as remote authorities, but women or men willing to put their influence and resources behind a good idea.

Spending time listening as people tell their stories of their actions and experiences is an investment in learning. We learn most when we test our ideas in action, but we also learn from listening to others and their experiences of action: what they did, how they did it, what they make of it. As we listen, we reflect on the differences and similarities, on our own ways of doing things – and on the alternatives.

Here are some questions for reflection and learning:

■ What actions did you take following the last meeting?

■ Did it go as planned?

■ What are your reflections on the actions and their effectiveness?

- If your actions were successful – why?
- If your actions were not successful – why?
- What could you have done differently?
- How did you/do you feel about the outcomes?
- What have you learned about leadership?
- What have others learned about leadership from this story?
- What do you want from the group on this occasion?
- Is there anything we could do that would make this group work more effectively for you?
- What actions do you plan to take before the next meeting?

Through this sort of reflection and learning we can come to take more effective actions.

You can get further guidance and help from Mike Pedler's *Action Learning for Managers* (Aldershot: Gower, 2008) and also from *DIY Handbook for Action Learners* (from Mandy Chivers at Mersey Care NHS Trust www.merseycare.nhs.uk).

Reference

Revans, R.W. (1998) *ABC of Action Learning*. London: Lemos & Crane.

The context of leadership

3

What do you see when you look at this picture?

In the picture above, the "candlestick" draws the eye, but look again at what shapes the candlestick. According to "Gestalt" psychologists, "the need organises the field"; that is: what we notice depends on what we need to notice. To a great extent, what we see or perceive, is what we want to see or construct.

Figure and ground

The candlestick can represent the leader, or a particular action or perhaps a change initiative in an organisation. Each of these is a *figure* and a focal point so that we may not notice what else characterises the situation. Yet, the field or *ground* around each figure is what shapes it, defines it and gives it meaning. Becoming aware of this shaping territory is to become aware of the context.

The challenges of leadership (Chapter 2) are the figures that first grab our attention; in this chapter we look at what grounds these challenges. In Chapter 1 we defined *context* as "the on-site conditions found in the challenge situation" and noted that this aspect is neglected in most leadership development programmes. Why is this so?

One explanation is that we live in times more influenced by the psychological than the sociological; that we are inspired more by individuals rather than by collective ideals. In the organisational world we tend to elevate personalities and make celebrities of our leaders. Consequently, most models of leadership are personality based, suggesting that the possession of personal characteristics such as vision, integrity, will or emotional intelligence is enough to guarantee success.

Context matters

Try this *thought experiment*:

> *Think of an admired manager or leader in your organisation. Think about why this person is admired and valued ... perhaps because of their achievements ... their track record? Think of how they are, how they behave. Perhaps there are particular stories about this person that resonate with you? Think about how you would describe this person ... what words would you use?*
>
> *Now think about the context and circumstances surrounding this person's success. What has shaped and supported them? How did they get started? Who else was involved? Under what conditions did they work? What were the forces at work – social, political, economic, technological and so on? Were they – and are they – in tune with the times?*

Long-term leadership success does not come about through force of personality or character alone. Sensitivity to context is vital in understanding what works and what doesn't. The leadership context includes the legacies of past leadership actions, previous and present organisational arrangements, patterns and networks of relationships and a host of other technological, social, cultural and political influences. To illustrate how these factors impact on any initiative, let's take the challenge of bringing about change – one of the most looked for requirements of leadership. Research from the UK's National Health Service shows that major change initiatives are only likely to succeed where the context is receptive.

Receptive and non-receptive contexts for change in the NHS

In their study in the UK National Health Service, Pettigrew, Ferlie and McKie (1992, pp. 267–299) suggest that organisational change is more likely to succeed in some contexts rather than others. These researchers found that there were eight contextual factors that supported organisational change in the health organisations that they studied. These were:

1. Quality and coherence of policy.
2. Availability and continuity in the key people leading the change.

3. Intensity of long-term environmental pressures, e.g. financial.
4. Supportive organisational culture, e.g. flexible working, open to new ideas, etc.
5. Effective relationships and mutual understanding between managers and clinicians.
6. Cooperative inter-organisational networks that support trading, boundary crossing and education.
7. Simplicity and clarity of goals and priorities.
8. Strategic fit between local change agenda and wider organisational environment.

These factors are specific to a particular service at a particular time and not an all-purpose shopping list; nevertheless this provide a useful model for thinking about the impact of any context.

Recent theories of work and action pay particular attention to the interaction between human beings and the non-human "actors" in the situation. Work involves both the people and the tools they use; accountants work with computer systems that keep running even when their human operatives are not there. The technologies available in any given situation partly determine what can and cannot be done in those particular circumstances. In his analysis of the D-Day landings in June 1944, Grint describes the crucial role of the tanks, landing craft and other specially designed items of kit as part of the leadership "system": "That missile or tank may be illegitimate in the eyes of the law, it may even be heading your way by accident, but it does have an uncanny ability to persuade most people to follow its lead and move" (2005, pp. 47–64; 51).

Context matters, it affects us in ways of which we are only partially aware. It impacts not only on what we do, but on how we are and how we present ourselves, including the language, symbols and metaphors we use. We sometimes feel we are not quite getting it right, but ... why?

Contextual intelligence ...

Robert Sternberg (1985) was among the first to talk about "contextual intelligence" and the importance of selecting from, adapting to and shaping the context. He suggests that contextual intelligence explains why some people, who score poorly on IQ tests, are nevertheless very *street smart*.

This means having a highly developed practical ability to understand what needs to be done in a specific setting and then to do it. There are two aspects to this:

- *Becoming aware.* Those seeking to influence events need to be aware of any circumstances or conditions that affect these events. To be relevant to the challenges of the time, any leadership effort must be attuned to the context. In this sense of *becoming aware*, context appears as a set of outside forces that impact us and from which we need to select the relevant intelligence.
- *Being part.* But when we set out to adapt to, and to influence the context, we also become part of it ourselves. This second aspect is more subtle and involves understanding that context is not something outside of persons and their actions, but actually "constitutive" of them, so that these various elements – persons, action and contexts – can be seen as parts of the same whole.

Seeing yourself as a part of the context can have a powerful effect on how you act. For example, when you see yourself as but one part of the context, rather than as a heroic leader determining events, it is easier to be aware of who else is acting in the situation. As Drath and Palus (1994, p. 5) put it:

> ... *you can think about leadership as a process in which everyone in a community is engaged. This is a way of viewing leadership as part of a context.*

And distributed leadership:

> *Being part of the context links naturally with the idea of distributed leadership, where many or of all the people involved in the situation are taking part. It seems obvious that it is easier to understand the ground or context of any leadership challenge when there are more people on the job. It's a bit like the pub quiz: you're a whiz on films and history, but clueless about music and politics. Because several heads are usually better than one, we often suggest in this book that you get together with your colleagues to tackle particular challenges, and this is especially so when it comes to understanding and "reading" the context.*

The idea of distributed or collective leadership is often misunderstood. A call for more rather than less people to get involved, does *not* mean that we can dispense with the positional leaders who can get so much attention. The quality of people in positions of "Headship" is of crucial importance, not least because of the impact they have on everyone else. The problem comes when we put everything on to this one person (and when that person takes everything on themselves); then as Gerard Egan has said: "If you only have one leader, you are very short on leadership."

In fluid and changing situations, leadership may need to move around. Who knows from where the right people for the times and conditions will emerge? Are you stuck with one person for all seasons, or does your organisation have strength in depth and the flexibility to harness all this talent?

Developing your contextual intelligence

No-one will enjoy long-term success in leadership without a sensitivity to context, without becoming what Mayo and Nohria (2005, p. 359) call a "first-class noticer". We are not born with "contextual intelligence", but it can be developed and fostered.

Many years ago in a pub in a small Derbyshire village, I met an old man who said he could not remember when he had last been to town. By town I assumed that he meant Sheffield, some 12 miles away, but he was thinking of Bakewell – just three miles away.

Because of the growth of travel and communications that have widened horizons and made many of us aware of so many different "worlds", people like him are harder to find these days, at least in the richer parts of the world. Yet positional leaders can often seem shockingly parochial; out of touch with how ordinary people live, and unaware of what goes on beyond the narrow confines of the city, often apparently blind to the critical issues of the wider society.

What is it that you need to notice to develop your contextual intelligence? Here are some starters:

- An interest in and appreciation of history – an ability to learn from the past helps put present challenges in context.
- Keeping abreast of developments – social, political, legal, international, technological, scientific.
- Getting out and about – visiting other organisations and places to learn how things are changing and developing.
- Networking with other employees, customers, clients, partners and competitors.
- Engaging in future thinking – by going to conferences or taking part in activities such as future searching and scenario planning which promote thinking that better prepares us for possible futures, opportunities and challenges.

Below is an activity to enhance your contextual intelligence and to help make you a first-class noticer. Like many of the activities in this book, you can do it alone or in a group of people. If you work through this with some colleagues, you are likely to get a richer picture than if you do it alone. But even if you only ever give this 10 or 20 minutes thought on your own, it will still widen your perspective and deepen your awareness of context. Use it from time to time to help you put challenges in context.

Picturing the context

To do this activity, first choose a current challenge on which to focus: what is it that you are trying to do? Pick a particular challenge that you are facing, and test your ideas for action by questioning them with all the contextual intelligence you can muster.

A context can be thought of as having several layers or rings, from local to global. Starting from our own local life context, we can extend the gaze to social, community and organisational settings, and then still wider to the global society and epoch in which we live.

- Personal: your life context.
- Organisational/community context.
- Gobal (era): historical, economic, social, political, technological, cultural, ecological and environmental influences.

We suggest working with a large sheet of paper (A3 or flip-chart size) or perhaps a whiteboard. Draw three pictures as a series of widening circles or concentric rings as in the illustrations below; start with the personal and work outwards to the global.

For each of the three layers, we have provided eight contextual factors that might affect the challenge you have in mind. Add in your own thoughts on the issues and how important they are. If you are working in a group, you could divide into three at this point and each take one aspect of the context to work on and to bring back to the whole group.

Remember: this is not about right answers, but a quick scan of the horizon – what's there that I should take into account? What in particular do I need to know more about? That sort of thing.

1. Personal context: your life

First, think about the personal context in which you do things. Think about the important aspects of your life that influence what you do.

Draw your own picture, like the example in Figure 3.1, to assemble these important qualities, relationships, aspirations and possibilities. Make sure you include the things that are most important to you.

Note: As there are two further contextual layers to come, remember to put your first picture in the middle of the page or whiteboard with plenty of space around it.

Now ask yourself three questions about each of these important areas of your life:

- What am I trying to do with this aspect of my life?
- What's getting in the way of I what I want at this time?
- What are the opportunities here to do something about this?

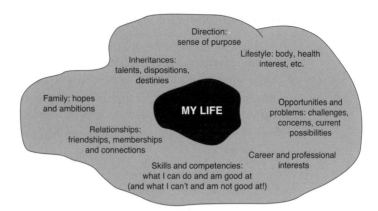

Figure 3.1 **Life context**

Make some notes about your answers. Use your picture to write on or make a list as in Table 3.1 below.

Table 3.1 Notes about my life context

Personal context: my life	Notes	Impact: H/M/L (high to low)
Inheritances: talents, dispositions, destinies		
Skills and competencies		
Family: hopes and ambitions		
Relationships: friendships, memberships and connections		
Career and professional interests		
Direction: sense of purpose		
Lifestyle: body, health, interests, etc.		
Opportunities and problems: challenges, concerns, current possibilities		
? (Add your own)		
?		

2. Organisational and community context

Now, think about your organisation and the communities in which you live and work: residential and professional. How do these influence what you can do? And what are the opportunities here to extend your influence?

Draw another layer to the picture you drew in Figure 3.1, to assemble these important qualities, relationships, aspirations and possibilities. Make sure you include the things that are most important to you.

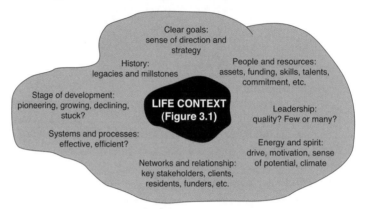

Figure 3.2 **Organisational and community context**

Again ask yourself these three questions about each of the important areas of your organisational and community context:

- How are we doing in this aspect of our corporate/community life?
- What are the prospects and likely future events in this area?
- How does this aspect affect what I/we want to do next?

Make some notes about your answers. Either put notes on the picture or make a list as in Table 3.2 below.

Table 3.2 Notes about my organisational and community context

Organisational and community context	Notes	Impact: H/M/L (High to Low)
Clear goals: sense of direction and strategy		
History: legacies and millstones		
People and resources: assets, funding, skills, talents, commitment, etc.		
Leadership: quality? Few or many?		
Networks and relationship: with key stakeholders, clients, residents, funders, etc.		
Systems and processes: effective, efficient?		
Energy and spirit: drive, motivation, sense of potential, climate		
Stage of development: pioneering, growing, declining, stuck?		
? (Add your own)		
?		

3. The global context

Now, think more widely about the world and the era we are in. What are the national, international, global and environmental influences that impact on your world?

Draw a third layer to the picture as in Figure 3.3, and consider some of the wider forces that are having an impact on what you want to do – in your life, in your organisation and in the communities to which you belong.

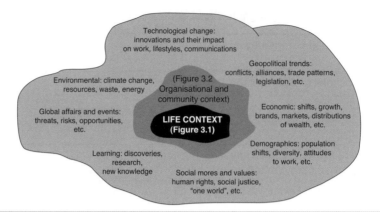

Figure 3.3 The global context

The three questions for the global context items are:

■ What's coming up in this area that bears on the current challenge?
■ What is there here that could help us adapt our response to this challenge?
■ What do we need to know more about?

Make some notes about your answers. Put notes on the picture or in Table 3.3 below.

Table 3.3 Notes about the global context

Global context	Notes	Impact: H/M/L
Geopolitical trends: conflicts, alliances, trade patterns, legislation, etc.		
Economic: shifts, growth, brands, markets, distributions of wealth, etc.		
Technological change: innovations and their impact on work, lifestyles, communications		
Environmental: climate change, resources, waste, energy		
Global affairs and events: threats, risks, opportunities, etc.		
Learning: discoveries, research, new knowledge		
Social mores and values: human rights, social justice, "one world", etc.		

cont'd

Table 3.3 Notes about the global context (*continued*)

Global context	Notes	Impact: H/M/L
Demographics: population shifts, diversity, attitudes to work, etc.		
? (Add your own)		
?		

Intuition and analysis

Contextual intelligence may be akin to intuition. Germany's "Iron Chancellor", Otto von Bismarck, placed great store by intuition and is alleged to have attributed his success to "the ability to intuit God's movements in history and seize the hem of his garment as he sweeps by".

The idea of this activity is not to engage in a too complex or detailed analysis, but to sharpen your contextual intelligence via a quick sensing or intuitive "ready reckoner". If you want to do more contextual analysis, there is an industry out there specialising in tools such as SWOT and PESTLE (look them up on the net) which appeared over 40 years ago and have been in continuous use since.

Conclusion

Why do some initiatives work while others, equally promising, fail? Why is a person's track record in one organisation such a misleading guide to their future performance in a different setting?

> *These leaders are not born. They emerge when organisations face new problems and complexities that cannot be solved by unguided evolution.*
>
> (Bennis and Nanus 1997, p. 17)

Guided evolution demands an understanding of the contexts in which we operate. There are an infinite variety of contexts and no right way to lead – except in the here and now – in this unique situation. Our chances of getting it right depend heavily on how good we are at noticing what's going on around us, on how sharp is our contextual intelligence.

References

Bennis, W. and Nanus, B. (1997) *Leaders: The Strategies for Taking Charge*. New York: Harper & Row.

Drath, W.H. and Palus, C.J. (1994) *Making Common Sense: Leadership as Meaning Making in a Community of Practice*. Greensboro, N. Carolina: Centre for Creative Leadership.

Grint, K. (2005) *Leadership: Limits & Possibilities*. Basingstoke: Palgrave/Macmillan.

Mayo, A.J. and Nohria, N. (2005) *In Their Time: The Greatest Business Leaders of the Twentieth Century*. Boston: Harvard Business School Press.

Pettigrew, A., Ferlie, E. and McKie, L. (1992) *Shaping Strategic Change*. London: Sage.

Sternberg, R.J. (1985) *Beyond IQ: A Triarchic Theory of Intelligence*. Cambridge: Cambridge University Press.

The characteristics of leadership

Leadership is about character.
Bennis and Nanus

The third domain of the "three Cs" model refers to the human qualities, attributes, abilities, competencies, skills, know-how and characteristics that contribute to leadership. Personal qualities and the "deployment of self" (Bennis and Nanus, 1997, p. 175) are a vital aspect of leadership, and the recognition of this truth has sparked a long quest for the characteristics, behaviours or competencies that signal a leader. From the trait psychologists of the 1950s to the competency modellers of the twenty-first century, this search continues to attract great human attention and energy.

Despite these efforts, no-one has as yet succeeded in compiling a list of characteristics that defines leadership. It's a bit like the encounter with the elephant:

> *In the ancient Indian story, six blind men encounter an elephant for the first time. The first touches the elephant's side and says "How smooth! The elephant is like a wall". A second man puts out his hand and touches the elephant's leg and says "How tall! The elephant is like a tree". A third man touches the elephant's trunk and says "How round! The elephant is like a snake". The fourth touches the elephant's tusk and says "How sharp! The elephant is like a spear". The fifth man touches the elephant's ear and says "How wide! The elephant is like a fan". The sixth man approaches and feels the elephant's tail: "How long! The elephant is like a rope". As they fall to arguing over who is right, a wise man, drawn by the commotion, says: "The elephant is big, each touched only one part. You must put all of them together to find the elephant."*

This story is told in different ways in different traditions in India, but the wise man or the Rajah always gets the last word by pointing out that the problem in describing the elephant is how the characteristics come together. In this chapter, we look at the recent history of attempts to define leadership in terms of characteristics and competencies and suggest a different way of looking at the contribution that human character can make to leadership.

The *Characteristic* domain is important, not just because "Leadership is about character" but because it inspires most leadership development programmes. Most large and many smaller organisations now have such programmes with global annual expenditure estimated at $37bn and perhaps £50m in the UK alone (Mabey and Ramirez, 2004; Burgoyne, Mackness and Williams, 2009). Lists of characteristics or competencies lend themselves easily to teaching, and allied to a training tradition that focuses on individual knowledge and skills, this has the effect of overemphasising individual character at the expense of *Challenges* or *Context*. This encourages an individualistic and universal, one-size-fits-all, approach to leadership. And even if leadership development based on competency models works well for personal development, does this produce leadership?

Character matters

The idea of leadership as an aspect of character is so common that it crops up in almost every part of our lives. We even attribute it to animals.

The Icelandic leader-sheep

The Icelandic sheep (*Íslenska sauðkindin*) are descended from stock brought in by the Vikings 1100–1200 years ago. In Iceland, it was necessary to graze sheep in winter and as a result, a small population of leader-sheep (*forystufé*) evolved to help the farmers manage the flocks. Most leader-sheep are coloured and horned – even four-horned in a few cases. They have slender bodies with long legs and are lighter than other sheep. They are graceful and prominent in the flock, with alertness in the eyes, normally going first out of the sheep-house, looking around in all directions, watching to see if there are dangers in sight and then walking in front of the flock when driven to or from pasture. They may even guard the flock against predators. There are many stories on record about their ability to sense or forecast changes in the weather, or refusing to leave the sheep-house before a major snowstorm. (Adapted from Wikipedia)

Because leadership is such a common notion, we all have our own opinions about it. What is the template against which you judge the quality of leadership? Try the following activity.

Activity 4.1: Leadership Characteristics

Think about your personal view of leadership and write down 10 words or short phrases that describe what leadership means to you:

_____ _____

_____ _____

_____ _____

_____ _____

_____

Now draw up a list of five people that you consider to be leaders:

1. _____

2. _____

3. _____

4. _____

5. _____

Now look back at your two lists. What do they have in common? And in what ways do they differ?

Most importantly, do all the people in the second list have all the qualities that you have put down in your template for what leadership means to you?

If leadership in humans were as easy to spot as in Icelandic sheep, it is a fair bet that all the people on your second list would be long legged, graceful and protective, etc. In other words, that they would share certain human characteristics that mark them out from the flock.

However, we suspect that the answer to this is "No". A list of 10 desirable characteristics is quite long. It probably comes from experiences with different people and from different situations – so perhaps most people will have some, but not all, of the qualities you would like to see? Additionally, some of those in the second list might have other qualities that would be useful in challenging situations. What of these?

Human leadership characteristics

Modern leadership research starts in the USA after the Second World War, much of it funded by the military or the government, alarmed by the apparent commitment engendered via communist or Marxist ideas both abroad and in trades unions and political parties at home. From the late 1940s researchers were looking for personality characteristics to differentiate "leaders" from "followers". The basic idea was that anyone who had these traits would be able to lead in any situation. In an era of reconstruction and new hope, leaders were needed in all walks of life, military, industrial and civic. If these qualities could be defined, leaders could then be selected for them and then trained in them.

The work of some of those twentieth century researchers still repays reading, but no-one came up with an agreed or definitive list. Despite what we have learned since that time, this way of thinking about leadership persists to this day. Most popular books on leadership will feature lists like the one you created above. We seem never to tire of creating lists of the qualities, behaviours, skills or competencies that we see as essential to effective leadership. Here is an example from a well-respected researcher, John Gardner:

- *Physical vitality and stamina.*
- *Intelligence and action-oriented judgement.*
- *Eagerness to accept responsibility.*
- *Task competence.*
- *Understanding of followers and their needs.*
- *Skill in dealing with people.*

- *Need for achievement.*
- *Capacity to motivate people.*
- *Courage and resolution.*
- *Trustworthiness.*
- *Decisiveness.*
- *Self-confidence.*
- *Assertiveness.*
- *Adaptability/flexibility.*

(Gardner, 1989)

Not a bad list. And funnily enough, it fits the Icelandic leader-sheep quite well too.

But there are all sorts of problems with such lists and with this sort of way of thinking about leadership. These are composite or "identikit" lists, drawn from many different examples, but describing no single human being. To expect to find them in individuals is to mistake the map for the actual territory. Secondly, and as noted in the last chapter, more recent research stresses the importance of context in defining what leadership qualities might be useful; leadership is more situational than formerly thought. A third criticism is that lists like Gardner's are a mixture of all sorts of things: skills and behaviours that might be learned, attitudes that might be acquired, but also other motivations and qualities such as physical vitality and need for achievement, that may be more to do with temperament or inheritance.

This third criticism provides a route out of the impasse for researchers: if it is now clear that there is no single set of leadership characteristics for all situations, perhaps there is a list of more behavioural requirements, or *competencies*, that define all leaders?

The competencies approach

Competence can be defined simply as the ability and willingness to perform a task. This emphasis on action and performance makes competency analysis different in principle from job analysis, which seeks to specify the "input" measures of knowledge, skills and attitudes to perform a task. Competency analyses are therefore about the "output" side and seek to combine all these factors and more in one measure of job performance. The aim is to isolate the dimensions of action that underlie job performance and then to specify the critical competencies that cause or predict superior performance.

The output focus of the competency approach is an advance on earlier thinking on leadership qualities. The difference is seen in the use of measures such as 360° feedback processes where colleagues provide feedback about actual job performance. As a result, the competency approach to leadership has become the norm for many large organisations who base their development programmes on models of what they see as the desirable qualities of managers and leaders. The NHS leadership competencies model is one example:

NHS leadership competency framework

There are 15 qualities within the framework covering a range of personal, cognitive and social competencies. They are arranged in three clusters.

Setting direction

- Broad scanning.
- Political astuteness.
- Intellectual flexibility.
- Drive for results.
- Seizing the future.

Delivering the service

- Leading people through change.
- Holding to account.
- Empowering others.
- Collaborative working.
- Effective and strategic influencing.

Personal qualities

- Self-belief.
- Self-awareness.
- Self-management.
- Drive for improvement.
- Personal integrity.

(Source breakingthrough@lead.institute.nhs.uk)

However, like the lists of leadership characteristics before them, there are a number of problems with models like this. The origins of the competency approach can be traced back to theories of psychological needs and many of the items on the NHS list refer to attitudes, motivations or inclinations to life as much as to abilities or capabilities. How would you recognise "Seizing the future" for example? How do you achieve competence in it? And does this quality or inclination mark out actually superior leadership performance?

Burgoyne (1989) has proposed eight challenges to the competency approach, which include the assumption that successful performance is divisible and can be broken down into component parts. Competency frameworks do not vary by context and assume universal applicability, to all people, in all situations. Yet if leadership is essentially unscripted, and defined as it is done in particular situations, how can it be pre-specified? Competency models largely emphasise the technical aspects of work and leave out the moral and ethical considerations; "leading people through change" for example, with no mention of who benefits or not from this change. Perhaps most importantly for this book, the focus of leadership competency models remains on the individual and not on the much bigger prize of finding ways to foster collective "competence" or performance.

Despite good intentions to be output focused, competency frameworks, once formulated and enshrined in selection and Assessment Centre processes, tend to become indistinguishable from other input measures. Competency models perpetuate the idea that leadership can be defined as a set of personal qualities, and in continuing this individualistic focus, are the latest incarnation of a line running from "Great Man" theory. If the message from leadership characteristics theory was "You've either got it or not", the message from the competencies approach is "Demonstrate these or else".

An infinite variety?

It seems unlikely that any list of characteristics or competencies, however long, can ever capture the range of qualities that human beings can bring to challenging situations. In their research, Bennis and Nanus found 850 different definitions of leadership in the literature and concluded from a study of 90 public and private sector leaders, that:

> There seemed to be no obvious patterns for their success. They were right brained, left brained, tall and short, thin and fat, articulate and inarticulate, assertive and retiring, dressed for success and dressed for failure, participative and autocratic. There were more variations than themes. Even their managerial styles were restlessly different. (1997, p. 24)

Leadership in human beings comes in all guises; people who show leadership are all shapes and sizes, and display the full range of human characteristics. And yet character really does matter. When leadership happens, those who display it stand out and demonstrate outstanding abilities.

Think about a recent situation where you, or someone else, displayed leadership qualities.

Activity 4.2: The Qualities of Leadership

1   Briefly describe the event or situation:

_____

_____

_____

_____

_____

2   What did you do?

■

■

■

■

■

3   Who else was involved and what did they do?

■

■

■

■

4   What qualities did you observe in people, including yourself, that made a positive contribution to leadership?

■

■

■

■

5   What qualities did you observe that had a negative impact on the situation?

■

■

■

■

It is interesting that we often recognise leadership qualities by their absence. Here are two teachers talking about their heads (from Aspinwall, 1998, pp. 132–133):

> *He is very pleasant, very personable, very easy to talk to. It really feels like he listens. But in a way that's the problem. He's like that with everyone; he agrees with everyone. One week he's very enthusiastic about one thing and the next week it's something quite different. It's as though there's no core.*

> *I know she's very able. I believe she will have found the best solution. I trust her judgement but I wish that I felt that she cares about what she's having to do.*

In both these cases, the teachers concerned can see that something is missing. Given the opportunity, perhaps they could make this contribution? When leadership doesn't happen or is seen to fail, those in positions of authority are usually blamed for being only too human, full of the frailties of character – weak, timid, partial, overconfident, greedy and so on. We can't say what might turn a failing situation until we understand what particular quality is lacking: impartiality to outweigh attachment and bias, generosity to shame cupidity and so on. We can't put them all into competency frameworks.

Leadership as a collective capacity

A better solution is not to try and capture leadership qualities or competencies in any list or framework. However carefully constructed, lists will always exclude qualities that might turn out to be useful, undervaluing them and undervaluing the people who might have them. Lists also take the focus away from outcomes and value.

This has always been true, but it acquires a new resonance in conditions that are both more complex than previously acknowledged but also more interconnected. As Bill Drath says:

> *In a world that is globally interconnected; that is networked electronically, economically, often culturally, and even spiritually; and in which differing views of life are held in a dynamic tension, the concept of leadership from a leader is much less workable than it was in a world where people stuck more or less in like-minded groups. Leadership from a leader still seems to make sense on the surface, but it often doesn't work as expected. And that's confusing.*
>
> *What people are looking for is a new source of leadership. It's a little like running out of a precious natural resource. Leadership is needed just as much and maybe more than ever before, but the traditional source – the individual leader – is drying up. A new source is needed, and I believe it's right under our*

> *noses: leadership can come from the activity of people making sense and meaning of their work together.* (2001a, pp. 7–8)

Drath describes three "sources" of leadership. The first of these is "personal dominance … when leadership literally involves going first, [and] everyone except the leader has someone to follow". This may falter as situations become more complex, with followers wanting to have their own ideas, and leaders not being able to "solve" the problems or handle the challenges alone. Personal dominance then becomes an inappropriate basis for leadership, and tends to be replaced by interpersonal influence, which:

> *opens up leadership to the participation of followers. The leader's voice is no longer solo and dominant. The source of leadership becomes the negotiation of values and perspectives between the leader and followers. The leader's voice becomes a* compound *voice that includes the voices of followers.* (2001a, p. 9)

Interpersonal influence allows people to make sense of situations in which there are differences in ideas, values and perspectives. However, where there are widely diverging world views its effectiveness is much less certain. In such situations, as Yeats said: "*Things fall apart; the centre cannot hold; Mere anarchy is loosed upon the world.*" In chaotic conditions, the "centre" or top of the hierarchy fails, and loses control. What should happen next? The top instinctively tries to regain control; but this may not work. But for "wicked problems", where there are conflicting but equally legitimate views among diverse stakeholder groups, it may be that the centre has to let go of its desire to hold on and to control everything. For example, on problems such as drug abuse or teenage pregnancy where social work, education and health agencies are unable to work effectively together, a grim clinging on to centralised power can itself cause things to fall apart. Central control in such circumstances generally demotivates staff, promotes subversion and leaves the original problems unaddressed.

For such wicked problems, Drath suggests a third source of leadership as "relational dialogue". This calls for different mind sets, assumptions, behaviours and competencies from those previously associated with "strong" leadership. These include the ability to switch consciously from personal dominance and interpersonal influence to relational dialogue but also the insight and willingness to move into this more collective approach to leadership and to develop these abilities within the group (Drath, 2001b; Palus and Horth, 2002).

Table 4.1 shows these alternative approaches.

Table 4.1 Three stances of leadership (Boydell, 2001)

	STANCE 1: CLASSICAL Personal Dominance	STANCE 2: MODERN Interpersonal Influence	STANCE 3: RELATIONAL Relational Dialogue
Leadership	*Doing things well:* Command and control	*Doing things better:* Winning hearts and minds	*Doing better things:* Making meaning together
Leaders	"Leaders as managers": top management setting mission, vision, objectives	"Managers as leaders": all managers create enthusiasm and commitment from their teams	Leaders as social architects – creating conditions for all to practise leadership as relational dialogue, having conversations across boundaries, between different world views
Assumptions about organisation's context	Simple, stable	Changing but relatively predictable	Complexity; interconnected needs and problems – addressing one requires organisation's addressing many others; apparent context solutions to one problem worsen/create problems elsewhere or later in time; social fragmentation – between individuals, groups, organisations, professions – gets in the way of collective action Turbulence, many voices wanting to be heard; many alternative purposes and courses of action becoming visible. "Joined-up-working", multi-agency, alliances, partnerships; use of networks Situations that cannot be handled simply by doing better that which we already do well
Organisational metaphor	Machine, clockwork, to be run smoothly	Organism, a problem to be solved	Network of conversations, to explore a mystery and create a story together
Mission, vision and strategy	Formulated by top management. Sometimes made available to others to the extent that this felt useful	Formulated by top management after consultation at all levels "Shared" with all employees inthat they are informed and strong efforts made to gain their enthusiasm	Continuously evolving through active engagement of many stakeholders Mission, vision and strategy of overall community defined so as to support the diverse legitimate missions and visions of all those stakeholders

cont'd

Table 4.1 Three stances of leadership (Boydell, 2001) (*continued*)

	STANCE 1: CLASSICAL Personal Dominance	STANCE 2: MODERN Interpersonal Influence	STANCE 3: RELATIONAL Relational Dialogue
Formulation of purpose	Located at the top of the hierarchy	Strategic purpose located at top of hierarchy Others buy in to this purpose and are committed to their own local purposes that must be aligned to the overall one	Appreciation that people want to achieve things together, to participate in the creation of an unknown future, while at the same time it is recognised that multiple stakeholders have their own legitimate diverse purposes and aspirations
Distribution of power	Is and should be held according to position in hierarchy – the higher the more power But many people have an "illegitimate" or "subversive" power to make things not happen	Strategic power held by those at top of hierarchy Employees given delegated power to make operational improvements; they are thus "empowered" to meet the purpose, objectives, etc. set by top management	Appreciation that diverse stakeholders have legitimate power within the overall community and can use this to make things happen as well as not happen
Distribution of risk	Assumed that the more senior you are in the hierarchy, the greater the risk you carry In practice many people "lower down" are heavily at risk in that their jobs and careers and pensions are all vulnerable to decisions over which they have no control	People have more control over how they do things, how they can improve performance, and therefore often feel less helpless than in Stance 1. Conversely employees often feel that by becoming more productive they are at risk of working themselves into redundancy – something that senior managers often ignore or deny	Appreciation that "we are all in this together" – we are all taking significant risks, we all need to support each other, in our endeavours to move on, to do better things
Distribution of knowledge	The more senior you are the more you are assumed to know In practice many "lower" employees have considerable knowledge which tends to be not acknowledged or ignored	Appreciation of local knowledge that is harnessed to determine the best way of achieving the hierarchically determined purpose	Appreciation of the value of the considerable amounts of knowledge in and between stakeholder groups Appreciation that different views, opinions and beliefs are valid to those who hold them

Conclusion

Personal qualities are a vital aspect of leadership, yet this truth has fuelled a wild goose chase. The obvious significance of personal qualities has sparked a modern quest for the "Holy Grail"; for the one set of characteristics, behaviours or competencies that signal a leader. This research tradition continues strongly into the present day, allied to a natural dependency that looks for saviours in challenging situations. Yet it is based on a myth or chimaera, that ancient fantasy that was made up of the parts of multiple animals.

In seeking a magic formula for the leader we are looking under the wrong lamp-post. Each of us can feel a part of the elephant, and believe that we have the whole truth, but in reality each only has a part of it. The *Characteristics* domain of the "3 Cs" model of leadership refers to the qualities, attributes, abilities, competencies, skills, know-how and experience of *all* the people who might contribute to leadership. If all these people are willing to put themselves into the leadership effort, then there are a huge variety of talents available for the common cause. What each of us can do in certain situations is only partially predictable, and, given support and encouragement, we can surprise ourselves. Acting together and in concert we will surely overcome any mythical creature, however fabulous?

We prefer the notion of leadership as collective endeavour. Leadership is a capacity not limited to the special ones, but one that is widely distributed and available among human beings. It is something enacted in a situation, and whether it happens or not depends greatly on the relationships between the people in that situation. The keys to releasing this collective capacity are the quality and extent of the leadership *practices* of any organisation or community. It is these leadership practices that become the focus of the next part of this book.

Robert Greenleaf's evocation of the practice of "servant leadership" makes the important point. His ethical perspective has also been reduced by some of his disciples to a list of 10 individual characteristics, but this is counter to his proposed "best test" for all leadership efforts:

> *Do those served grow as persons? Do they, while being served become healthier, wiser, freer, more autonomous, more likely themselves to become servants? And, what is the effect on the least privileged in society? Will they benefit or at least not be further deprived?* (2002, p. 27)

This is an output measure and a collective one; and the best test of any leadership.

References

Aspinwall, K. (1998) *Leading the Learning School*. London: Lemos & Crane.

Bennis, W. and Nanus, B. (1997) *Leaders: Strategies for Taking Charge*, New York: HarperCollins.

Boydell, T.H. (2001) *Doing Things Well, Doing Things Better, Doing Better Things*, electronic publication on demand via tboydell@inter-logics.net.

Burgoyne, J.G., Mackness, J. and Williams, S. (2009) *Baseline Study of Leadership Development in Higher Education*. Lancaster: University of Lancaster, April.

Burgoyne, J.G. (1989) Creating the managerial portfolio: building on competency approaches to management development. *Management Education and Development* **20**(1): 68–73.

Drath, W. (2001a) The third way: a new source of leadership. *Leadership in Action*. **21**(2): 7–11.

Drath, W. (2001b) *The Deep Blue Sea: Rethinking the Source of Leadership*. San Francisco: Jossey Bass.

Gardner, J. (1989) *On Leadership*. New York: Free Press.

Greenleaf, R. (2002) *Servant Leadership: A Journey into the Nature of Legitimate Power and Greatness* (25th Anniversary Edition). Toronto: Paulist Press.

Mabey, C. and Ramirez, M. (2004). *Developing Managers in Europe*. London, Chartered Management Institute.

Palus, C. and Horth, D.M. (2002) *The Leader's Edge*. San-Francisco: Jossey Bass.

Part 2

7 Leadership Practices

Introduction to Part 2

The *7 practices of leadership* are at the heart of this book and make up the seven chapters that follow. This preface introduces the idea of *practice* and explains why it is so important for leadership.

If leadership is seen as a social activity, it can be described as an everyday *practice* or set of practices. This opens up many possibilities: it means that everyone who wants to can engage in leadership; it means that we can learn from doing it and get better at it; and thirdly, it means that we can do all this together with other people.

The idea of practice has two important dimensions: a *reflective practice* dimension that connects doing with learning and a relational or *connective practice* dimension that links individual doing with collective performance.

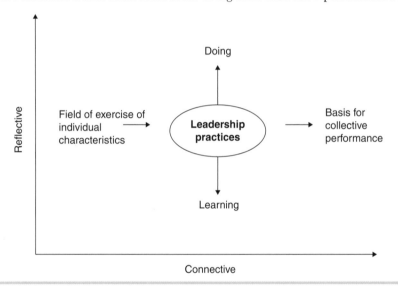

Figure A **Practice as reflective and connective**

The *reflective practice* dimension denotes practice as something that is done and also that can be learned from on a more or less continuous and lifelong basis. This is important because it makes leadership – or any other practice – learnable. This learning is never complete and is subject to continuous re-interpretation and development.

The *connective practice* dimension shows leadership as something which is both personal and individual; and also as something done with other people, as part of a leadership community of practice, and as a contribution to a collective effort.

These two dimensions highlight three important meanings or properties of the practice idea that run throughout this book: doing, learning and connecting:

- Practice as *doing* comes from the Greek *praxis*, which also means a combination of thinking and doing, as part of each other. Practice is what you do as a teacher, plumber, financial controller, and as a leader. For any practitioner, what we do is also an important part of our identity: of who we are and what we have become. So a practice is more than a collection of skills, competencies and personal characteristics, it is something that you do and are. It is both professional and personal; to some extent, I *am* my practice.
- In its second meaning, practice implies *learning*. We practise something in order to get better at it. This is particularly important in leadership work, where choices must be made and decisions taken, despite inadequate data. In such circumstances, leadership must act, for action creates information, which provides the clues for the next steps. This shows especially when actions turn out wrong; good learners react and recover faster. Leadership goes first in order to learn – not only for self but on behalf of others.

  Learning especially happens through "reflective practice" (Schön 1983), which involves reflecting *on* action, or after the event, but also *in* action, that is, while doing it. Minzberg (2004, p. 266) has pointed out that reflective practice can be a social process as well as an individual one, by involving all the participants in a situation.
- In its third meaning, practice is a *connecting* word. It connects knowing and doing in the person and also connects individuals to tasks. Nurses, builders and leaders all use their practice skills to tackle their work tasks and challenges. As well as connecting us to tasks, we can also connect with everyone else involved in the situation through these leadership practices. The practice of leadership brings people together to address the challenge in a joint effort at action and learning.

It is through this third meaning that leadership becomes a collaborative and shared activity. If you think of leadership in terms of particular skills, competencies or personal characteristics, this tends to individualise the idea and make it as a property of particular people. This can result in attributing leadership qualities *only* to those people, and thus excluding others with different qualities. In using the word practice, leadership can be both individual *and* collective:

- My leadership practice: my personal way of working.
- Our leadership practice: the professional community of practice.

A leadership community of practice is where many people are encouraged to take part and add value through their leadership. Whilst each person must develop their own practice, based on their unique qualities, as with any craft or trade, this is best done among other people with similar aims and purposes. Together, these individual and collective efforts at leadership constitute a service to other people, which creates a third "level":

■ The practice of leadership: a recognised service for valued human purposes.

Developing a shared practice of leadership has many benefits. In Revans' phrase, it promotes *the wisdom of peers* rather than a reliance on experts and other authority figures to provide the answers. A shared practice of leadership can generate honest and collaborative enquiry in the face of the doubts, confusions and risks that characterise leadership situations. It builds trust in our abilities to resolve our own problems and create our own opportunities.

References

Minzberg, H. (2004) *Managers not MBAs: A Hard Look at the Soft Practice of Managing and Management Development*. San Francisco: Berrett-Koehler.
Schön, D. (1983) *The Reflective Practitioner*. New York: Basic Books.

5

Practice 1: Leading yourself

The process of becoming a leader is much the same as becoming an integrated human being.
Bennis and Nanus

Whether you are an aspiring or experienced manager, a new team member or a highly trained professional, you may be asking yourself questions such as:

- I'm good at what I do, but am I a leader?
- Leadership is clearly the future, but how can I contribute to it?
- Do I want any part in leadership?

Many people have an ambivalent attitude to leadership. We know that it is vital at times, we complain about it when it is missing, but at the same time we have our doubts. Arrogance seems so easily to follow success and we distrust people with too much power. We don't like to push ourselves forward too much and to become like that. Perhaps also we have doubts about our own abilities – "am I up to it?"

Part of this doubt comes from our association of the idea of leadership with the deeds of "Great Men". We are told that the company was founded by great men, we are still taught that the nation was shaped by great men, and we continue to learn that all the big ideas come from great men. Histories are constructed on the assumption that the events and milestones of the past are the outcomes of the actions of outstanding individuals. Not only are these outstanding people nearly always men – which rules out half the potential resource – but they are depicted as so exceptional that ordinary folk can never hope to emulate them.

This is a legacy that we need to question. It is holding us back. The current era offers more opportunities and challenges for leadership than any number of exceptional individuals could handle. Successful action is made up from the efforts of the many and not just the few. Modern leadership research dates back to the Second World War, and its voluminous history makes it plain that there is no one model for leadership, no single quality or set of competencies. What you can bring to leadership depends on who you are, the circumstances you find yourself in, with the colleagues you find there. What you can offer depends on who you are, what's important to you, how you see the world and how well you can learn.

This book defines leadership from the "outside in", as pulled by the task or challenge. We emphasise that it is the collective performance that matters: leadership is effective action in the face of the challenges facing organisations and communities. Individuals have a critical role in relation to these challenges – noticing them, choosing them, moving towards them or away from them. What this means is that although leadership is a collaborative process, it is also a deeply personal matter: you can only influence others when you believe in what you are doing. What is it that you want for yourself and for other people?

Leading yourself is the first leadership practice because it underpins all the others. The leadership practices of *purpose, power, risk, challenging questions, facilitating* and *networking* are all practised with and between people, but leadership starts from within. It requires what Bennis and Nanus have called "the deployment of self". If you have already prioritised some leadership challenges in Chapter 2, then you have already taken a first decisive step in leading yourself.

In this chapter you will find ideas about *leading yourself* and with how leadership is learned. A reflective practice of leadership is proposed as a way to deal with some of the factors that prevent and obstruct learning in organisational life. The centrepoint is a DIY 360° feedback tool that enables you to seek the views and opinions of others about your leadership approach and capabilities. The chapter contains three activities for *leading yourself*:

- Activity P1.1: What I Can Do; What Others Can Do.
- Activity P1.2: DIY 360° Feedback.
- Activity P1.3: My Leadership Resolutions.

These activities are found at the end of this chapter.

Learning leadership

Leading yourself starts inside, in knowing yourself, what you want and what you can do – and can't do. In the face of any challenge, each of us must decide for ourselves whether to step forward, backwards or to the side. Everyone can learn to contribute to leadership by stepping up:

Helena fulfilled an important ambition when she was promoted to a senior management post at the age of 33. This was something she had worked for in the 12 years since she left university. Now that she had her top job she was experiencing new pressures. She found that the requirement to "be corporate" was difficult to reconcile with the informal style of leadership on which she had always prided herself. This was compounded by the fact that she found her boss' style unhelpful and irritating. Although privately very frank, in public Graham always delivered the party line without hesitation. He appeared to believe every word he said and showed no imagination or sympathy for those charged with implementing the new policies. Helena found this unacceptable as a model for her own behaviour, and she struggled to find a way of remaining true to her own values while being a member of the senior team.

Learning leadership involves adapting to new roles, tackling demanding tasks and using power in organisations. It also means learning a lot about yourself. Helena needs to know who she is, and to understand her values and purposes. She needs to know what she is good at, less good at, and how can she get better. It would help a lot if she knew how other people see her. How is she seen to be doing the job, say, compared to Graham? In order to lead in the way that she wants, she needs to know how to learn.

Leaders as learners

No plan survives its first encounter with the enemy.

(Von Clauswitz)

It has become increasingly obvious in recent years that a person's capacity to thrive and survive in both leadership and management is greatly enhanced by their ability to learn.

The skills of leadership overlap with those of management, but emphasise the more relational and personal skills. Leaders need to be good listeners, confident in themselves and in building good relationships with other people. They need to be open to new ideas and tolerant of different views and able to give up positions when circumstances change. They need to be able to look beyond personal needs and become coaches of other people. They will sometimes have to take hard decisions that are painful for themselves and others and deal with the consequences of this. This means that they must practice emotional resilience and seek to maintain themselves in good physical and psychological health.

These sorts of capacities and qualities can be learned but not taught, except by example. Many people report that they learned most about themselves and about leadership from the most difficult and personally challenging times.

Leadership is learned through the processes of challenge, risk taking, feedback and reflection. When old practices do not work, it takes insight and courage to recognise this and confront reality, receive feedback, and to try some new ways of being and doing. This can take time and is greatly helped by support from others.

What stops leaders learning?

Learning while working and leading is difficult because people are too busy and engaged to take time out, reflect and question what they are doing. We all tend to hang on to cherished beliefs that have served us well, but which may no longer be valid. For Revans there are four characteristics of managers and leaders that may hinder learning:

- ■ *The idolisation of past experiences* – as interpreted and recalled.
- ■ *The charismatic influences of others* seen as successful.
- ■ *The drive to act* – the urgencies of the moment drive out the long term.
- ■ *The need for all to know their places* – the hierarchical principle which undervalues people (1998, pp. 47–50).

We can scarcely escape these characteristics: work is after all necessarily driven by deadlines, facilitated by functional hierarchies, and reliant on tested routines. At the same time all these aspects can block learning, discourage experiment and consistently underestimate the capabilities of all people to respond to challenges and opportunities. Learning leadership, including any programme for leadership development, must face this contradictory reality.

A reflective practice

No-one ever becomes an expert leader, except in books, but everyone can improve their leadership practice. The idea of *practice*, as discussed previously, means that learning and improving are an integral part of working and taking action. This can only happen if you reflect on what you are doing and why. Like any other skill or ability, learning to provide leadership is a process of adaptation and improvisation on the basis of ongoing assessment: How did that sound? Where did that behaviour come from? Knowing yourself, listening to yourself, observing and listening to others, knowing enough about our own biases and preferences to make a balanced judgement are all vital on the practice front line.

A reflective practice of leadership starts with understanding your own skills and abilities. Think of a current challenge in your work or life and do this simple activity:

See Activity P1.1: What I Can Do; What Others Can Do.
(At the end of the chapter.)

Analysing challenges in this way is a good habit to acquire: *it is a contribution to leadership in itself*. We admire the person who keeps a cool head and who sees clearly in a crisis. This does not mean that they are always the most able to act to bring the crisis under control. Learning leadership means understanding the requirements of situations and harnessing the coalition of resources and talents needed to resolve the problem or seize the opportunity. In the narrower terms of leading yourself, working with challenges in this way develops transferable skills. As you develop your leadership practice in contributing to current challenges, so you increase your abilities to contribute to new ones in the future. Working on and strengthening this leadership practice will also develop you as a person.

A reflective practice of leadership means "using yourself as data" (Heifetz, 1994, p. 271). We are a rich resource to ourselves and there are many possible directions for inquiry and learning. Here are just a few areas for exploration that may be useful for your leadership development:

- How you learn – your learning style, habits and preferences.
- Your purposes and values.
- Your personal preferences and constructs – your ways of seeing and interpreting the world.
- Self-awareness and how others see you.
- Looking after yourself – your health, fitness, work/life balance and emotional resilience.
- Managing your career and reputation.
- Deepening your leadership practice – the three levels of leadership: as doing things well, as doing things better and as doing better things.
- Exploring your understanding of the wider world of social and economic trends.

You may already be familiar with some or all of these ways of looking at yourself and leadership. This depends largely on the opportunities you have had for your own personal development thus far. If you are not familiar with any of these areas for personal exploration, some sources for development are listed for each of them in *further resources* at the end of this chapter. Additionally Chapter 12 of this book is devoted to leadership development, which is a field of study and practice in itself. Here you will find more ideas both for your own development and that of your colleagues.

The next part of the chapter looks at a most important source of data for *leading yourself* – how other people see you and your leadership. This activity is the complement to the one you have just done, where you assessed the contribution that other people can make to a challenge. Here you are asking people to assess you and your contribution.

With a little help from your friends ...

360° Feedback is a process for eliciting feedback from a range of sources – colleagues, managers, your own staff, customers and clients. Done well, this can be one of the most useful tools for leadership development because it generates views on your approach and performance from all angles. A questionnaire is sent out to a range of people who are asked to respond to certain questions. To protect the informants, the feedback forms are often sent anonymously to a third party, often to an external consultant or perhaps to someone in the Human Resources department, who processes and summarises the data.

However, the 360° feedback process does not need to be so formal: you can do it yourself. Where there is reasonable trust between you and those people you plan to ask to give you feedback, it is a technique that you can initiate yourself and it does not need to be anonymous. The idea of anonymity is that it encourages openness as well as protecting the informant and the relationship you have with them. However, it is surprising what people will say and do if you ask them. If you display honesty and openness – the same qualities you are looking for in them – then you just might get it back.

Choose some people, check if they are willing to take part, and then ask them to be as honest as possible. If they are prepared to put their names to constructive feedback then this opens up the possibilities for fruitful conversations after your survey.

See Activity P1.2: DIY 360° Feedback. (At the end of the chapter.)

Scoring and analysing the feedback from your 360°

When you receive the questionnaires back, they are likely to contain much useful information. Hopefully there are two types of data to analyse: Part A contains quantitative scores, while Part B is more qualitative.

Starting with Part A, plot the scores from the seven rating questions onto the grid shown in Figure P1.1: Plotting your 360° feedback to give overall scores that combine *importance* and *capability*. This is done by totting up the *importance* and *capability* scores given by each of your informants, dividing each total by seven to get the average score, and then plotting these on the grid.

Figure P1.1 below illustrates a worked example where the ratings from six questionnaires have been aggregated. The person being rated in this example is seen as being very good at *Leading yourself* (P1); *Facilitation* (P6) and *Networking* (P7), but much less good at the practices of *Working with power* (P3) and *Living with risk* (P4). As these last two are seen as more or less equally important to the first three at this time, then they might be the obvious candidates for this person's leadership development.

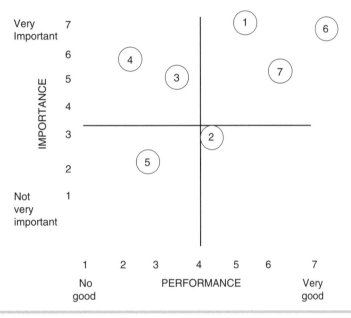

Figure P1.1 **Plotting your 360° feedback. (Adapted with permission from Boydell and Leary, 2005, p. 182.)**

Analysing your returns to Part A of the questionnaire will give you a snapshot of how others see you against the model of the *7 core practices of leadership*. This should give you some valuable insights into what you are *seen* as being good at and as not so good at, and into those things that you could improve on.

The more qualitative data from Part B cannot be analysed in the same way, but it might provide the basis for some deeper insights into your leadership and also for improving your relationships with the people who have responded to your questionnaire. If people have put their names on the questionnaires, or have let it be known that they are happy for you to talk to them about what they have said, then you have the basis and the excuse for some very useful conversations. For example, in asking a person why they want you to do more of a certain thing, you can also say what you would appreciate more from them.

For leadership purposes, the 360° feedback technique is often a more appropriate way of getting feedback than from formal appraisal systems. Less hierarchical and perhaps less connected to organisational control systems, it is much more appropriate to flatter structures and teamworking situations. In our DIY version, the 360° is also self-managed, and you are much more likely to take advice when you have initiated and controlled the process than when you are subjected to it by others.

What are the three most critical insights to come from your 360° feedback?

1

2

3

My leadership resolutions

Most programmes for leadership development encourage you to write a *Personal Development Plan* (PDP) which sets out what you have learned from activities such as the 360° feedback process and other diagnostic exercises, together with some learning objectives and targets for those things that you would like to get better at and develop further. It can be a useful way of continuing your effort to learn and to be supported in this, perhaps by a coach, mentor or action learning set.

You can find a briefing on how to create a format in Chapter 12 on *leadership development*. This can be used both personally for yourself and for any group of people working together. As noted in Chapter 12, we have some reservations about PDPs and how they are used in some organisations. The key point is that any development plan needs voluntary commitment to be a worthwhile undertaking. This is because learning itself is a voluntary activity and all of us at different times refuse to learn new things – that is our choice. While it might be reasonable to make certain forms of learning more or less compulsory, for example concerning health and safety matters, leadership can never fall into this category. The difference between cooperation and commitment is a big one.

Whether you want to develop a PDP or not, it will help if you write yourself some *leadership resolutions*. This takes far less time than a PDP but such resolutions are the cornerstones of any effort to develop yourself and your leadership practice. A leadership resolution is *a statement of intent in the face of a challenge*, for example:

> *I resolve to improve my use of power with my colleagues by being less timid and more assertive.*

or

> *I resolve to get involved in the forthcoming merger of my department by volunteering to be part of the working party, with a view to learning about leadership in change management situations.*

What are your resolutions for your own practice of leadership? In what directions do you want to develop and improve? What are the important challenges for you and how will you develop the strategies to deal with them?

See Activity P1.3: my leadership resolutions. (At the end of the chapter.)

Leadership is always forward looking, its purpose is in finding a better place. Like all resolutions, leadership resolutions have to be made in good faith and with the intention of carrying them out. Whether you decide to create a more formal plan for your leadership development or not, writing out some resolutions will help you to find the right direction to go in next.

Activity P1.3: my leadership resolutions suggests some options for action on the basis of what you have written. Choose one of these or another of your own devising and give yourself a chance of success.

Good luck.

Leading yourself

Leading yourself means adopting a learning attitude to everything. For every action you take, you wonder what you will learn from it; from everything you see happening you ask what lessons can be learnt; for every person you encounter, you consider what you can learn from them; for every problem or opportunity you meet, you think: how can I learn to do this better?

The senior civil servant's story

> *In the final stage of his career, a senior civil servant resolved to develop a new leadership style. He has already more or less stopped going to formal meetings or reading e-mail attachments. He has decided that he will only write six briefing papers this year, and then of not more than two sides apiece. He has also decided that he will only wear a tie on 10 occasions at most throughout the year. These apparently fancy gestures are part of a deliberate attempt at what he calls "undoing the hierarchy" in order to bring about more effective relationships.*

So, how does he do this? "By having constant conversations with people, by introducing people to other people, by finding out what people are doing and then trying to support them in what they are doing. By saying 'we' and not 'I'." He describes taking a new administrative secretary to an important meeting with ministers: "I took her partly because I wanted to get to know her, and the long train journey helped immeasurably with that, but also because I wanted to introduce her to people – people who are important in getting this work done. It is about giving authority away and trust and letting go and all that, but it is not about dumping it on people."

Leading yourself is a life-long preoccupation with personal and professional development.

The suggestions in this chapter for generating feedback and information about your leadership will add to the priorities that have already emerged from Chapter 2. The next six chapters of this book will add further by considering your leadership practice in each of the other *seven core practices of leadership*.

As the first leadership practice, leading yourself has three strands:

- practising leadership – by seeking out and contributing in challenge situations
- learning leadership – by finding time, space and good companions to reflect on your actions and improve your capabilities
- valuing leadership – knowing your own values and relating these to those of the other people involved in leadership challenges.

Without the first of these you will not be doing leadership at all; without the second you will not get any better; and without the third, you will lack conviction when it really matters.

References

Boydell, T. and Leary, M. (2005) *Identifying Training Needs.* London: Institute of Personnel & Development.

Heifetz, R. (1994) *Leadership without Easy Answers.* Cambridge, Mass: Belknap Press.

Revans, R.W. (1998) *ABC of Action Learning.* London: Lemos & Crane.

Further resources

This aspect of leadership development is rich in resources. Below are some starting places for each of the eight areas for exploration listed earlier in this chapter.

How you learn – your learning style, habits and preferences. Honey and Mumford have developed inventories for checking out your learning style based on David Kolb's learning cycle of Experience, Reflection, Ideas and Action. For the latest versions and information go to: www.peterhoney.co.uk.

Your purposes and values. The next chapter of this book, on purpose, is devoted to this theme and also contains further resources on these aspects.

Your personal preferences and constructs – your ways of seeing and interpreting the world. Much of the work in this area stems from Carl Jung's theories of personality and George Kelly's Personal Construct Psychology (PCP). Of the many psychometric questionnaires and development activities available, one of the most widely used is Myers Briggs Type Indicator (MBTI) based on Jung's theories. This is only available to licensed practitioners but there are likely to be one or more of these in your organisation. Jenny Rogers' *Sixteen Personality Types at Work in Organisations* (London: Management Futures Ltd, 1997) provides an excellent summary of the MBTI approach. Alternatively you can get a do-it-yourself version via the Kiersey Temperaments Sorter from David Keirsey's *Please Understand Me II: Temperaments, Character, Intelligence* (Del Mar, CA: Prometheus Nemesis, 1998) or on the web at www.keirsey.com. On PCP Fay Fransella's *The Essential Practitioner's Handbook of Personal Construct Psychology* (Chichester: Wiley, 2005) and Devi Jankowicz' *The Easy Guide to Repertory Grids* (Chichester: Wiley, 2003) are good sources.

Self-awareness and how others see you. Both MBTI and PCP work will help here together with the 360° feedback activity given in this chapter.

Looking after yourself – your health, fitness, work/life balance and emotional resilience. Mike Pedler and Tom Boydell's *Managing Yourself* (London: Lemos & Crane, 1999) will help with all these and generally with taking charge of yourself. Harvard Business School Press also has a collection called *Managing Yourself* (2008) which includes useful ideas on "managing your energy, not your time". A self-development group or a mentor is also indicated here – and for most of these areas for development. This is because many aspects of self-development are assisted by ongoing support over time and are unlikely to be achieved by one-off efforts.

Managing your career and reputation. Managing your career involves understanding how organisations handle succession and development as well as your own aspirations. John Burgoyne's *Developing Yourself, Your Career and Your Organisation* (London: Lemos & Crane, 1999) will help you with all these aspects. These are also proper questions for your Human Resource Development department or adviser. If you are suffering during a downturn then Harvard Business School Press' *Managing Your Career in a Downturn* (2009) might help.

Deepening your leadership practice – the three levels of leadership. This is a whole theory of leadership in itself, and about learning at each of these three levels. It is available as an e-book, called *Doing Things Well, Doing Things Better,*

Doing Better Things from Tom Boydell: contact him at tboydell@inter-logics.net.

Finally, *Exploring your understanding of the wider world of social and economic trends* can be pursued by cultivating reading, study and research habits. Taking one of the "broadsheet" newspapers or the magazines specialising in such affairs is a good start. Searching on-line is a very good way of accessing this sort of information, which is often very specific to markets, industries or areas of concern. For example, an Amazon search under "Trends" produces almost 6000 references ranging from Music and Asian Markets to British Social Trends.

Activities

- Activity P1.1: What I Can Do; What Others Can Do.
- Activity P1.2: DIY 360° Feedback.
- Activity P1.3: My Leadership Resolutions.

Activity P1.1: What I Can Do; What Others Can Do

The activity will help you to think about what you have to offer in a particular challenge situation. It will also help you to analyse the challenge situation, to understand the leadership required, and to assess the part your colleagues can play in providing this.

1 Think of a current challenge in your home or work life. What is required to tackle this challenge? What knowledge, skills or personal qualities will help? What power and resources are needed?

Write down all the requirements you can think of in the left-hand column – not neglecting the importance of basic functions such as communicating with people, making contacts, doing research, organising meetings, etc.:

What this challenge Requires:	What I can do	What others can do
1.		
2.		
3.		
4.		
5.		
etc.		

2 When you have fully scoped the requirements of the challenge, ask yourself where these abilities and resources will come from. Fill out the middle column for all the things that you can offer. Come back to this column once you have completed the next step.

3 Now fill out the contributions that you think that your colleagues can make, or any others that you can think of, in the right-hand column.

4 Revisit the middle column and add any extra things you can offer. One key ingredient is: who will contact and get together the resources of the people in the right-hand column? Could this be you or could you be part of this?

Activity P1.2: DIY 360° Feedback

1 First choose a range of people to ask to take part in this feedback activity. Choose people who interact with you from different perspectives, for example, your boss, someone who works for you, a colleague, a client, a business partner and so on. You can include friends or family if you think this is appropriate. About six people is a good number.

2 Having chosen your people, ask each of them if they are willing to take part in a *DIY 360° feedback activity* to help you improve your leadership capabilities and performance. If they are reluctant don't force them, but say that you would value their opinion and anything they are prepared to suggest. If several people turn you down then you may have to widen your net – and also reflect on what this is telling you.

3 Now send a simple questionnaire to those willing respondents and ask them to return it to you by a given date – say, by the end of the week.

The questionnaire can be based on any measures that you think are important. What are the aspects of leadership against which you would like to be rated?

You could brainstorm your own criteria with a colleague or two or ask around your professional network for possible criteria and formats. Alternatively, perhaps your organisation has a model of leadership that is used to select and develop people?

When you have decided on your criteria, you need to format them into a questionnaire. Here is a sample questionnaire based on the criteria of the *7 core practices of leadership* as used in this book:

Dear Colleague

Please fill out this questionnaire on my leadership capabilities. The purpose of this is to help me improve in my performance, so please be as honest as you feel able to be in answering the questions. In return, I promise not to be thin-skinned. Your replies will be confidential to me, and, with your permission, I may want to discuss them with you at a later date.

Please return this form to me by _____ (Date)
Many thanks for your help in this.
_____ (Your name)

Part A

Please rate me as you experience me on the following seven aspects of leadership:

1. *Leading Myself: my general ability in self leadership, self-initiating and learning*
   How good am I at this?
   No good   1 2 3 4 5 6 7   Very good
   How important do you think this is for me in my leadership?
   Not important   1 2 3 4 5 6 7   Very important

2. *On my sense of Purpose: my capacity to be focused and purposeful; to pursue goals but with a deeper sense of purpose and direction*
   How good am I at this?
   No good   1 2 3 4 5 6 7   Very good
   How important do you think this is for me in my leadership?
   Not important   1 2 3 4 5 6 7   Very important

3. *How I use Power: my skills in using power in all its forms and in a positive way so that other people are not oppressed or victimised*
   How good am I at this?
   No good   1 2 3 4 5 6 7   Very good
   How important do you think this is for me in my leadership?
   Not important   1 2 3 4 5 6 7   Very important

4. *How I live with Risk: my ability to estimate, manage and take appropriate risks to achieve important purposes*
   How good am I at this?
   No good   1 2 3 4 5 6 7   Very good
   How important do you think this is for me in my leadership?
   Not important   1 2 3 4 5 6 7   Very important

5. *Challenging Questions: my skills in asking good and critical questions which surface underlying issues and lead to creative outcomes*
   How good am I at this?
   No good   1 2 3 4 5 6 7   Very good
   How important do you think this is for me in my leadership?
   Not important   1 2 3 4 5 6 7   Very important

6. *Facilitation: my capabilities in helping other people to get their work done – individually and in groups*

How good am I at this?

No good   1 2 3 4 5 6 7   Very good

How important do you think this is for me in my leadership?

Not important   1 2 3 4 5 6 7   Very important

7. *Networking: my ability to connect with other people to get access to information, resources and potential allies*

How good am I at this?

No good   1 2 3 4 5 6 7   Very good

How important do you think this is for me in my leadership?

Not important   1 2 3 4 5 6 7   Very important

PART B

Now, please complete the three sentences below:

(i) "In your relationship with me, I find the following things that you do to be very helpful, so please continue to …

(ii) "However, I would prefer it if you stopped or did less of …

(iii) "And it would be good for me, if you could start or do more of …

That's it. Many thanks for taking the time to respond to this. Please send this form back to me at: _____ (*Address*)

Activity P1.3: My Leadership Resolutions

Like New Year resolutions, leadership resolutions should be made in good faith and perhaps include those things that you have had in your mind for a while.

Also like New Year resolutions, leadership resolutions can become quickly neglected, so don't create a long shopping list, but do think about one or two things that you would really like to see yourself do.

Fill out the *my leadership resolutions* box below. When you have made your list, look at the following text for some ideas for how to use it:

My Leadership Resolutions

I RESOLVE …

These are my Leadership Resolutions. They are my statements of intent in the face of the challenges I see around me. Their purpose is to help me contribute to leadership around here and to develop my leadership practice.

I resolve to …

1.

2.

3.

4.

5.

etc.

Signed: *Date:*

What to do with your leadership resolutions:

1 Put your list in your right-hand drawer where you will see it every time you look for your stapler.
2 Stick it above your desk, headed with a bold "I resolve …".
3 E-mail it to your coach or mentor.
4 Post it to a friend and ask them to send it back to you at the end of each of the next three months.
5 Give a copy to your partner and ask them to check out how well you are doing against your leadership resolutions from time to time.
6 Read them, memorise them, screw them up and throw them in the bin.

Whatever you do with your leadership resolutions, the act of writing them and committing them to paper is an important start. At the very least you have made a statement to yourself. If you choose one of the publication options, you invite discussion with others perhaps including those with whom you work. Who knows what this might do; it might help you recruit allies, or bring you useful feedback – and it may well contribute to the personal leadership development of others.

6

Practice 2: Being on purpose

Introduction

Purpose lies at the heart of any enterprise. Beyond any specific goal or aim, a successful venture requires a deep and enduring *sense of purpose*. This long-term direction is rooted in what is most valued; it is what makes the risks of leadership possible and worthwhile. Leaders do things "on purpose".

A sense of purpose reminds us what we are for as well as what we are against. Without clarity of purpose, without that deep sense of what we want, our actions can be erratic or capricious, driven by short-term, even random, influences.

But purpose can be hard to find at times, and at other times it may be hard to hold on to. We can lose heart and purpose as the urgent drives out the important, or as success continues to elude us. Churchill defined leadership as "the ability to go on from one failure to another" and this demands much more than the popular notion of vision. Without determination, persistence and sheer force of will, visions remain dreams.

Like other leadership practices, finding direction and purpose can be learned and developed. The aim of this chapter is to help you to understand your purpose and to develop your own practice of being "on purpose". Understanding what you want and what you are about will help you to contribute to leadership in any challenging situation. It also aims to help you find collective or common purpose with colleagues and other people. This ability to develop the collective capacity to do useful things is a vital aspect of organisational life and a critical competence in all leaders.

This chapter addresses three related questions:

- What is a sense of purpose?
- How do I find my sense of purpose?
- How can I create common purpose with others?

In pursuit of this last question, three main ideas are offered to help you and your colleagues get "on purpose":

- A learning approach to strategy.
- Scenario thinking.
- Storytelling.

This chapter also includes six working activities to use in order to develop your leadership practice of *being on purpose*. These are referred to at appropriate points in the text and are then assembled for ease of use at the end of the chapter, following the references and further resources.

What is a sense of purpose?

There are many words used to describe this central aspect of the practice of leadership. According to Bennis and Nanus:

We cannot exaggerate the significance of a strong determination to achieve a goal or realise a vision, conviction or even a passion. (1997)

But these things are not the same as one another; a goal is not necessarily a passion; yet, neither are they completely different – purpose has three aspects:

- *Direction* is the immediate intention, aim or goal, the desired objective in this situation. It embodies the desired vision for the future in specific circumstances. Direction gives point to purpose in particular situations: what do we intend to do? What is the goal here?
- *Sense of purpose* is a deeper pulse, the internal compass. It is connected to core values and closely coupled with identity. It is concerned with the questions: What am I here for? What is our work? It is the quality that underlies the will and which keeps us going in discouraging circumstances and over the long run.
- *Will* is the drive, determination, persistence, energy and effort to make things happen. It is the force that translates impulses and directions into practice. Will is often neglected in discussions of leadership that prefer to emphasise vision or values but miss the importance of persistence and determination. It is the quality sought when people talk about "empowerment" and "engagement", but the will is not easily bidden.

Following your sense of purpose means much more than pursuing a goal. In an era of target setting as the principle means of motivation, it can be difficult to keep in touch with the deeper sense of purpose. Clear goals are relatively easy to specify, and this is an important task for managers. But in complex circumstances, where direction is not clear or is disputed, the imposition of clear goals may not help very much. The feeling is: "I know what the goal is, but is it what am I here for?" and "Do I have the will to pursue it?"

Many of us find it hard to follow directions that run against our sense of purpose. If we must do so then we might tend to work without enthusiasm, and perhaps, over the longer term, become stressed.

Being on purpose

Being "on purpose" means being clear what you are aiming to bring about in the world. Here is an old story:

> *A traveller arrived in a small town and came across a group of bricklayers. He asked each of them what he was doing:*
>
> *"Laying bricks" said the first,*
> *"Building a wall" said the second,*
> *"Creating a cathedral" said the third.*
> *A fourth, working a little way off, said "Serving God".*

This fable reminds us of the different ways of interpreting and making sense of our purpose. The four bricklayers create a hierarchy, from the mundane to the sublime, from an immediate purpose or goal to a deeper sense of purpose or moral compass. They all seem to be doing the same work, and can apparently collaborate well, yet their purposes are very different.

To get an idea of your sense of purpose, try Activity P2.1: My Purpose

Leadership involves choices and commitments: Which side are you on? What do you stand for? What are you committed to? As with the bricklayers perhaps, most of us have multiple purposes – lower, more specific purposes can co-exist with higher, broader ones. But it is the higher sense of purpose that is most "portable" and which is likely to sustain us in difficult times.

The how–why ladder

The hierarchy of purposes can be seen as a ladder that we can move up and down (see Figure P2.1).

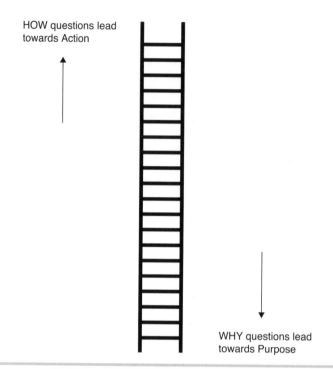

HOW questions lead
towards Action

WHY questions lead
towards Purpose

Figure P2.1 **The how–why ladder**

In any situation, "How" questions such as:

- How can I resolve this problem?
- How can I get help with this?
- How can I fit this into my busy schedule?

take us up the hierarchy or ladder, to a concern with action and implementation. Perhaps we are culturally inclined to ask these "how" questions because most of us are employed to be active and get on with things. The "why" questions connect us to our deeper sense of purpose:

- Why should I resolve this problem?
- Why would anyone want to help me with this?
- Why should I change my busy schedule to focus on this?

The rephrasing in these questions changes the whole direction of inquiry, taking us down the ladder to the bigger issues. These are the leadership questions. You can check your sense of purpose compass by asking the "Why" questions from time to time. But it is often difficult to keep doing this in organisational life. The pressure is always on to decide quickly and act without hesitation, which can result in behaviour of the "Ready, Fire, Aim" variety. In such situations it is especially important to be aware of the compass of higher purpose, for this is the key not just to good leadership but also to learning how to act differently.

Purpose, leadership and learning

Laying bricks is a valuable activity, but if that was all that we did, cathedrals would never be imagined and designed. The "laying bricks" line is often easier to take in life, but where is the leadership in that? Leadership involves posing the difficult questions about problems that need to be faced, those that Heifetz calls the "adaptive challenges":

> ... *problems for which there are no simple, painless solutions – problems that require us to learn new ways.*

(Heifetz, p. 2)

Adaptive challenges are the prime responsibility of leadership: from uncompetitive, inefficient or corrupt businesses to the problems of public health, poverty, housing, drugs and child abuse, the issues have no simple answers. They demand novel solutions that involve changes in our own attitudes and behaviour. This can only be done via questioning our own positions, re-assessing our current practices and learning new ways. Leadership and learning are closely coupled.

Finding a sense of purpose

Yet a sense of purpose is not always easily found. It may take a considerable time for a person or a group to identify the pulse within and discover how to bend their energies and work to this purpose.

The starting point is often to be found in the everyday questions: What am I trying to do? What is stopping us from doing this? How can we move forward? Here is a group of people trying to do their work better.

The community midwives' story

A group of community midwives began meeting informally to improve the care in their city for women and babies with HIV/AIDS. This started when two of them met for coffee and to talk over a difficult situation that one of them was experiencing. This led on to a further meeting, to which the other midwives were invited. When this second meeting proved valuable, they decided to meet on a regular basis.

Over several months, the group became more widely known about and influential. Having come together informally to talk about their concerns they had created a forum for an important aspect of health care that had not previously existed. Without intending it, they had become a useful part of the public health system. The Strategic Health Authority then asked the group for advice on policy and also for help in implementation. Not all the group were keen on this idea. Is this the sort of group we want to be? Will this help our women and their babies?

In this example, leadership and direction emerge as a normal part of working together. It starts from one person with a question, which leads to the discovery that others share her concern. The common or shared purpose in this group develops out of this shared interest without any forcing. A dilemma arises when the group is offered a role by a powerful authority that may not fit with this purpose. The future of this group and its capacity to do useful work will depend on how this conflict is resolved.

However, purpose sometimes takes much longer to find. The consultant and writer David Casey described the wide differences to be found in management teams:

> The speed of arriving at the answer to the question "What is this group for?" varies enormously. Sometimes the answer is clear, universally agreed and forthcoming. Other times it is extremely obscure – every member of the group offering a different answer to the question and in the end the role of the group appears to be anything and everything from information exchange, decision-making, mutual support, strategy formulation, social chit-chat, monitoring performance, exacting revenge and nurturing habits, to providing a platform for the Chief Executive to ride his favourite hobby horse. In one organisation I got on their nerves by persistently asking the question "What is this group for?" over a period of nearly eight months. (1993, pp. 50–51)

These examples show that individual and group purposes are two different things. They may easily coincide, as with the community midwives, or they may be at odds and hard to reconcile, as in the management team described by Casey. While we can work with other people's purposes without being aware of our own, understanding *my* purpose is an essential part of doing things "on purpose".

My sense of purpose

A simple but effective activity, based on Personal Construct Psychology (PCP), can put us in touch with our sense of purpose. George Kelly's PCP holds that each of us perceives, understands and construes the world via a set of unique personal constructs. Kelly took a "critical realist" view that there is a real world out there, but that each of us only perceives certain aspects of that reality, and moreover, perceives them differently, depending on our personal constructs. He devised several useful tools based on his theories, one of which – *laddering* – helps to locate the sense of purpose in any situation.

At this point try: Activity P2.2: Finding My Sense of Purpose.

The laddering activity helps you to understand and be in touch with your sense of purpose. You can also use it with other people to help them think more deeply about their purpose in any situation. We now turn to the question of how to find purpose and direction with a group or organisation.

Creating common purpose

For groups or organisations facing difficult and adaptive challenges, a more collective effort at leadership is likely to be more successful than reliance on a few heroic individuals. Individual purposes are vital, but common purpose is needed to align our efforts:

> *The opposite of purpose is aimless drifting. But it can't be any old purpose that will animate, galvanise and energise the people. It has to have resonance, meaning …. Without a sense of alignment behind that common purpose, the company is in trouble.*

> (Bennis and Nanus, 1997)

In some organisations, purpose is not an issue. Only when the business fails through lack of energy and vitality do we realise that we have been drifting for some time. Addressing the question of how to find common purpose first requires us to think of all the different purposes that people have in a situation. Each of us has our own individual sense of purpose, or could have, given the chance to think about it, but these are not usually taken into account.

"Collaborative advantage" accrues when we manage to harness many individual purposes without submerging them. The compelling argument for a more relational view of leadership comes from the need for each of us to share our ideas, knowledge and learning as the basis for wealth and welfare creation in a knowledge-based era. This sharing work is most naturally done not in hierarchies but in communities of peers, where common purpose is found in relationship and in a dialogue of all those concerned.

Activity P2.3: Mine; Ours and Theirs – A Matrix of Purposes can be done here to provide a framework to think about what is involved in establishing a common sense of purpose.

Understanding all the different purposes in a situation may look to be complicating matters unduly, but it is the starting point for creating common purpose and direction. There are various ways to do this, and the rest of this chapter offers three tools or ways of engaging individual purposes and forging common purpose:

■ A learning approach to strategy.
■ Scenario planning.
■ Storytelling.

A learning approach to strategy

The fish rots from the head. (Old Chinese saying)

In many organisations, setting strategy and direction remains the province of great men or top teams – and their consultants. Yet these top teams are not always good examples of teamworking themselves:

> A management consultant reflected on a long experience of working with senior teams on strategy: "I spend a lot of time encouraging them to collaborate … because they spend so much of their time using their strategic abilities to compete with each other." He continued: " I often wonder if I'm right in this because they live in such a competitive world and they do need to hone their competitive skills; the problem is that they can't give it up even in this team. This means that they can't listen to each other in the right way and they can't learn from each other."

This inability to learn is a cause of premature death in organisations. It is hard to get it right first time, but if we are confident in our abilities to learn, then we can adjust, flex and move quickly to change. Traditionally strategy work is mainly about *thinking* and *planning*, e.g.:

■ analysing the organisation's environment and planning to take an advantageous position in it
■ forecasting the future and creating rational strategic plans to fit
■ understanding the core competencies and internal resources of the organisation
■ identifying the big decisions that matter, etc.

While such activities are useful they do not anticipate the question of learning. A learning approach to strategy does not over-analyse but sets a broad direction of travel and then aims to react swiftly and creatively to emerging situations and to take advantage of any new opportunities. The ideas of challenges and dialogue are central to this approach:

■ *Challenges*: what situations are we facing that require us to stretch ourselves and develop new capabilities? These situations challenge us to go beyond where we are now, so that energy is released by our joint efforts to achieve this. Goals are set and modified as we go along, as various innovations and discoveries allow us do things we have not done before.
■ *Dialogue*: leaders to orchestrate discussions to share understandings and commitments. Dialogue involves open discussion of purposes and projects and about what is being learnt about progress and from actions. Leadership sets up the frameworks and structures for dialogue and encourages everyone to take part in it.

A learning approach to strategy develops a collective conversation about the future, and undertakes concerted action learning on this basis. Leadership creates space for learning, intelligence sharing and for review and improvement processes. The vision is of people as partners in strategy implementation, with everyone networked together to form a powerful collective intelligence.

There are eight elements of a learning approach to strategy (Pedler, Burgoyne and Boydell, 2000):

1. *Space*: giving individuals space for learning and responsible experimentation.
2. *A Big Picture*: explaining the strategic context of work and plans.
3. *Feedback*: seeking and passing on comments on strategies in the light of implementation experience.
4. *Participation*: facilitating participation while ensuring decisiveness.
5. *Holding framework*: creating a climate where existing working methods can be challenged and changed in a coordinated manner.
6. *Experiment*: enabling responsible experimentation and sharing of learning.
7. *Learning*: encouraging a "solve and learn" rather than a "blame and punish" approach to problem solving.
8. *Personal example*: personally and visibly modelling a learning attitude and approach.

See Activity P2.4: A Learning Approach to Strategy Questionnaire is based on these eight elements and will enable you to check your, your team's or your organisation's standing in this respect.

Scenario thinking

If something can go wrong, it will. (Murphy's law)

Scenario thinking is a second tool for creating common purpose. This is a "What if" activity that can sharpen our perception of the future challenges and how we might respond to them. The traps of prediction, extrapolation and too much certainty await those who over-rely on planning. This can be avoided by looking at possibilities and alternatives that "express uncertainty in structured ways". This is strategic thinking rather than strategic planning.

Scenario thinking helps groups of people – from small teams to large stakeholder conferences – to start thinking about future directions. This process of participation is perhaps more important than the outcomes. Some valuable options may come out of these discussions, but more significantly they help to create a general readiness and orientation to the future.

A simple form of scenario thinking takes three basic positions or cases:

- *Middle ground*: "The future will be much like the present".
- *Best case*: environmental conditions favour us.
- *Worst case*: environmental conditions work against us.

Figure P2.2 illustrates these positions graphically:

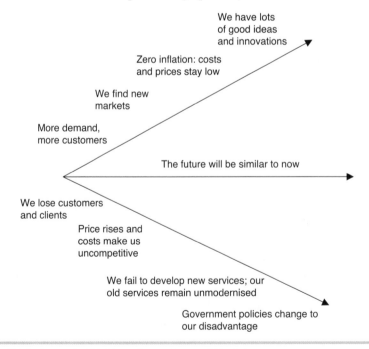

Figure P2.2 Scenario thinking: three views of the future

You can try your hand at scenarios in Activity P2.5: Scenario Thinking at the end of the chapter.

The value of scenario thinking is that it demonstrates that different futures create different challenges. This is very helpful in terms of preparation for alternatives and contingencies, by helping to develop the "mental muscles" for finding direction in complex circumstances. Above all it shows the importance of the ability to learn from experience, which is the best safeguard of future success.

Scenario thinking is not complicated and the brief in Activity P2.5 is enough to get you and your colleagues started on the process. There are many elaborations on this basic form, and larger groups in particular can generate multiple scenario options that add to the richness of the picture. If you are keen to go further, there are plenty of resources available, some of which can be found at the end of the chapter.

Storytelling

Once upon a time ... All of us have been brought up with stories. They carry knowledge and wisdom across borders and generations, and they can also help us deal with changes and even to make changes ourselves.

Telling your story can be the first step in a journey. In action learning groups, each person tells their story of what is happening to them. Encouraged by the others, they also talk about what they would like to happen, what they would like to do and what perils and dangers may be stopping them. If the story touches on core purposes, and the group meets for long enough, over time new episodes are added and the narrative moves on, being rewritten and reinterpreted.

Action learning stories lead into dialogues and reflections with colleagues, who can provide us with the support to change ourselves and what goes on around us. Stories can also be co-created in groups – generated and developed by the group as a whole. Here is an activity that can be done in a group of, say, five to 12 people.

See Activity P2.6: storytelling in a writers' circle.

Storytelling can be used in all sorts of situations. If it is used as part of a change process, it may help to assuage anxieties and allow people to contribute to ideas about what they would like to see happen. It can also help people come to terms with the personal consequences of changes and work out how they want to respond. Storytelling can be a valuable way of summing up or evaluating any change effort; the glimpses or critical incidents produced by a writers' circle can often catch the essence far better than any number of questionnaires.

Conclusion

The critical work of leadership requires people who do things on purpose. Finding our own purposes in life and work is an important part of being able to contribute to leadership. Negotiating common purpose within the diversity of views within a community is essential for effective action and learning.

The message of this chapter is: find your own sense of purpose, develop it and strengthen your practice or purpose. This is a philosophy for people who serve their purposes and not just their employers. It is important to find and build the communities that support you in your purpose, for without these others you are unlikely to achieve what you want to bring about.

As the first leadership practice, the question of purpose is always present whenever a significant challenge appears. Like the other core practices in this book, being on purpose is both a personal characteristic and also a means for forging alliances with other people. It is an inclination and an ability that is strengthened in action and learning; do things on purpose, and you will learn to do them better.

References

Bennis, W. and Nanus, B. (1997) *Leaders: Strategies For Taking Charge*. New York: Harper Business, 2nd edition.

Casey, D. (1993) *Managing Learning in Organisations*. Milton Keynes: Open University Press.

Heifetz, R. (1994) *Leadership without Easy Answers*. Cambridge, Mass: Belknap Press.

Pedler, M., Burgoyne, J. and Boydell, T. (2000) *The Learning Company Toolkit*. Maidenhead: Peter Honey.

Further resources

There is a great deal written on purpose, much of it from a religious or philosophical perspective, and surprisingly little from an organisational or leadership perspective.

Purpose is about finding both meaning and direction and if you don't know Jim Collins' *Good to Great* (London: Random House, 2001) then this is a first starting point. The distinguishing feature of Collins' "Level 5 leaders" is their personal modesty allied to "intense professional will". *Purpose: The Starting Point of Great Companies* by Nikos Mourkogiannis (Basingstoke: Palgrave Macmillan, 2006) makes the obvious point: a strong sense of purpose is essential to success in any field. In the "Good to Great" tradition of Jim Collins this book identifies four kinds of possible purpose for your organisation: Discovery, Excellence, Altruism and Heroism.

Beyond Reason: Using Emotions as you Negotiate by Roger Fisher and Daniel Shapiro (New York: Penguin, 2006) is a recent development of the famous Harvard Negotiation Project and is a useful slant on using purpose in conflict situations. This slim and clearly written book shows that understanding all the purposes in the situation can work positively in reaching agreements.

On purpose as finding direction, Kees Van den Heijden's *The Sixth Sense: Accelerating Organisational Learning with Scenarios* (Chichester: Wiley, 2002) builds on the author's previous work and the work on scenario development done at Shell. *Leading Change: A guide to whole systems working* by Margaret Attwood, Mike Pedler, Sue Pritchard and David Wilkinson (Bristol: Policy Press, 2003) gives a whole systems thinking perspective on developing strategy and leadership, and will help particularly in working with big groups and conferences.

The importance of stories in making sense and finding meaning has long been recognised. Dave Snowden works with the idea of storytelling as part of sensemaking approaches to knowledge management He has written a number of books and papers on the topic: http://www.cognitive-edge.com/articlesby davesnowden.php.

Activities

The six activities in this chapter will help you to locate your own sense of purpose and to develop a common purpose with others. They are:

- Activity P2.1: My Purpose.
- Activity P2.2: Finding My Sense of Purpose.
- Activity P2.3: Mine; Ours and Theirs – A Matrix of Purposes.
- Activity P2.4: *A Learning Approach to Strategy* Questionnaire.
- Activity P2.5: Scenario Thinking.
- Activity P2.6: Storytelling in a Writers' Circle.

Activity P2.1: My Purpose

1 Think of a recent event in which you were influential. This could be a work project where you got some good results, or perhaps a party or a trip that you organised, or a conversation you had with someone.

Now thinking of your sense of purpose in that experience, consider the hierarchy in Figure P2.3 below. Put an × in the third column of the hierarchy to represent the level at which you believe you were operating:

Fable	Your translation	Your level of operation
Bricks		
Wall		
Cathedral		
God		

Figure P2.3 **A hierarchy of purposes**

To do this, you may need to translate bricks, wall, cathedral and God into your own situation – perhaps as ...

- personal "brownie points"
- good teamwork
- enhancing the company's reputation, and
- contributing to the wider society?

Whatever labels you choose, the underlying hierarchy remains – we always have this choice of purpose.

2 Looking at where you have put your ×, and thinking generally about what motivates you, consider the following questions:

- Would you say that the position marked is typical of you or not?
- Does your sense of purpose move up and down the hierarchy depending on the particular situation or would you say that it was usually at this level?

Activity P2.2: Finding My Sense of Purpose

This activity is best done by two people working together, although it can be done alone – by questioning yourself using the prompts and questions below and writing down your responses. (*It's a good idea to write down your responses anyway so that you can study them later*.)

Working in a pair, one person can concentrate on responding and on recording their responses to the questions in seeking to locate their sense of purpose. The other person can help by asking the questions until the possibilities have been exhausted. A skilled helper will vary the wording of the questions to match the nature of the responses, but their essential character remains the same.

Start this activity by eliciting a *personal construct*. Personal constructs are bi-polar in form, as in warm – remote, but are not simple opposites. Constructs may be described by single words or by short phrases, e.g. "comfortable to wear" – "restricting". To elicit your constructs, you first choose three objects or subjects, perhaps three objects in the room, or three people you know, or three items of clothing, and then use these three apparently mundane items to get at what is really important for you personally.

Here is a worked example that you can follow.

Kath's sense of purpose

Kath is facing a challenge and does not quite know how to act. She has decided to do this activity to get clear in her own mind what she wants in the situation. She responds to prompts and questions put by a colleague, and her responses to the questions are in italics.

■ Look at three pieces of furniture in the room.
   OK – curtains, rocking chair and table.

■ Name one way in which two are the same and one is different.
   Two of these are mobile; one is static.

■ Now, which do you prefer: mobile or static?
   Mobile.

■ So, what is it that is important about being mobile for you?
   More potential.

■ And, what for you is the opposite of more potential?
   Stuckness.

■ So, which of these two do you prefer: more potential or stuckness?
   More potential.

■ And what is it that is important for you about more potential?
   Because it is about hope and possibility.

■ And, what for you is the opposite of hope and possibility?
Despair.

■ That sounds like it – do you agree?
Yes: this is me – I am always looking for hope and possibility.

You can tell when the sequence is finished when you begin to repeat words or synonyms and when there does not seem anywhere else to go. The effect of this process is to move you remarkably quickly from the concrete particulars of any situation to your personal core constructs and values. This is why the activity is called *laddering*, and its effect is to put you back in touch with what is important to you. In this example, Kath goes very quickly from inanimate objects to personal values. Some people may need to persevere longer than this.

In this simple example, Kath has clearly found a touchstone, something that can guide her in the situation she faces. Of course, tackling the challenge will still not be easy, but at least she knows what she is for and what she wants to bring about. Now try it yourself, perhaps keeping in mind a current leadership challenge facing you: what are you trying to bring about here?

Eliciting a personal construct
1 Choose any three things or people that you know:

(i)

(ii)

(iii)

2 Now, describe a way in which two of these are the same and one is different:

Now you have a personal construct that can be used as the basis for the laddering activity. Work carefully through the questions below, writing down your responses before moving on.

Laddering questions
3 Which of these two words do you prefer?

4 What is it that is important for you about the preferred word?

5 And what for you is the opposite of that preferred word?

6 Then again, which of these two words do you prefer?

7 Now, what is it that is important for you about the preferred word?

Continue to repeat the sequence in 3, 4 and 5 above as long as new material keeps emerging. This involves the repetition of the three questions:

- which of these two words do you *prefer*?
- what is it that is *important* for you about the preferred word?
- what for you is the *opposite* of that preferred word?

And so on. You can try using three different objects to see if you get different words or phrases. What you are trying to establish is a sense of your own core constructs – those that you take around with you everywhere you go; those that determine what you see and how you make sense of things.

Activity P2.3: *Mine; Ours and Theirs* – A Matrix of Purposes

This activity uses the same hierarchy of purposes from Figure P2.3, but with added columns.

1 Think of a current project in which you are involved. This could be a work project or one involving friends or family.

2 Thinking of your own sense of purpose for this project, put an X in the Mine column of the hierarchy in Figure P2.4 below to represent the level where you wish to operate:

Fable	Translation	Mine	Ours	Theirs
God				
Cathedral				
Wall				
Brick				

Figure P2.4 Mine; ours, theirs – a matrix of purposes

Again to do this, you may need to translate the terms in the hierarchy to fit this current project. In this situation what would be a good way to describe:

■ Bricks?
■ Wall?
■ Cathedral?
■ Society?

3 Now, thinking of all the other people and colleagues involved with you in this project, put an × in the Ours column to represent where you think this group wishes to operate in terms of its collective sense of purpose.

4 Thirdly, now think of all those who are not directly involved, but who will be affected or impacted upon by the outcomes of this project. Put an × in the Theirs column to represent what sense of purpose would best fit their aspirations.

5 Finally, looking at where you have put the preferences for the three different groups, consider the following questions:

■ Are the various purposes clear?
■ To what extent do we have common purpose?
■ How accountable are the people engaged on this project to the other interested or affected parties in the Theirs column?

Activity P2.4: *A Learning Approach to Strategy* Questionnaire

This questionnaire is based on the eight elements of *a learning approach to strategy*. You can use it either as a self-rating questionnaire for individuals and teams, or as a more general survey of the style of strategic leadership in an organisation.

You can do it here and now for your own benefit, but the best results come from talking over the results with other people. It takes only a few minutes to complete and score the questionnaire but considerably more to discuss the findings and implications.

Rate yourself on each of the following 24 questions using the five-point scale below:

I rarely or never do this = 1 – 2 – 3 – 4 – 5 = *I always or regularly do this*

Try to avoid using 3.

1	I encourage others to undertake new projects to widen their experience	1 – 2 – 3 – 4 – 5
2	I always explain the big picture behind current projects	1 – 2 – 3 – 4 – 5
3	I ask for feedback from stakeholders on the strategies we are following	1 – 2 – 3 – 4 – 5
4	We try to involve everyone in arriving at decisions	1 – 2 – 3 – 4 – 5
5	I encourage all team members to question our ways of working	1 – 2 – 3 – 4 – 5
6	People are encouraged to work in small groups for learning purposes	1 – 2 – 3 – 4 – 5
7	We treat crises and problems as opportunities for experiment and learning	1 – 2 – 3 – 4 – 5
8	I publish my own personal development plans to my team	1 – 2 – 3 – 4 – 5
9	All our people are expected to have plans for their personal development	1 – 2 – 3 – 4 – 5
10	We take time out to take a "helicopter view" of what we are doing	1 – 2 – 3 – 4 – 5
11	I always want to hear how strategies are working in practice	1 – 2 – 3 – 4 – 5
12	As much as possible, I involve all those people concerned with a problem in arriving at a solution	1 – 2 – 3 – 4 – 5
13	Anyone who wants to change the way we do things can give it a go	1 – 2 – 3 – 4 – 5
14	When people try things out which work – or don't work – we all want to know about them	1 – 2 – 3 – 4 – 5
15	When someone makes a mistake, we know it will start a good discussion	1 – 2 – 3 – 4 – 5

16	In team meetings, I make it plain what I am learning from what we are doing	1 – 2 – 3 – 4 – 5
17	When I meet with colleagues I always check on what they have been learning recently	1 – 2 – 3 – 4 – 5
18	I have a strong sense of strategic direction and communicate this	1 – 2 – 3 – 4 – 5
19	My team is keen to pass on to our bosses how well they think implementation programmes are going	1 – 2 – 3 – 4 – 5
20	Up to the deadline, everyone around here can have their say	1 – 2 – 3 – 4 – 5
21	People consciously think about how they are working on a regular basis	1 – 2 – 3 – 4 – 5
22	We make time for the regular transfer of knowledge across teams	1 – 2 – 3 – 4 – 5
23	When a problem crops up, there is competition for who gets to work on it	1 – 2 – 3 – 4 – 5
24	I maintain the space for my own learning in spite of the pressures	1 – 2 – 3 – 4 – 5

Scoring

Add the scores from the 24 questions in the eight vertical columns:

QUESTIONS:	1	2	3	4	5	6	7	8
	9	10	11	12	13	14	15	16
	17	18	19	20	21	22	23	24

TOTALS:	[ ]	[ ]	[ ]	[ ]	[ ]	[ ]	[ ]	[ ]
	1	2	3	4	5	6	7	8

The Learning Approach to Strategy Questionnaire is based on the eight elements of:

1 Space

2 A Big Picture

3 Feedback

4 Participation

5 Holding Framework

6 Experiment

7 Learning

8 Personal Example.

What this means to you in your team or organisation is a matter for reflection and discussion; there are no right and wrong answers. However, if this way of working appeals to you then a score of …

- 7 or less on any element indicates that you might need to make greater efforts here, whilst a score of less than 4 indicates considerable grounds for concern
- more than 9 on any element shows that you are making good progress here
- more than 12 indicates that you are setting a fine example for others. Well done!

Review

Before moving on, you might like to take time out to reflect on the findings from *The Learning Approach to Strategy Questionnaire*. Here are some review questions to think about or discuss with colleagues:

- What are your strengths as a strategic leader?
- How do your responses to this activity compare with those of your colleagues?
- What one thing could you do to develop yourself in this context?
- What would you say are the strengths and weaknesses of your organisation as a whole?
- How could you encourage the development of your organisation along these lines?

Activity P2.5: Scenario Thinking

This is one that is hard to do alone, and you need a group of at least three people. Groups of 12–20 people work very well.

Divide the group into three, then either allocate, or ask the sub-groups to self-select from, the three scenarios in Figure P2.2 (reproduced below for you).

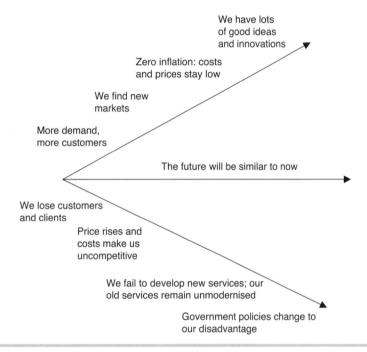

Figure P2.2 Scenario thinking: three views of the future

If you want to encourage diversity and maximise the options, you could divide the group into as many teams as possible (three or four per group is probably the minimum to get good creative thinking). You can have more than one team working on each option

Set the date for five or seven years into the future. The trick is to get people to think as if the future had already happened.

1　Brief everyone as follows:

"It is 20 __ [5 or 7 years from now], how are we leading strategic change and its implementation in this organisation?

(i)　What has changed for our:

- clients or customers and their level of service and satisfaction?
- staff and their commitment and motivation?
- business partners and the relationship we have had with them?
- other stakeholders, including the communities we work in?

(ii)　What have been the critical issues since 20 __ [today]?"

NB Put yourselves into the future, work from the perspective of 20 __ [5 or 7 years from now] and talk about now in the past tense. However, when you refer to yourselves, use "we" and not "they", as you are still here directing the organisation.

2　The groups should then disperse to their own space with whatever materials they might find useful: flipcharts, coloured pens, collage materials and so on.

Fix a time for them to come back with their findings and ask them to present these in whatever way they think will have most impact.

3　At the appointed time, have the teams present their scenarios. Encourage the other teams to support rather than compete by asking questions only for clarification.

4　When all the teams have presented their scenarios, facilitate a whole group discussion around the question:

What are the strategic themes and issues that we should be pursuing now in order to maximise our chances of getting to where we want to be?

This question helps to avoid pointless competitiveness and puts the focus on the challenges and common purposes.

Activity P2.6: Storytelling in a Writers' Circle

This activity can be done in any group of five to 12 people.

1   Choose a current change situation, and ask each person to think about an experience of this that is significant for them. For example, the theme might be health at work, or working in a team, or merging with another department. Ask everyone to think of a story and write some notes on:
   - When and where did this take place?
   - What happened?
   - Who was involved?
   - Why have I remembered it?

2   Now ask each person to tell the story of their experience. If the group is large, this might be best done in smaller groups or continued over more than one session. While the storyteller is speaking, everyone else should:
   - listen without interruption
   - show appreciation but not pass any judgements on other people's stories
   - when the story is finished, ask questions to clarify things, if they wish
   - join in discussion afterwards on general issues.

3   Once all the stories have been told, ask everyone to join in co-creating a story of this theme in the future organisation.

   This can be done in lots of creative ways. You can write stories or draw pictures alone or in pairs. A fun way to write is to do it as a joint story in a writers' circle:
   (i)   Ask each person to start off a story by writing two or three sentences about this theme in the future company, say, in five or 10 years' time.
   (ii) When everyone has done this, pass the paper to the right and ask the next person to add two more sentences to the story. Encourage people to be imaginative – creative, funny, pessimistic – however they feel; but also to be serious by adding what they think is important.
   (iii) Pass the story on to the next person and ask them to add two more sentences. Repeat until the story comes back to the originator. This person should now add the final sentence.
   (iv) Each person reads out "their" stories in turn. Enjoy them and allow them to settle briefly before moving on.
   (v)   When all the stories have been read, ask: What are the common themes arising from these pictures of the future? What would we like the future to be like?

Practice 3: Power

7

*Be not afraid of greatness, some men are born great, some achieve greatness,
and some have greatness thrust upon them*
William Shakespeare, *Twelfth Night*

Introduction

Studied and pondered endlessly throughout human history, power remains a subject of fascination. We learn that it is both a highly desirable and also a dangerous thing, associated with high risks. Some are tempted by it, try to acquire it and monopolise it; others are wary of it and seek to deny it even when they hold positions of formal authority.

Yet, power is an everyday thing; it is the ability to do or to act, to get work done, to make things happen. However, beyond this simple definition, power is hard to pin down. It is omnipresent in human society, and has many aspects, effects and guises. For example, think of all the words that can be coupled with power:

- influence
- freedom
- control
- responsibility
- authority
- politics
- compliance
- resistance
- conflict
- corruption, etc.

If the first part of this list reminds us why we want it, the second reveals the long shadow cast by power. This should prompt a proper wariness. Leadership must and should embrace power, but needs to do so wisely and responsibly. The responsible use of power is one of the more testing challenges of being human, and if purpose is the first practice of leadership then power lies close behind.

The aim of this chapter is to provide a starting point for the sensible, responsible and positive practice of power in leadership. It contains:

■ A *Power Index* for assessing your own sources and use of power.
■ A model of the sources of power in organisations.
■ An exploration of the "dark side" of power and powerlessness.
■ How to build positive power in assertive individuals, high-performing teams and powerful organisations.
■ References and further resources.

Are you a powerful person?

Power is usually defined as the ability to get something done or the capacity to influence the actions of other people. But any dictionary will reveal many meanings, from physical force and energy, to aspects of mathematics to the powers of authorities and states. So, first thinking about yourself, consider three questions:

1. Are you a powerful person?
2. And, do you want to be?

The first of these questions appears factual or empirical, the second more to do with moral purposes. These two are always intertwined: the pursuit and use of power in leadership comes with accompanying moral considerations and responsibilities. This is in part because of a third question:

3. How can I work with others, in teams, groups and organisations to realise our power and use it well and wisely?

So, back to question 1: are you a powerful person? You might hesitate over this; perhaps it all depends on the type of power we are talking about? Perhaps it is a question that only makes sense in a certain context? So, are you a powerful person:

■ In this group?
■ In this business?
■ In this family?
■ In this community?

These everyday situations are all stages on which actors seek to influence each other to get things done. Getting and using power is a normal thing.

The second question seems obvious, and easy to answer; but the reality usually turns out to be trickier than it looks. Power is slippery, dangerous stuff, as much in the perception as in the actuality. The holding of power in particular situations doesn't always deliver what we want.

The third question is the important one for leaders. Leadership requires an understanding of power, how it works, where it comes from, what is available in a particular situation and how this can be used. But it also requires a moral authority in using this knowledge and capacity. In all social groups and situations power is usually unequally distributed; some people have more of it than others. Yet because there are many types and sources of power, there are ways of compensating for weakness or for balancing one sort of power with another. The deliberately unequal distribution of formal power in work organisations is designed to give some people the right to direct others, but it also gives rise to the mobilisation of alternative power sources, often operating in less visible political processes.

Where does power come from?

Understanding the sources, uses and effects of your power is a first step in this leadership practice. Now, consider three more questions:

1. What is the basis of your power? Where does it come from?
2. Do you understand the different sorts of power available to you? Do you prefer to use some sorts of power rather than others?
3. Do you use your power in a positive way? Does your use of power result in an increase in the power available in the system or not?

> *To find the answers to these questions, you can start by looking at how you use power with your colleagues; try Activity P3.1:*
> *The Power Index to investigate this*

The *Power Index* is based on a model first proposed over 50 years ago by two social scientists: French and Raven (1959). In this view, some sources of power derive from the *position* we hold in an organisation whilst others are more do with us as *persons*.

There are three types of POSITION power:

■ *Role power* derives from your role and status and the perception that you have the right to exercise influence because of this. This kind of power is linked to the hierarchical structure of an organisation and defines the scope of your authority.

- *Coercive power* is based on the use of fear. It depends on other people thinking that you can punish them if they do not comply. Examples of this might include strong measures such as formal reprimands, the withdrawal of promotion or privileges, the allocation of unpleasant duties and even dismissal. But there are many highly effective and subtler forms of coercion such as disapproval, withdrawal of friendship, exclusion from key meetings and so on.
- *Reward power* is the twin of coercion – the carrot to go with the stick. *Reward power* is based on the perception that you have the ability and resources to reward the compliant. There are many ways to reward people including praise, recognition, increased responsibilities and the granting of individual privileges. Pay, promotion and the allocation of desirable work are other possibilities.

There are also three types of PERSONAL power:

- *Expert power* which is based on your competence or special knowledge in a given area. Expert power is based on credibility, and the value attached to the particular field in which you can show competence.
- *Personal power* is based on the influence that comes from your personal attractiveness to others. It is the power which comes from your personal characteristics and charisma, your reputation, the respect of others and the esteem in which you are held. Personal power is sometimes called referent power because it is based on the psychological identification of others with you.
- *Connection power* derives from networks and relationships. This kind of power can be used to build political knowledge, gather information, gain personal support and feedback, or build trusted alliances. Connection power was not in French and Raven's original list, but it has become increasingly important as a way of getting things done in a networked world.

The *Power Index* is a simple way of checking your use of the different types of power. It will be helpful to discuss your results with a trusted friend or mentor. Here are some questions to consider:

- Which sources of power do you have access to in your organisation?
- Are there sources of power that you are overusing?
- Are there sources which are available to you but which you are not currently using?
- How can you increase your power to bring about what you desire?

But as well as assessing your use of the different sources of power, the *Power Index* also measures how happy you are with this current pattern or practice of power. Your scores can also help you to ask answer the questions:

■ Does my current practice work for me?
■ What do my friends and colleagues say about how I use power?
■ How could I improve my practice of power to achieve more valuable results?

The dark side

A message from the Dark Side there is. (Yoda, *Star Wars*)

Before looking at the positive side of how to build power in yourself and others, consider first the negative aspects. Two aspects of the dark side of power are represented here: the dangers of bullying and the deleterious effects of powerlessness. Recognising and avoiding these downsides of power is a key part of developing your leadership practice.

What do you do with your power? Do you use it to:

■ Enhance your own position?
■ Advance the purposes and goals of your friends?
■ Benefit your organisation or community?
■ Serve a higher purpose?

This question leads back to purpose. Why do you want power and what will you use it for, are important questions because power is as easy to abuse as to use. Bullying and oppression are part and parcel of the "high performance" culture so prevalent in many organisations today. And this is not confined to the City. Abuses of power and bullying happen in public service agencies and even more ironically, in charitable and other "third sector" agencies focused on redressing power imbalances in the outside world.

They also happen in voluntary and community groups, in golf clubs and in families. They happen where people live and work together, wanting to get things done with limited resources – money, time, love. Who among us has never been bullied? And, who among us has never resorted to bullying to get their way?

Bullies: victims or oppressors?

The relationship of bully and victim is familiar from fairy stories and from our own lives. Recalling and reflecting on past episodes where we have been bullied or victimised can be unsettling, but unless we can find ways of breaking out of this pattern of relationship then we might be condemned to repeat it. Oppressor and victim is a dance with two partners. To break free from such slavish patterns is one of the basic purposes of personal development, and it is a vital stage in the emergence of wise leadership.

In one sense, bullying starts in our perception that power resides in individuals. We see people as powerful or less powerful, influential or ineffective. But power in organisations is a mainly relational affair, generated and located in relationships, rather than being a property of individual persons. This is not to discount the existence of big, charismatic or wise people, but to emphasise on the whole that people in organisations are powerful because we agree to be influenced by them. If we are not impressed by the general's epaulettes, then they have no power over us, or with us.

The problem is of course that it may cost us if we choose not to be swayed. Bullies exist because of our fears of being battered or disappointing those we, however misguidedly, love and respect. We conform, acquiesce, comply, obey, abide by and go along with all sorts of influences to preserve our bodies or our lifestyles. In crisis and law and order situations, conformity may be appropriate, but if conforming is what we learn to do, how well will this quality of relationship deal with the challenges that demand concerted and creative effort from all concerned? To work well together usually needs more than compliance and conformance. Leadership involves understanding what sort of relationships can generate positive power, and also recognising those which drain it away. Will we be able to step up for that? Will we know how?

Figure P3.1 shows a polarised relationship with an oppressor at the top and a victim at the bottom. These two positions are chained together in a double loop.

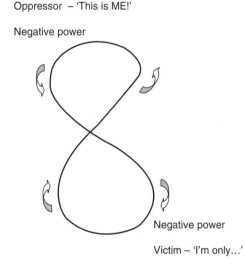

Oppressor – 'This is ME!'

Negative power

Negative power

Victim – 'I'm only...'

Figure P3.1 **Abusing power**

Now, put yourself on this double loop and then move round it, pausing to remember at particular points when you felt like this:

■ What does it feel like to be on top – *the oppressor?* Perhaps childhood experiences come to mind as you think of how you dominated and threatened other children to get your way? When have you done this recently at work?

■ Now move down to the bottom – you are now *the victim.* Is this familiar? How does this feel? What does it remind you of? Remember the times when you were weak and powerless – "I'm only ..." "If only ..." "I can't ...."

Now turn to Figure P3.2 and try a journey around this new double loop. Start in the middle and move round, but now with awareness, avoiding the outer parts of the loops beyond the centre circle.

■ What does it feel like to be in the middle – avoiding the traps of both oppressor and victim? Think of a relationship where you have this balance with another person or group. How does that feel? When have you done this at work recently?

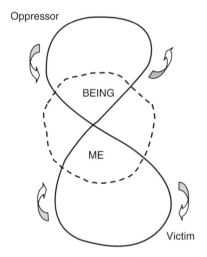

Figure P3.2 **Using power positively**

The way to avoid the oppressor/victim trap is in working to enlarge the circle in the middle of Figure P3.2. The secret of using power positively is to stay in and build up that area where both parties can be themselves to influence and be influenced without coercion. This is very hard to do sometimes, because these habits can be engrained; some of us are chronic victims or bullies and some are both – easily moving from one to the other position and finding it hard to stay in the middle.

Start by being aware of your relationships with people, and aim to stay out of the territory at either end of the loops. Learning to develop positive power relationships with other people and groups is a vital leadership skill. Use your responsibilities to lead *with* others, feeling on top only when they are feeling good too and taking a positive view of themselves and what they can do.

This is not always possible. If exercising power could always be morally justified then many of the dilemmas of this leadership practice would disappear.

Powerlessness

Powerlessness corrupts. Absolute powerlessness corrupts absolutely.

(Rosabeth Kanter, 1977)

A culture of bullying and victimisation can result in a widespread loss of power that makes it harder and harder to get anything done. We may deplore those testosterone-soaked boardroom battles, decry the back office chicaneries, and despair at the machinations of politicians, yet the absence of power can be even worse. It has been said that nature abhors a vacuum, and too little power can be as corrupting to our purposes as too much of it. Powerlessness saps the will and makes of us all victims and slaves.

The Abilene paradox

Jerry Harvey (1996) tells the tale of a Texas family who take a nightmare trip on a hot summer afternoon. With nothing to do and nowhere to go, people are listless and bored, and someone suggests going to Abilene for an ice cream. The day is hot, the road is dusty, the air-conditioner is broken, and the trip takes far longer than forecast. Even the ice cream disappoints. It subsequently turns out that no-one really wanted to make the trip – including the person who made the suggestion. This turns into a dire experience for which everyone blames each other. How does this happen? Why have …

> … *four reasonably sensible people, of our own volition, just taken a 106-mile trip across a godforsaken desert in a furnace-like temperature, through a cloud-like dust storm to eat unpalatable food at a hole-in-the-wall cafeteria in Abilene*, when none of us had really wanted to go?

You can probably think of examples of *the Abilene paradox* operating in your organisation. Harvey suggests that groups and teams often take actions in contradiction to what they really want and thereby defeat the very purposes they are trying to achieve. Individuals privately agree on what they want to do, but do not communicate this and, on the basis of misperceptions and invalid information, take decisions which no-one really wants. Not surprisingly, people are fed up about this and tend to blame each other and especially any leaders.

A variation on this theme can be seen in the media design team in a large publishing group.

The media design team

The media design team are a talented bunch of folk. They work to a properly structured and focused agenda, but they lack the collective desire to manage it well. The relationships between members are fractious and cliquey, and behaviour is poor; team members commonly:

■ make political statements
■ manoeuvre for positions
■ self-market themselves at the expense of others
■ show off and generally try to impress
■ put other people down
■ show distrust and even dislike of colleagues
■ openly compete for work with clients.

Because of the difficulties experienced in reaching consensus, the media design team has started to vote on issues. But people tend to vote for their allies irrespective of technical know-how and professional arguments, and there are lots of poor decisions. Customers complain but are fobbed off or ignored.

The media design team is an example of a blight that can especially affect teams of professional and "creative" workers. Here, the collective output is actually worse than the individuals working alone could achieve: $2 + 2 = 3$ or even less. There are frequent experiences of the Abilene paradox, where decisions are taken on behalf of the whole that nobody really wants.

Struggling teams are a major source of power loss in organisations. They are "energy sinks" absorbing more than they produce, divided by various disintegrating forces:

■ fighting for "turf" within the team
■ individuals avoiding anything that will make them look bad
■ avoiding disagreement and plain speaking
■ going along with "consensus" decisions that nobody wants
■ quality of leadership
■ poor personal relationships
■ unresolved conflicts.

Groups like this have not developed a positive politics of teamwork. Until they feel more confident and positive about using their power with one another instead of against one another, they will all continue to be losers.

Building positive power

Every generation needs to learn democracy anew. (Kurt Lewin)

Guarding against bullying, victimisation, powerlessness and the other disorders of power is an important aspect of the stewardship role of leaders. What is the distribution of power among people, teams and in the whole group or system? Who has it and how are they using it? Where is power being generated and where is it being absorbed and dissipated? Where there appear to be but a few powerful barons, the overall effect might be a widespread powerlessness:

> … a monopoly on power means that only very few have this capacity, and they prevent the majority of others being able to act effectively. Thus the total amount of power – and total system effectiveness – is restricted, even though some people seem to have a lot of it.
>
> (Kanter, 1977, p. 166)

Leadership should be less concerned with individually powerful people and more with enhancing the total amount of power in a system. Because power is a relational phenomenon, and happens *between* people, developing the total power of the organisation means ensuring that everyone has access to the tools and resources they need to get things done. The three sections below are concerned with the leadership practice of building positive power in:

- assertive individuals
- high performing teams
- powerful organisations.

Assertive individuals

With teams like the media design group, individuals may be helped by some assertiveness training. Being assertive means pursuing your purposes and exercising your powers, but not at the expense of others. Being assertive means striking the balance between your purposes and those of other people.

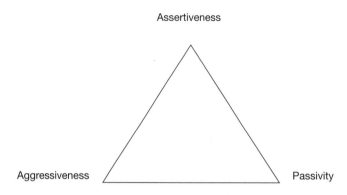

Figure P3.3 **The assertiveness triangle**

It is easy to get this wrong. Assertiveness is easily distinguished from passivity, but less easily from aggression. When we say someone is being "assertive" in everyday life, we often mean that they are insisting on their own rights or getting their own way *against* other people. The word assertiveness is often associated with "pushiness" or aggression, but in the assertiveness triangle it means pursuing your goals *and* the goals of the other people in the situation.

The aim is to get into the top of the triangle and to avoid the two bottom corners, drawing everyone away from the other poles by taking all their goals and purposes seriously. A team that can operate in this zone will get positive results in difficult situations by avoiding the traps of pushing too hard or holding back and letting things go. Again, Rosabeth Kanter puts it so well:

> ... *the meaning of power here is closer to "mastery" or "autonomy" than to domination or control over others. Empowering more people through generating more autonomy, more participation in decisions, and more access to resources increases the total capacity for effective action.*
>
> (Kanter, 1977, p. 166)

The myth of empowerment

The unequal distribution of formal power in organisations makes it easy for us to fall into the traps of passivity and aggression, oppressor and victim. Perhaps, like chickens, we also have some tendencies to form hierarchical pecking orders. Whatever the pattern, power relationships in organisations can either enhance or seriously hamper performance, and it is the job of leadership to do something about it.

It has been popular to talk about "empowerment", as in "I empower you to … ". But this sort of empowerment is a myth if it does not alter pay, position or authority. If you disagree, try the following test:

Think of when you last "empowered" someone: what power did you actually give them? And, if you did give them some actual powers, when did you take these back?

Without real power attached, empowerment is a confidence trick. The notion is also faulty because power can't easily be given away and has to be taken. Enlightened leaders and monarchs can help to create the conditions, but freedom, democracy and autonomy have to be achieved.

Taking power positively

Bad experiences with power can cause passivity and withdrawal even at very senior levels. Wary of getting our fingers burned again, we may prefer to avoid the risks. A friend told us the story of a chief executive who did not like to exercise her formal and legitimate power:

Make it so!

The chief executive was explaining a difficult situation to her personal consultant. It concerned a recent team meeting where the decision under discussion was a difficult and controversial one. The chief executive was trying to give everyone their say and becoming irritated in particular with one person who was taking a strong position. After listening for some time, the consultant interrupted, and the following exchange took place:

Coach: "It sounds to me as if you were trying to facilitate your team rather than lead it?"
CEO: "Just what do you mean by that?"
Coach: "It means that you were acting as a facilitator for a group and trying to bring about a consensus decision".
CEO: "And …?"
Coach: "Well, in these circumstances, and if all the knowable information is available, you have to lead the team and make the decision."
CEO: "And how would I do that in this case?"
Coach: "After a suitable length of discussion, you could stop the proceedings and ask each person in turn for their recommendation. Then you could say something like 'Thank you for your views – they are very useful. After listening carefully, I have decided to do it like this. I realise that some of you will not like this, but I think this is the best decision in the circumstances.' End of conversation."
CEO: "Yes. …"

The coach makes the obvious suggestion that the CEO should acknowledge her legitimate position power and make the decision. Facilitation might be useful in some circumstances, but here, where a decision is needed on the basis of what is known, leadership means taking the power and acting. The simple rule here is: "Don't defer a decision … unless there is an unknown that is knowable." The CEO knows this really, but in practice she holds back because of her prior experiences.

High-performing teams

So even the chief executive might need help in being assertive with colleagues. If she is able to do this more then there is a chance that not only will she become more effective, but that the team as a whole might become more powerful. Assertive individuals make their best contribution in high-performing teams.

High-performing teams have developed their own good habits for working and performing. Because they are able to be assertive with each other, saying what they want and trying to take each other's wants into account, they are also often able to be self-critical and to regularly review their own performance. This means that they are unafraid and open to learning, and perhaps have their own arrangements for personal and team development. They might even have a regular consultant, but they are not dependent on such outside assistance. These teams do not need much leadership attention beyond recognition and reward – which is important. (Perhaps you also need to watch for signs of complacency, exclusivity, competitiveness, customer condescension and all the other trappings of success!)

However, lots of teams are like *the media design team*, not struggling as such but doing "OK".

The first question to ask about these teams is whether there is a need to do anything? Are you happy with them being OK? Or could they do better? And if so, how can you bring this about?

The "OK team"

The OK team were encouraged by their leader to look at customer evaluations of "adequate", "satisfactory" and "provided us with a 75% solution" and were asked how they felt about these comments. It emerged that the project brief had not been entirely clear and that communications with this customer had been minimal. It was also clear that some team members thought they could do better. Following this discussion the customer was invited to a full-day meeting. The team prepared the questions they wanted to ask and sent a note to the customer explaining this and suggesting that it might be good preparation for them too.

The customer was pleased to be involved and responded enthusiastically to the questions. What surprised the team members most was that although the customer was critical about some aspects of their performance, he was "on their side" and clearly wanted to help them do better. The OK team had not seen the customer in this light before.

The OK team may know deep down that they are just OK, and may be concerned by this. If so, this make the leadership task far easier. Just suggest that they carry out a simple customer survey to learn about how their performance is seen from the outside.

> *See Activity P3.2: The Customer Survey for a simple tool to provide the data and feedback that can start to build the power of any team.*

The view from outside is always the best check for a healthy reality inside. A stubborn group may take some time to come round to this, but a stubborn leader can keep raising the question. Sooner or later, doubts about performance, or a desire to improve, will provide the spark that helps the team to start on building better performance.

Support *and* challenge for high performance

> *Warmth comes before light.* (Reg Revans)

While asking challenging questions, leadership must also provide lots of support to individuals and teams to help them improve. Support and challenge look to be different qualities, but these are actually twin virtues that belong together. It is obvious that people find it easier to speak up and ask questions if they are encouraged to do so; but it is also the case that it becomes easier to raise a challenge in a group when the level of support is high rather than low.

Figure P3.4 shows four combinations of these twin virtues. As the figure suggests, some teams may appear to be highly supportive but are low on challenge. This apparently feels safe and secure, but this is a security that is never tested, and may turn out to be illusory. This is not a powerful team. By contrast, in teams with high challenge but low support, it feels unsafe to take risks. The consequences of getting it wrong are unknown or too great, and it feels as if you are out on a limb with no back-up. This is not a powerful team either.

High performing teams need a high balance of both challenge and support. A high level of support provides everyone with a level of security and confidence for risk taking. The ability to face challenges on the outside, ultimately comes from inner strength.

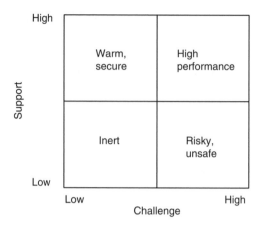

Figure P3.4 **Support and challenge**

There are many ways to build support and challenge. Start with support: this is the warmth that prepares the ground for the light that might be seen via a good challenge. Nothing supports more than listening to people; and nothing challenges more than a good question that makes you think about what you're trying to do. These practices are simple enough to grasp, but need to be developed in any team. Power in a team can also be built by practising action learning as described at the end of Chapter 2. You can also read more about how to do this in the following leadership practice chapters: Chapter 9 on *Challenging Questions*, Chapter 8 on *Risk* and Chapter 10 on *Facilitation*.

Powerful organisations

However difficult in practice, the work of helping individuals and teams to realise their power seems relatively straightforward compared with the work of building powerful organisations. This is a much more complex and long-term endeavour, and one that requires a "whole system" perspective of how the whole organisation works and fits together.

Again, a useful first step is to become aware of the current distribution of power: where is it, who has it and how is it being used? However, this is easier to say than to do; in organisational life, things are not always as they seem. Take the organisational chart for example: this has a value as a "Who's who?" but may not be the best guide to who really has influence and power around here.

The invisible organisation

A hospital doctor told the story of his arrival in a new hospital. After a few weeks he was approached by a colleague and invited to join the local masonic lodge. Cautiously he asked for some time to think about it. During this time he noticed that various people sought him out, introducing themselves and giving him words of advice and encouragement. What surprised him most was that these tended to be people that he either did not know at all or those who would not normally stop and talk with him. After a while it was obvious that these people were linked in some way, and also that some people who were quite junior in the hospital seemed to be in quite senior positions in the lodge.

When he eventually decided not to join, these encounters stopped immediately. The people who had been contacting him melted away. But for a while he had glimpsed a completely different organisation.

It is obvious from this story that taking the organigram as a true map of how things happen here would be the leadership equivalent of going to the stores in search of a left-handed screwdriver. Much power in organisations is bound up in networks such as this masonic example. Networks are interest groups of connected individuals whose purposes may or may not coincide with those of the formal system.

The significance of networks has become increasingly recognised in recent years, along with an emerging view of the organisation as "a network of networks". As Chapter 11 *Networking* implies, working with and around these networks has become a leadership practice in its own right.

Of course, the lines and boxes of the organisational chart still matter; these are the visible and formal structures of the organisation. They are the rational aspects of organisation upon which managers concentrate their managing efforts. They are also the things that tend to get changed when people at the top decide that change is needed. However, from a social constructionist standpoint, these lines and boxes are just a skeleton that is brought to life by the people who inhabit it. These people, and their everyday actions and relationships, *produce* and reproduce the organisation on a daily basis in line with their purposes, values, connections and cultures.

This view suggests that vitality of the organisation as a human construction is influenced but not directed by the shaping effects of formal structure. In *Figure P3.5 The Organisational Iceberg* conceals most of its bulk below the surface. Above the waves are the formal structures, but much of what you bump into when you are trying to do things is concealed below this level. These invisible, less acknowledged aspects are less available to scrutiny, rational analysis and change but they constitute the energy sources for action.

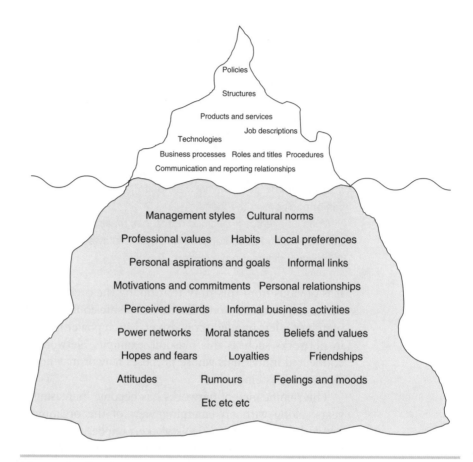

Figure P3.5 **The Organisational Iceberg**

Leadership dilemmas

It is obvious from the *Organisational Iceberg*, that intervening or interfering in the workings of organisations as wholes is far more problematic than suggesting a course of action to an individual or a team. Nevertheless, directions and future possibilities can be raised and discussed; projects and initiatives may be sponsored and facilitated; relationships and linkages may be orchestrated and encouraged.

The lessons here are to do with what to say and do and what to leave up to other people.

Effective leadership means providing a big picture that enables others to make sense of their own worlds. This means suggesting directions of travel but also offering some "holding frameworks" within which other people can decide what should remain the same and what needs to change. This has been described as "getting on the balcony":

> Business leaders have to be able to view patterns as if they were on the balcony. It does them no good to be swept up in the field of action. Leaders have to see a context for change or create one. They should give employees a strong sense of the history of the enterprise, of what's good about its past, as well as an idea about the market forces at work today and the responsibility people must take in shaping the future.

(Heifetz and Laurie, 1997, p. 125)

The challenge here is to get the balance right between direction and letting people get on with it; between speaking and listening. In any situation in which you want to influence events in the "whole system" ask yourself:

- How well do I listen to other people's views?
- Do I show respect for different opinions to mine?
- How clear am I in my views about the best approach to difficult problems?
- How well do I communicate my personal bottom lines about the future direction?
- Do people have a clear sense of the direction in which we are going?
- Are people's freedoms and their responsibilities clearly spelled out?

And, am I getting the balance right between speaking out and leaving things to develop?

Political skills

In leadership roles, it is often necessary to work subtly and indirectly:

> The union representative met with her members to discuss a dispute about training opportunities. The representative was more or less delegated to express the group's position, which she thought was ambitious. She then met with the Human Resources department over several meetings and worked out the bones of a possible deal. However, at the branch meeting where she was due to report back, she announced less favourable terms than she had in fact negotiated. She was told quite forcefully to go back in and do better. She did, and after a couple more meetings with HR, came out with an improved offer that was finally accepted by the members. She could have announced this same deal at the earlier Branch meeting but she didn't.

How do you see this leadership behaviour: as manipulative and dishonest or as smart and politically aware? Getting things done in organisations, where different groups and networks can be expected to have different interests and positions, calls for political awareness and sensitivity. You can waste a lot of energy, and create a lot of negative energy and resistance, by not understanding how these interests stand and line up. We have lots of words to describe this political ability – we call it being *street-wise, savvy, clued-up, on the ball* – and recognise it in people who have it. Test your skills in Activity P3.3: *Political Skills*.

> ***Activity P3.3: Political Skills will help your political awareness and increase the likelihood of your taking skilful action.***

Whether you regard the union representative in the case above as skilful or manipulative – or both, Activity P2.3 will help you to avoid some of the obvious pitfalls, but it will not tell you what is the right thing to do. The moral dilemmas of using power can't be analysed or rationalised away. Some people are very quick to claim the moral high ground for dubious acts, and this is one of the reasons that political skills are regarded both with admiration and distrust.

On the other hand you don't want to be a donkey. Kim James and Simon Baddeley offer a very useful model of political skills based on what they call "Reading" and "Carrying". Reading is how well you understand the situation, whilst Carrying is more to do with your moral *intent*. The Fox reads the situation well but sets out to manipulate and trick; the Owl reads well and has the high ambition of achieving the best solution that can be achieved for all concerned. Obviously in this model you want to be an Owl – and not a Sheep, who doesn't really know what is going on, or what they want to achieve, and certainly not a Donkey, who wants to manipulate but reads it all wrong.

However knowledgeable or skilled you are in your own field, you can't get things done without knowing how the organisation works. The Owl, Fox, Sheep and Donkey are all political options in organisational matters. It is quite easy to recognise the political innocents among us who seem to have very little idea of what is going on. And also those clever people who enjoy gameplaying as part of the fun of being in the organisation. Yet, whilst the Foxes are admired for their skills and while innocents can exhibit a kind of wisdom, we would only use the word wise of someone who manages to combine political awareness with integrity.

Endpiece: the mirror and the window

Nothing gets done without power. And power is exercised most effectively by those with a strong will and determination to bring about what they believe should be done. The importance of will, determination and persistence in leadership can hardly be overstressed. It is the combination of this will to see something happen with the power to bring it about that marks off the successful from the less successful.

The key to handling power wisely lies in a combination of the personal and the professional. In *Good to Great*, Jim Collins' "Level 5 leaders" are characterised by a blend of "intense professional will" and personal humility. The word "professional" suggests an ambition beyond the personal, in service to some wider or higher purpose. Using this great willpower in a responsible way requires a paradoxical personal humility. When things go wrong, the Level 5 leader:

> *Looks in the mirror, not out of the window, to apportion responsibility for poor results, never blaming other people, external factors or bad luck.*

But when things go well, he or she:

> *Looks out of the window, not in the mirror, to apportion credit for the success of the company – to other people, external factors and good luck.*
>
> (Collins, 2001, p. 36)

Larger-than-life celebrity leaders who dominate the financial gossip columns do not usually fit this bill. According to Collins' research, neither do they achieve great results for their organisations.

References

Baddeley, S. and James, K. (1987) Owl, Fox, Sheep or Donkey: political skills for managers. *Management Education and Development* **18**(1), 3–19.

Collins, J. (2001) *Good to Great*. London: Random House.

French, J. and Raven, B.W. (1959) "The bases of social power" in Cartwright, D. (ed.) *Studies in Social Power*. Ann Arbor, Michigan: Institute for Social Research.

Harvey, J. (1996) *The Abilene paradox and other meditations on management*. San Francisco: Jossey-Bass.

Heifetz, R. and Laurie, D. (1997) The work of leadership. *Harvard Business Review*. January–February.

Kanter, R.M. (1977) *Men and Women of the Corporation*. New York: Basic Books.

Further resources

Although it is central to leadership, few books give proper attention to how power is used. A major exception is Ronald Heifetz, *Leadership Without Easy Answers* (Cambridge, Mass: Belknap Press, 1994). This excellent book is suffused with sophisticated understandings of power and its working especially in government and professional settings, and remains one of the best resources available.

Also from the Kennedy School at Harvard University is a new offering *On Leadership: Definitive Writings on Power, Authority, and Influence* edited by Barbara Kellerman (New York: McGraw-Hill, 2010).

There are lots of books on assertiveness. A popular classic is *Assertiveness at Work: A Practical Guide to Handling Awkward Situations*, by Ken Back and Kate Back (Maidenhead: McGraw-Hill, 2005). A simple approach is presented by Mary Hartley in *The Assertiveness Handbook* (London: Sheldon Press, 2005)

In case you found this chapter a little naïve for your taste, Robert Greene is a modern Machiavelli who believes that "power is a game of constant duplicity". His *The 48 Laws of Power* (London: Profile Books, 1998) is a provocative read described as "amoral, cunning, ruthless, and instructive". He also blogs at *Power, Seduction and War. Robert Greene's Blog.*

Activities

The three activities in this chapter will help you to read the organisational political map, to understand the bases of your power, and to use it wisely. They are:

- Activity P3.1: The Power Index.
- Activity P3.2: The Customer Survey.
- Activity P3.3: Political Skills.

Activity P3.1: The Power Index

This activity is based on a model of six power sources. It will help you understand where you get your power from, which sources you favour and which you might be underusing.

1 *Think of a recent experience at work.* Pick a particular situation to keep in mind as you answer the following questions. It could be a project you worked on over several months, or a particularly dramatic episode that sticks in your mind. It could also be a relationship that you have with some person or group of people. It does not matter which as long as the experience is significant to you and is related to useful work outcomes.

2 *Complete the power index.* Work through the following questions. For each question choose one of these four options that seems to best describe your use of power in that situation:

■ little
■ sometimes
■ usually
■ always.

When you have decided which of these best describes your use of power in that situation, mark this with a × in the appropriate column of the table below.

In this situation, I influenced people and events by ...

Item	Little	Sometimes	Usually	Always
1 using my formal power and position in the organisation				
2 warning of the consequences of certain courses of action that I don't like				
2 praising people and recognising their contributions				
4 relying on my specialist knowledge and expertise				
5 working well with people that I like				

Item	Little	Sometimes	Usually	Always
6 linking people to other sources of data and resources				
7 being senior in the organisation				
8 suggesting that things could be difficult for them if I make an adverse report				
9 offering people what they want in exchange for their cooperation				
10 my credibility and experience in the field				
11 helping people to reflect and learn from my personal experiences				
12 making suggestions for alliances and connections with other people and groups				

3 Now, consider *your preferred forms of power*. You have now completed the power index on the basis of your behaviour in a recent experience, project or relationship. Now go back through the Index and think about how you would *ideally* like to act in any similar future situation. What is your preferred form of power?

To do this you need to use a different opening statement. Instead of "In this situation, I influenced people and events by …" use:

In future, I would prefer to influence people and events by …

This time mark your choice in the appropriate column with a ✓.

4 *Scoring the index*. The *power index* is based on six major sources of power and influence. In the table below, these are listed together with the relevant index item numbers.

Assess your actual use of power by scoring each × depending on where you put them:

Little   = 1
Sometimes = 2
Usually   = 3
Always   = 4

So, for example, if you put your × for Item 1 in the "Always" box, and for Item 7 in the "Usually" box, you would score 7 for Role and position power.

When you have assessed your "Actual" use of power, now add up your "Preferred" scores in the same way:

Source of power[a]	Actual (×)	Preferred (✓)
Role and position [1 & 7]		
Coercion [2 & 8]		
Rewards [3 & 9]		
Expertise [4 & 10]		
Personal [5 & 11]		
Connections [6 & 12]		

[a] Numbers in brackets correspond to items in previous list.

5 *Review*. The numerical scoring of the *power index* is a simple way of displaying difference in the use of the different types of power. There are two main types of difference:

■ the different sources or forms of power
■ the difference between what you actually do and what you would prefer to do.

Looking at your scores, ask yourself these questions:

■ Am I using all the forms of power that I could?
■ Do I overuse one particular form of power?
■ Does this pattern work for me or could I improve my practice by developing other forms of power?
■ What do my friends and colleagues say to me about how I use power?

Activity P3.2: The Customer Survey

The customer survey is a simple tool to build the power of any team. There is no better health check on performance than the view from outside.

1 In any team, *first agree that you are all "up for this"*. Unless there is at least a consensus (a general agreement where those who do not agree at least have had their voices heard) the survey results are unlikely to be "heard".

2 *List all the customers*, clients or end users served by this team. You can divide these into internal and external, new and old – whatever classification makes sense.

3 The third step is to *rank order* the clients or customers by importance to this team.

4 Now make arrangements to *survey your customers*. You can do this by sending them a questionnaire or paying a market research company to do telephone interviews – this will provide you with feedback and may impress your clients – but you might learn more by doing it yourselves. There are all sorts of ways of doing it yourself; you could:
   - Divide the key customers among the team and agree to interview them by telephone
   - Form into pairs and have each pair choose two customers off the list. Ensure that the team as a whole is covering the most important clients.

   And there are lots of other variations. The reason why it is best to do it yourself is because nothing impresses people more – team members and customers alike – than personal contact. If the customer thinks you really want to know what he or she thinks – then they might just tell you!

5 *Interview or survey your clients and customers*. Ensure that the following questions are covered:
   - How much do they know about us (your team)?
   - What do they want and expect from you?
   - What do they think of what they are getting now?
   - How would they like to see their service improved?

6 Meet again to *share the data*. Go round the team and hear all the stories. When all have been heard, classify the findings of your joint research under the questions as in 5 above.

7 Finally and importantly, *agree*:
- What have we learned about ourselves?
- What are the implications for this team?
- What actions will we now take (i) each individual? (ii) as a team?

Activity P3.3: Political Skills

This activity does not guarantee wisdom, but it might help you to become a little more street-wise around your organisation.

1 *Think of a change that you want to make – small or large.* Even small changes – such as in paperwork systems, furniture layout, meal times and so on – will illustrate the effects of power and politics very nicely. However, make sure the change is important to you and that you do intend to make it.

2 *Map the people, their interests and their power.* Take a piece of paper and divide it with two vertical lines to make three columns as below.

Name of group or person	Interests	Power +, ++, +++
1.		
2.		
etc.		

■ List in the left-hand column all the people and groups who are involved in making the change or who will be affected by it.
■ Now list the *interests* of each of these people or groups in the centre column; consider:
  – *vested* interests – salary, resources, career prospects, territory, advantages, perks, etc.
  – *ideological* interests – political or philosophical commitments
  – *self*-interests – personal values, sense of personal and professional identity.
■ Now note in the right-hand column what you see as the main sources of power of each, using the classification from Activity P3.1, i.e.
  – role and position
  – coercion
  – rewards
  – expertise
  – personal
  – connections.
You could also denote the strength of this power as you see it, using +, ++ or +++.

3 *Orientation*. Now take another piece of paper, divide it into four labelled quadrants as below, and consider the orientation of each of these people or groups in terms of the two dimensions:

- Support/resist – is the person or group supportive of or resistant to the change?
- Power – does the person or group have high or low power in this situation?

Powerful and supportive	Powerful and resistant
Weak and supportive	Weak and resistant

Put your people or groups into the quadrants. You can assign them simply to one of the quadrants or you can grade them carefully with regard to the vertical and horizontal scales of power and support.

- To which of these groups and people do you need to pay special attention? Mark any group that needs particular attention.

4 *Action*. How does your chart look? Does it show a critical mass of support for your change or solid ranks of resistance against it? If the latter, should you rethink your ideas or reconsider your plans? If the picture is more evenly balanced, what could you do to increase support for your change? For example, you could:

- find out why the resisters are resisting. Do they understand fully the proposed change? What are their objections?
- ask powerful supporters to approach powerful resisters to try to "get them on board" or at least to reduce their resistance.
- help those who are supportive but weak become more powerful. Perhaps these people could be brought together to develop a joint position?

Make yourself a short *action plan* – a "back of the envelope" list rather than a detailed plan – what do you think you should, could and might do? Who could you discuss this with before acting? Who can help you with this action?

8

Practice 4: Risk

Leaders get attacked, dismissed, silenced and sometimes assassinated because they come to represent loss.
Heifetz

Along with purpose and power, risk is the third defining characteristic of leadership. So central is risk to leadership that the popular literature is saturated with clichés and tales of the "with one bound Jack was free" variety. Heroic theories of leadership continue to thrive on the legendary capacity of exceptional individuals to rise to historic challenges. Yet, despite these fabulous stories of the celebrity CEOs, the presence of risk makes leadership an often dangerous activity. To be in authority means being in the place where the hard decisions, the tough dilemmas and the extraordinary contingencies end up. In any hard decision there are losers, and leadership must carry this risk.

Risk is also a critical aspect of entrepreneurship, the ability to undertake pioneering ventures. It is said that successful entrepreneurs have often failed several times before achieving their ambitions, and perhaps that some aspects of risk-taking may therefore be learned. At the personal level, risk-taking is associated with the characteristics of the creative person, imaginative, willing to challenge the *status quo* and to tolerate ambiguity. It is an ability or quality that enables us to act without permission; but also one that demands that we must be equally able to seek forgiveness.

This chapter includes the following:

- Taking the heat – and staying visible.
- Estimating and planning for risk.
- Managing risk.
- Going public.
- Staying alive.
- The risk imperative.

It also includes three activities for estimating and managing risk, together with proposals for sharing and living with risk:

- Activity P4.1: Personal Risk Assessment
- Activity P4.2: Planning for Risk
- Activity P4.3: Facing the Feelings.

Taking the heat

The buck stops here. (Harry Truman)

All tough decisions entail risk. Unlike purpose and power, the upside in taking risks is always in the unknowable future, whilst the uncertainty and pain is *now*:

The merger

Two "third sector" charitable organisations agreed to merge. They shared the same field of activity and the business case for pooling their resources and streamlining their joint operations to save costs was convincing.

Yet the process was long and painful. Despite the apparent similarities there were big differences in the way these two went about their business. Founded by very different groups of people, they had developed different strategies and cultures. One was close to the commercial world and frequently appeared in corporate promotions; the other began in opposition to the business world.

The sense of loss and betrayal was strongest in the second charity. To many people it was their work that was important and it did not matter that their organisation was no longer growing. They distrusted the new venture and suspected that the values of the "corporate" organisation would take over.

Unlike many such ventures, this merger was no CEO ego trip. The leadership of the two charities had a clear purpose for the project, a strong business case and were able to explain what they were doing. They communicated a view of the future that was meaningful and made sense. They were surprised by the unhappiness they saw around them.

These sort of leadership decisions carry big risks. There may be obvious gains but there are also considerable losses. There is a huge potential loss of purpose when a merger takes place. Expect people to say "I didn't join this organisation to see it taken over", "If I had wanted to work for them, I would have applied there" and "So what have we been working for all this time?" Expect people to ask "Who are we – now?" Tough decisions generate unhappiness and anger in the losers.

Being visible

*The irony of leadership (is that) it is often avoided
where it might seem most necessary.*
Keith Grint

The question is: will it work out OK? No-one can be sure. In the merger situation, loss of purpose and loss of identity might lead to powerlessness and negativity. Good leadership will try to tackle this head on. They will communicate a view of the future that is new and better, they will be able to explain how things will work after the decision. They will be aware of the urgency of the task of turning around the negativity and of finding a way to create new meaning. They must do this in spite of their own uncertainties. They must take the stand and be very visible.

However, one of the ironies of leadership it that it is often absent when most needed; the impact of risk and its dangers frequently induces invisibility on the part of those who should be showing leadership:

> *With problems as tough as jobs, health and economic diversification, it is no wonder that everyone expects authority to make the decision. That seems our inclination – to look to someone or some agency to take the heat in choosing what to do. Ordinarily these expectations act as constraints on people in authority, inhibiting them from exercising leadership.*
>
> (Heifetz, 1994, p. 98)

The absence of leadership is a failure both of those in authority and those who have expectations of them. We expect those in charge to resolve the intractable problems without pain or loss to ourselves, so that authority figures are stuck in this way with impossible expectations – better services, but no more taxes; economise but make no job cuts. This explains why authorities are often preoccupied with maintaining equilibrium and are seen as averse to change. The argument is that you're damned if you do and also if you don't: take the decision and you risk unforeseen consequences; avoid it and you may be blamed – or blame yourself – for missing the opportunity. These sorts of pressures intimidate us into choosing safety first.

In situations of risk, the locations of leadership and authority may be quite different. When not exercised from high office, leadership can appear from "the foot of the table" or from the women's position, as Heifetz puts it. The critical challenges that demand our attention, and that require change and learning to address them, generally come first to light through informal leadership, especially those "perceived as entrepreneurs and deviants, organisers and trouble-makers [to] provide the capacity within the system to see through the blind spots of the dominant viewpoint" (p. 183).

Some of the personal risks of leadership lie here: do I question the system and risk disfavour? Will I risk my career by speaking against the accepted view? There are always good reasons for the prudent to stay invisible; which is where the "entrepreneurs, deviants and trouble makers" come in. To stay alive in leadership territory, it is important to become familiar with risk, its nature and its effects. The fears may never be fully overcome, but like climbers who tolerate exposure better through familiarity, the practice and the performance of risk can be developed.

Calculating risk

Given that risk is part of the territory of leadership, then how can it be assessed or calculated? As with all of the leadership practices, the first step is to know yourself, and how you respond to different situations. How does your personal attitude to risk impact on your contribution to leadership?

Think of a risk you have taken recently. Buying a new car, speaking up at a meeting or approaching another person for help in difficult circumstances. It need not have been a very big risk, but big enough that it made you stop and think and weigh the options.

Now try the following activity: Activity P4.1: Personal Risk Assessment to test your personal attitude to risk.

What did you learn about your personal attitude to risk?

■ Are you a person who carefully thinks through the consequences of risk, systematically reviews the options and seeks to weigh the outcomes of each? Or do you prefer a more intuitive, action-oriented approach, relying on an ability to learn quickly from initial consequences?
■ Do you generally imagine the worst possible outcomes? Or can you maintain an optimism that things will turn out well? (The best decisions may require some of both.)
■ Are there some circumstances where you are willing to act more riskily than others?

These are important questions for anyone contributing to leadership. Given that we tend to act on the basis of "justifiable risk", this involves first assessing the risks of action in advance and sharing our perceptions with each other. The calculation of justifiable risk varies from situation to situation and from person to person. You might not even notice what is for me a highly significant risk: I am not afraid of heights but I hate to be seen to be failing; you are happy to make a fool of yourself, but always avoid conflict and so on.

Identifying and facing up to leadership challenges involves the acknowledgement and *management* of risk. In Activity P4.1, what was your purpose in trying to manage your risk – discovering, avoiding, concealing or addressing? Are you inclined to take risks in these sorts of situations or not? Are you are more cautious and risk-averse or do you see yourself as willing to take a fair measure of risk whenever opportunities present themselves? Managing risk involves knowing our own and each other's propensities in chancy situations.

Managing risk

The public practice of risk management is a big and growing business. Running a hospital or a railway demands good quality risk management processes and procedures as a basis for day-to-day working.

Avoidable risks?

A recent US survey suggests that 100,000 people a year die as a direct result of medical mistakes partly due to the faulty prescribing of medicines. A UK study of prescribing in a London teaching hospital found that mistakes occur in 1.5% of the 1300 drug orders written each day. These included the overprescribing of a heart failure drug by a factor of 10 times the recommended dose. Perhaps that figure doesn't sound too bad: 1.5% mistakes means a 98.5% success rate – a figure that would delight train operators. But supposing the pharmacists also make mistakes? Another study concluded that pharmacists misread prescriptions in no less than 17% of cases. Then the overall error rate is multiplied.

The managerial control of safety, confidentiality, individual and professional accountability, competency and training are all key aspects of the effective organisation. Making sure that safety systems are in place, that lines of accountability are clear, that people are properly trained for what they are doing and so on, is the very essence of good operations management.

The preoccupations of leadership overlap with these concerns, but are different. Leadership issues and questions are less well defined, and there are fewer systems and procedures at hand to handle an emerging crisis. Consider, for example, the challenges for public health leadership from the confident predictions that we are overdue for a global influenza pandemic:

"Swine flu"

Concerns about "swine flu" [swine influenza virus (SIV) or H1N1 flu] swept the globe in 2009, breaking out in Mexico and spreading rapidly via returning holidaymakers. Concerns were magnified by previous scares including "bird flu" and respiratory illnesses such as the SARS (severe acute respiratory syndrome) outbreak in 2003 that caused the World Health Organisation to warn travellers not to go to Toronto. Underlying these scares are the persistent public health predictions that sooner or later the world will suffer a pandemic such as the one after the First World War, which caused far more deaths than that terrible war itself.

Bird flu and other new respiratory illnesses now seem to regularly erupt in an increasingly mobile and networked world. They create risks for individuals, businesses and governments. Universities, for example, recruit more and more of their students from all over the globe. When the students go home on holiday and come back a few weeks later, their international student residences create the ideal conditions for the incubation of a potential world pandemic. What precautions should the individual university authorities take? Should they develop their own procedures or leave it up to the public health authorities?

The potential impact of an influenza epidemic is one example of the sort of situation that defines the need for leadership as distinct from management. Here there are no "best practices" to take the risk out of the situation. Some procedures and systems may be available to deal with previously defined risks, but who decides what this risk is now and what should be done about it? The trade-off between prudence and risk produces very difficult decisions: do we take this child from its family or run the risks of child abuse? Do we allow this elderly person to stay at home with the associated risks of falls and burns or do we take them into residential care at the risk of them losing their independence and spirit?

Wicked problems

These sorts of dilemmas are "wicked problems". In Grint's threefold model (Figure P4.1), the progression from "critical" to "tame" to "wicked" problems is marked by an increase both in uncertainty about solutions and the need for collaboration. "Critical" problems are the domain of *command*: crisis situations such as heart attacks, train crashes or natural disasters demand swift action, leaving little time for procedure or uncertainty. "Tame" problems, though they be very complex, such as timetabling a school, planning heart surgery or building a new hospital, are essentially amenable to rational tools and constitute the natural domain of *management*. "Wicked" problems defy rational analysis and are the domain of *leadership* (2008, pp. 11–18).

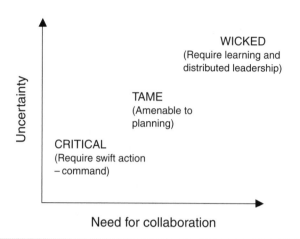

Figure P4.1 **Three types of problem**

Wicked problems are not just complex and ambiguous, but messy, circular and aggressive. Problems of drug abuse, crime, homelessness or how to engage the full energies of people in organisations are never straightforward. These problems are tricky to deal with, they change shape as you work on them, and often prove contradictory because of complex interdependencies of factors. Attempts at single actions and partial solutions tend to produce even more complex and tangled problems.

A risk-averse leadership may choose to focus on the tame problems, and ignore the wicked ones. Although these are the very situations most in need of their talents and resources, they require different qualities and skills. These include not rushing to solutions, asking questions, taking deliberate risks and learning from this process. Wicked problems demand a concerted effort by many people working together.

Above all, tackling the wicked problems needs courage.

Balancing courage and caution

The heroic stories of risk takers are inspiring because they exemplify qualities that we admire – guts, fearlessness, the sheer determination not to be beaten. The entrepreneur and the pioneer are leaders in the sense of going first, but to tackle the more intractable and wicked problems, lots of people and groups have to encourage each other and generate a collective effort. The heroes might be the right people to follow in a crisis – if it happens that they know what they are doing – but following this sort of lone ranger can also easily lead us astray. For example, those formerly conservative citizens, the bankers, recently embraced this vision to such an extent that they handed out 125% mortgages to people with poor credit records. Survivors of the earlier Enron scandal recalled that the company had become so "bold" that insiders had lost the power to discriminate between right and wrong. The bankers and the Enron folk thought they were highly entrepreneurial, but they lacked a proper caution.

Examples of excessive caution also litter the business world. Alongside the heroic tales of leadership we also savour those fatuous examples of the over-application of "risk management". The three men who come to change the light bulb or the health and safety rules that prevent the resolution of simple problems by those on the spot. This sort of silliness does not lead to the sudden catastrophic losses of excessive "courage", but over the long term it can sap productivity and smother initiative, creativity and innovation.

The ability to take courage and then balance it with caution is the true mark of leadership. It is easy to get it wrong and to err on one side or the other. Handling this dilemma means not choosing one over the other, but valuing two, equally desirable, qualities. A *Helvig Square* of values shows the complementarity of these apparently contradictory qualities (see Figure P4.2).

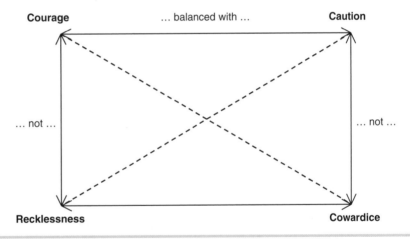

Figure P4.2 A Helvig Square of courage and caution

In the Helvig Square the two complementary qualities on the top line retain their value only when the tension between them is balanced. For an increase in courage, a similar rise in caution is also required. If the balance on the top line is not maintained, these good values can become debased and turn into the deteriorated forms on the bottom line, where courage becomes recklessness and caution degenerates into avoidance. Courage and caution are not opposites – the diagonal lines show the true opposites – but partners in leadership.

Recklessness is not a mark of wise leadership. The practice of risk should embrace proper preparation and planning.

Planning for risk?

If anything can go wrong it will! (Murphy's law)

In his book *Up the Organisation*, Robert Townsend estimated that, as managing director of Avis, some 40% of the decisions he made were wrong. He did stress that this meant that 60% of them were right. The important point was that he made the decisions in the knowledge that he might well be getting it wrong. This takes courage, but is not necessarily foolhardy, because in uncertain conditions, the decision, and the action that follows, creates new information, and information reduces uncertainty.

This does not mean that taking decisions on the snap is a good idea. The calculation of risk involves the estimation of the possible consequences for any given action. This provides the basis for a risk management where the obvious perils are avoided, while safety nets, fall-backs and contingent options are prepared for the unavoidable or unforeseen hazards.

This general approach to thinking about risk will help whatever the outcomes, as long as it does not supplant or undermine the urge to action. In uncertain situations, although things are not likely to go to plan, the planning activity helps to prepare us for action and its consequences. Activity P4.2: Planning for Risk is an example of the rational approach to estimating risk and planning for contingencies. This activity is applied to a personal decision but more elaborate and organisational versions can be found in the many sources available on risk management (see further resources).

Now try Activity P4.2: Planning for Risk to help you build options for contingencies.

However well armed with analyses and options, the action still feels risky.

The incalculability of risk

The alternative to the rational approach is to proceed on intuition, acting on hunches. The advantage of the intuitive approach is that you are not blinded by plans and preparations that might lead to false and favourable interpretations of any new data that emerge. The intuitive risk taker stays alert and open to new information because these associated qualities help with quickness and balance. Act on hunches and it is easier to abandon that direction and take a new one; work to a well-prepared plan and you feel you should complete it like a course of antibiotic.

Handling leadership risks may often benefit from a combination of the intuitive and the rational approaches. The value of the two will vary by the particular situation: how much planning before action? How quickly to get into action? But there are several other problems with an over-reliance on the rational approach. The lack of evidence does not indicate the absence of risk. If risks are not predictable, a rational approach may induce a sense of false security. Rational analyses can also be employed to conceal; as in the public rationalisation of risk through the measuring and reassurance of the easily measurable, whilst the indeterminate are ignored and unmentioned. This "technical concealment" features in some business prospectuses and also in reports and enquiries of the CYA (Covering Your Arse) variety.

Yet this knowing concealment underestimates the problem. For Ulrich Beck, the calculability of risk is a modern myth. In seeking to estimate the possible consequences of any action, by engaging in elaborate exercises of risk analysis, risk assessment, risk management and all the other controlling words now coupled with risk, we are calculating the imagined effects of some probable scenarios, and not the *actual* risks of taking that action:

> *The studies of reactor safety restrict themselves to the estimation of certain quantifiable risks on the basis of probable accidents. The dimensions of the hazard are limited from the very beginning to technical manageability. In some circles it is said that risks which are not yet technically manageable do not exist – at least not in scientific calculation or jurisdictional judgement. These uncalculable threats add up to an unknown residual risk.*
>
> (Beck, 1992, p. 29)

Because so much has been invested in systems of risk management and because we are easily impressed with science and numbers, we can delude ourselves into thinking that these estimates are assessments of actual risk. The better we get at risk estimation the worse we make it. Risk management is a proper responsibility of good management, and at its best tells us something of the possible risks. With considerable "unknown residual risks", risk management is ineffective and can become an evasion of responsibility for unforeseen consequences. A courageous response in this sort of situation is to go public.

Going public

Mark, a social services manager, was charged with cutting £400,000 from the £2 million budget for the transport system for disabled people. Such a large cut was not possible through incremental savings and demanded a radical approach – and it had to be done in this financial year.

This was a tough situation. In his analysis Mark considered the various options open and also the possible risks, threats and consequences. Stopping the transport would have a severe social impact because people relied on the system to get them from home to workplaces and day centres. Asking them to pay would hit the poorest and most vulnerable people in the city.

Mark decided to talk with the people who used the service. He held a meeting with some of them and put forward various options including using existing public transport, charging for the service at a full rate or charging at a subsidised rate. What surprised him was the willingness of the service users to pay for the service – they were willing to pay the subsidised rate or in some cases even a higher rate. Either of these scenarios would make a significant contribution to meeting the savings required.

Another surprise was the source of the fiercest resistance. This came from two sources. First were the parents of children with learning difficulties. These parents were paid the transport allowance to allow them to run cars to transport their children to and from the day centres. They needed this allowance to run their cars even though many no longer took their (now adult) children to the centres.

The strongest opposition came from the minibus drivers and the attendants who accompanied the children. They wanted to maintain the *status quo* and were reluctant to accept additional duties such as collecting fares. The trades unions were swiftly mobilised. The dispute led to splits and disagreements within the majority political party, with the members responsible for the social services budget having stand-up rows with those responsible for transport, many of whom were sponsored by the drivers' trade union. This disagreement between two groups in the same party over which was most important – the drivers' conditions or the ability of social services to modernise and make savings – was the biggest issue in the whole process.

Without taking the risk of going public, Mark would not have learned those things that eventually led to the resolution of this situation. Sitting tight in his office and carrying out risk assessment and management procedures could not have produced this outcome. On the other hand, going public produced surprises and risks that he could not have anticipated. Once he had decided to take this risk, Mark had several surprises, some of them pleasant, but some of which posed more difficulties than he had seen at the outset. Surprises, both pleasant and unpleasant, are likely to be part of leading in uncertain conditions. You can't stay safe and still lead in these situations. In any case, so-called "safe options" often turn out not to be safe after all.

Because leadership is sometimes about taking risks and not playing it safe, people in leadership positions must find ways of sharing risks and finding sources of support. In this case, among Mark's pleasant surprises was his discovery of new allies. His actions in going public had the effect of spreading or sharing the risk by involving users, and engaging staff and political allies. Although "risk sharing" can be "spun" to become a euphemism for job cuts, wage reductions and so on, true risk sharing (and risk management) involves leadership visibly sharing the costs and engaging in a process of learning.

This risk sharing may be as simple as telling friends or colleagues about your situation. A special form of this move is action learning, an approach devised to help people learn from tackling difficult problems and reflecting on their experiences with a few trusted colleagues (see Chapter 2). Going public can also mean using stakeholder involvement processes and conferences, which are discussed in Chapter 10.

Towards public learning

The two strategic leadership principles involved in going public are:

- identifying the adaptive challenge – diagnosing the situation and suggesting what learning is needed to meet this
- giving the work back to the people – to the stakeholders and the people with the problem (Heifetz, 1994, p. 128)

In the social services example above, Mark made the challenge public and also made it plain that he did not know how it could be met. He then set out to involve others in working towards solutions by going to talk to them and listening to their viewpoints. He could not know what he would do next until he had absorbed this information. "Giving the work back to the people" who can learn and resolve the situation involves the risk of not controlling and of letting go. Leadership …

> … *requires an experimental mindset – the willingness to work by trial and error – where the community's reactions at each stage provide the basis for planning future actions.*

(Heifetz, p. 243)

This asks a great deal of people in leadership situations. In many cases, such risks are covered up, avoided or suppressed. It may be right for leadership to carry these burdens alone for a time, but for what purpose and to whose ends? One of us worked as a consultant to a bakeries group, which was reducing capacity and closing local bakeries at the rate of four a year. Everyone in the company knew that this was happening, but the locations of the doomed plants were kept secret. The unlucky ones came to work on a Monday and were told the plant would close on the Friday. The argument was that a long period of notice to allow people to find new jobs and to adjust would be counter-productive; productivity would drop and machinery might be damaged. In any case a sudden death was better than a long-drawn out one. Although this case comes from some years ago, this type of thinking and behaviour is alive and well in some leadership circles.

Contrast this with the example of William Ruckelshaus, Head of the USA's Environmental Protection Agency, when faced with problems at a copper plant at Tacoma in Washington. Arsenic emissions from the ore were a public safety hazard but the plant was the major employer in the town and an important part of the state economy. Ruckelshaus could have played safe and ruled on emissions, yet he

> ... cut against the grain when he insisted that the public realise that the job of regulating pollutants was not simply a technical matter of setting safe thresholds of emission. Trade offs would have to be made that involved value conflicts not amenable to scientific analysis. And if those trade offs between jobs and health were to be faced, then perhaps new adaptations might be achieved in the face of loss.

(Heifetz, p. 98)

As with the earlier social services example, the local people in Tacoma showed that they could share responsibility for managing this risk and that they could learn, in this case, about the enormous costs of "cleaning up" the environment. We can only begin to learn about living and working with this sort of risk by being given the opportunity to deal with the difficult situation. Here the role of leadership is to push us to face realities that require change and adjustment. This learning and change can have effects that we cannot anticipate. In the Tacoma case, the learning spread beyond the locality as part of a wider national debate on managing environmental risks. Activity P4.3: Facing the Feelings contains some ideas

Activity P4.3: Facing the Feelings for some ideas on how to go public.

Risk sharing through public or stakeholder engagement and learning is no easy ride and from a strategic standpoint, it may not be that easy to include everyone anyway. Sometimes parties must be excluded from the problem-solving process, because the disruption potential is just too great. In extremely difficult circumstances such as those in Northern Ireland or Palestine, delicate alliances have to be built before negotiations are even possible.

Staying alive

Leading in risky situations demands great emotional resilience. Keeping going forwards requires agility and personal survival skills:

> *a leader stays alive not by "playing it safe" but by taking deliberate risks based on his on-going assessment of the territory, knowing that corrective action will almost always be necessary. He takes the risk of challenging people, directly or indirectly, slow or fast, soft or hard, guided by his comprehension of and sensitivity to the changes people have to make in their lives as they take account of the questions he raises.*

(Heifetz, p. 243)

This sounds very masterful, and sometimes the adrenaline can more than compensate for the stress. Adopting this approach to change demands a great deal in terms of courage and confidence from the leadership of any organisation. Yet the costs in emotional energy can be very high. Driven by personal survival needs, many people are not up to it. Take this story from an advertising agency:

The fish rots from the head (old Chinese saying)

The directors of an advertising agency commissioned a development process to help the agency respond to feedback from its major clients and stakeholders. Extensive staff and customer surveys were followed by a large conference for all employees where the survey data would be fed back. However when the consultants submitted the conference design, the directors removed all references to "dialogue" between the conference floor and the leadership team. They wanted to hear the views of staff, but were not prepared to discuss issues openly in public.

Unsurprisingly, given the circumstances, the views expressed from the floor during the conference were not as forthright or explicit as they might have been. The directors concluded that people were more or less happy with how things were in the agency and that there was no strong case to change their own actions and behaviour. (Adapted from Attwood *et al.*, 2003, Chapter 9.)

As noted earlier, developing the right sort of visible leadership is often one of the most difficult things to achieve in any change situation. The climate in many organisations inhibits everyone from risking actions that seek to change things. Here is a group of public service managers:

> *"We have the responsibility but not the authority."*
> *"I'm a middle to senior manager and I don't feel empowered to act."*
> *"We have disempowered a whole raft of people."*

"We've created a top-down culture – we always need permission to do even the smallest things that would improve the service."

As in most work organisations, people are busy, often excessively so, but what are they doing? An evaluation of a change project in the NHS proposes a distinction between two types of action:

Type 1 actions are everyday actions that occur as people perform their normal tasks ... Type 2 actions are more demanding and involve actually implementing an idea or changing a system.

(Pedler, 2007, pp. 11–12).

Type 1 actions require less effort and are less risky, and are therefore perhaps unlikely to result in much significant change or learning; Type 2 actions require new energy, are more risky, and much more likely to lead to service improvements and learning.

The people in the senior leadership roles set the tone, but they are the guardians of the organisation, and as in the agency example above they incline towards the established order. This truism of organisational life is often tackled by changing the people at the top, in the hope that the new will drive out and reform the old. This may not work.

The three envelopes

On being appointed, the new CEO seeks out the old chief for advice. The deposed leader is wary, unwilling to proffer advice. "Please" urges the new man "there must be something that you can pass on to help me?" Finally the old leader says "OK", and hands over three numbered envelopes, "when times are bad, open these in order and follow the instructions".

The new leader thanks him and takes the envelopes. After six months, with the honeymoon wearing off, questions arise about the direction of the organisation. As these get louder the new CEO decides he must act, and opens the first envelope. Inside is a slip of paper bearing the words: "Blame your predecessor." "Hmmn" thinks the chief executive, "good idea." Accordingly, he puts it about that the problems of the present are due to the ideas of the old leader. This has the desired effect. But a few months later the unrest returns, now with increased volume. After some sleepless nights, the CEO opens the second envelope, to find a slip bearing one word: "Re-structure." "Excellent!" he thinks, and immediately announces a major reorganisation, and stipulates a complex process of working groups.

As people become busily engaged in organisational redesign, all energies previously devoted to questioning and complaining are channelled into the crafting of new models and the debating of their relative merits and demerits. Everyone is busy and happy, up to and beyond the point of the installation of the new structure. This structure is better in some ways, but there are also several unanticipated problems. Soon, the questioning and muttering return with even greater force – "Is our leader really up to the job?" After seeking to weather this storm for a few months, the CEO turns to his last envelope. The slip now reads: "Prepare three envelopes …".

The joke suggests that the senior leader's focus is on staying alive at all costs. So, resolving the challenges of change by replacing the leadership may not produce new actions and responses. The new leaders may feel the need to act precipitately rather than wisely; to make their mark, rather than engage with the difficult and adaptive problems.

In whole systems development approaches (Attwood *et al.*, 2003), the problem of "resistance to change" is overcome by including all those who need to have a voice in the change process. This "big tent" approach is demanding for leaders, but is an alternative route to staying alive. To bring it off, leaders have to learn to share their power with other stakeholders in the future of the enterprise. This relieves them of the burden of having to be right all the time, but it looks riskier and demands a visible and committed presence.

The risk imperative

> *… the very origin of learning lies in the recognition of risk or ignorance.*
>
> (Revans)

Blinded by their examples of visionary and exceptional individuals, few leadership books even touch on the practice of risk. Heifetz and Revans are exceptions who share an interest in helping people to act in challenging situations characterised by conflicting facts and by the presence of risk and fear. In his critique of business school teaching practices, Revans termed this "the risk imperative".

> *These attacks, whether upon problems or upon opportunities, must carry significant risk of penalty for failure. Those who are not obliged to assess the risk to themselves of pursuing, or of trying to pursue, such-and-such lines of action cannot, by their indifference to the outcome, explore their own value systems nor identify any trustworthy pattern of their own beliefs.*
> (1998, pp. 8–9)

> *A man* may well learn to talk about taking action simply by talking about taking action (*as in classes at a business school*) *but to learn to take action* (*as something distinct from learning to talk about taking action*) *then he needs to take action* (*rather than to talk about taking action*) *and to see the effect,*

*not of talking about taking action (at which he may appear competent) but of
taking the action itself (at which he may fall somewhat short of competent).*

(Revans, 1971, pp. 54–55, original emphases)

In risky situations, sound judgement is often a more useful quality than high
intelligence. Any amount of intelligence will not tell us what to do. Action
learning improves the quality of judgement in assessing, taking and learning
from risk. More details on this approach can be found in Chapter 9, P5: Asking
Challenging Questions.

Risk and risk management are modern facts of organisational life. Increasing
service standards and targets, together with high visibility and threats of
litigation, raise the pressure not only to manage risk but to be seen to be doing
so. This makes essential systems for risk assessment and risk management, but
it also means that risk avoidance and concealment are likely to flourish. This
imperils good leadership and entrepreneurial risk-taking. For these pursuits,
risk is not an option, but a stock in trade.

References

Attwood, M., Pedler, M., Pritchard, S. and Wilkinson, D. (2003) *Leading Change:
A Guide to Whole Systems Working.* Bristol: Policy Press.

Beck, U. (1992) *Risk Society: Towards a New Modernity.* London: Sage.

Grint, K. (2008) *Leadership, Management and Command – Rethinking D-Day.*
Basingstoke: Palgrave.

Heifetz, R. (1994) *Leadership Without Easy Answers.* Cambridge, Mass: Belknap Press.

Helvig, H. (1951) *Characterologie.* Stuttgart: Ernst Klett Verlag.

Pedler, M. (2007) Introduction: the pathology action learning programme. In
Modernising from Within: action learning solutions for pathology. London: Department
of Health, May 2007.

Revans, R.W. (1971) *Developing Effective Managers.* New York: Praeger.

Revans, R.W. (1982) *The Origins and Growth of Action Learning.* Bromley: Chartwell-
Bratt.

Revans, R.W. (1998) *ABC of Action Learning.* London: Lemos & Crane.

Further resources

There are dozens of books on risk management, often specialising, for example,
in finance or environmental issues, but not many on risk and leadership. The
practice of risk really shows up the difference between managing and leading:
managing risk is a rational planning process to try and avoid any risk, whereas
leadership implies unavoidable risk.

Limiting and avoiding risks is an essential aspect of managerial life in all walks of organisational life. There are very many books on risk management and also on project management that give good advice on this aspect of risk. *The Book of Risk* by Dan Borge (New York: Wiley, 2001) is readable, comes from a financial perspective and takes the complex risk-management theories employed by major global companies and distills them down to simple principles for applying the systematic tools of risk management to your "risk investment in life". Chris Chapman and Stephen Ward's *Project Risk Management: Processes, Techniques and Insights* (Chichester: Wiley, 2nd edition, 2003) is a detailed look at assessing and dealing with risk in projects. By the same authors, *Managing Project Risk and Uncertainty: A Constructively Simple Approach to Decision Making* (Chichester: Wiley, 2002) works on the principle of "constructive simplicity" and uses "10 tales" to illustrate how different risk management techniques can be applied to actual cases. Jacqueline Reynes' *Risk Management: 10 Principles* (London: Butterworth-Heinemann, 2001) is much more basic but may be useful for a first grasp of the ideas. Finally, Douglas Hubbard's *The Failure of Risk Management: Why It's Broken and How to Fix It* (New Jersey: Wiley, 2009) helpfully distinguishes between uncertainty (unavoidable) and risk (avoidable) and how to prepare for both.

A great deal has also been written on risk and leadership, much of which is rather heroic in flavour. In the USA tradition of leadership as "character", Bill George's *Seven Lessons for Leading in Crisis* (San Francisco: Jossey Bass, 2009) is a slim, easy to read, practical guide to navigating through crises. Using exemplars from all walks of life, the advice is basically to find your "true north" or the internal compass of values and purpose that can help you deal with the crises, which are where leadership quality is truly tested.

Kouzes and Posner's *The Leadership Challenge* (San Francisco: Jossey Bass, 2008) is the fourth edition of an excellent book that first appeared in 1990. As with Heifetz's *Leadership Without Easy Answers* and Revans' *ABC of Action Learning* (see References), this makes risk central to its perspective on leadership, treating it not as a topic, but as integral to the territory.

Activities

The three activities in this chapter will help you to assess risk, plan for it and share it with other people. These are all part of the leadership practice of risk.

- Activity P4.1: Personal Risk Assessment.
- Activity P4.2: Planning for Risk.
- Activity P4.3: Facing the Feelings.

Activity P4.1: Personal Risk Assessment

Think of a risk you have taken recently. It need not be a very big one, but big enough to make you stop and think and weigh the options. Perhaps you hesitated over it for a time, unwilling to commit. Work through the following questions, reflecting on your experience, and getting a sense of your personal attitude to risk:

1 *Why was this a risk for you?*

2 *What were the possible outcomes that you thought about in advance?*

   (i)

   (ii)

   (iii)

   etc.

3 *In making your decision, did you attempt to assess:*

   ▧ the likelihood of each outcome? – yes/no

   ▧ the seriousness of the consequences of each outcome? – yes/no.

4 *In the process of making the decision did you:*

   ▧ act impulsively in the face of the incalculable odds? – yes/no

   ▧ vacillate in a fit of indecision for a long time, before deciding? – yes/no

   ▧ avoid making a decision and let nature take its course – yes/no.

5 *How did things turn out?* (tick one)

■ Better than I could have expected?

■ As I had hoped?

■ Not as I had hoped?

■ Disastrously?

6 *Thinking back on this risk-taking situation, what was your main motive of your risk assessment or risk management thinking? Was it about ...* (tick one or more)

■ *Discovering risk?* – looking to see what risks might exist

■ *Managing risk?* – deciding how to deal with risks you knew were there

■ *Avoiding risk?* – changing what you planned to avoid identified risks

■ *Concealing risk?* – keeping the risk quiet rather than changing plans

■ *Acknowledging risk?* – openly accepting that certain risks existed.

7 *In general terms, sum up your personal attitude to risk on this seven-point scale:*

Risk	1	2	3	4	5	6	7	Risk
averse?								addicted?

Review

Reflect on the following questions. Talk them over with a close colleague:

1 What did you learn about your personal attitude to risk?

2 Are there some circumstances where you are willing to act more riskily than others?

3 How does your personal attitude to risk impact on your contribution to leadership?

Activity P4.2: Planning for Risk

Choose a decision facing you or your organisation. For practice purposes it can be any decision, however small, as long as it is surrounded by some uncertainty about the outcomes. It could be a purchase decision, a personal relationship or some aspect of organisational policy making.

1 *Describe the decision to be made:*

2 On the basis of Murphy's law – "If anything can go wrong it will!" – *brainstorm and list all the possible outcomes*, good and bad:

Good *Bad*

3 Now, taking just the bad outcomes, *estimate the level of danger* of each of these risks, using the formula:

$$R = P + S$$

Where:

R = the *size* of the risk – Level 1 [(low), Level 2 (medium) or Level 3 (high)]

=

P = the *probability* of this happening (low/medium/high)

+

S = the *seriousness* of the situation, if it does happen (low/medium/high)

(two lows for P & S = a level 1 risk; a high plus a medium = a level 3 risk and so on)

Put *L*, *M* or *H* against all your *bad* possible outcomes in (2) above.

4 Look at your level 3 risks. *What contingency plans can you put in place?* Brainstorm some options for each of your level 3 risks – what back-up plans can you invent? What safety nets can you devise?

Activity P4.3: Facing the Feelings

Going public with a difficult dilemma or challenge is a risk in itself. You may be afraid of losing face in the eyes of some people, or they may not take up the challenge and refer it back.

However, if you decide to take this chance, there is the possibility of a surge of energy and a pooling of resources based on the sharing of risk and the giving of "the work back to the people".

There are many ways to do this but do not overlook the simple calling of a meeting and the straightforward telling of the story. Good intent is probably more important than elaborate design.

Tell the story
This is the starting place. This is what everyone wants to know first. Telling the story so far creates an opportunity for people to listen, reflect and acknowledge their feelings about the situation.

Publish any existing decisions and stick to them
Be honest up front. Bluntness is better than having the rumour mill grind out a more lurid version of the story.

Face up to the feelings
Ask about the reactions and feelings. How do people feel? Talk about your own feelings in meetings. Feelings carry potential energy. How you acknowledge your own feelings and take account of them in your actions is a model for others. How can the energy of the feelings be put to good use?

Acknowledge and build on the past
Past stories of the company and the biographies of those who have worked here are the prime source of current values and beliefs. What are the stories that should be told again now? What new stories shall we tell?

Offer a "holding framework" and partial map of the future
It helps to know that there is a plan, even if the details are unclear and the content is yet to be worked out. Make public the road map or change architecture and show people what will happen when. What will happen when? What can be said with certainty? What is the plan for keeping everyone informed? What can be said about what is not clear? How will we get from here to the new organisation? Who will be involved and how?

Engage people in creating the future
Give the work back to the people. Most of us feel better when we have something to do. What is the plan for engaging people in thinking about the future and working on tasks to bring it about?

Keep talking ... and listening

Too much information is probably better than too little. In the absence of information we tend to make it up. Talking and engaging with people provides new information that gives us more to talk about, speculate over and respond to. Keep talking.

There are many ways of "facing the feelings" and working with them, including the scenarios and stories described in Activities P2.5 and P2.6. Other approaches to working with the whole system can be found in Attwood *et al.* (2003).

9

Practice 5: Challenging questions

The essence of action learning is to pose increasingly insightful questions from an origin of ignorance, risk and confusion.
Reg Revans

Even simple questions have great power to open up new avenues of thought and action:

An old training film shows a group of naval officers engaged in an animated conversation while poring over a map. Each makes different points and does not listen to the others. Suddenly, one voice silences the rest: "Just a minute, where exactly are we trying to go?"

The memory of this stagey old film still makes us laugh. The point was a rather heavy-handed one about the importance of setting objectives. The point here is that, in conditions of confusion and risk, a sense of direction is more likely to come from one good question than from an avalanche of proposals for action. The ability to pose challenging questions – those that challenge current thinking – is a critical leadership practice. This practice is key to making sense of the world and also to learning and innovation. It is the originating point for fresh ideas and directions.

This chapter starts by considering the *power of questions* and their function, especially with regard to *complexity, knowledge* and *learning*. It introduces the action learning idea of the question as the source of *questioning insight* in the search for new ways in difficult circumstances in the context of *leadership as a reflective practice*. It concludes with a discussion of the traps that await the unwary questioner and *the most valuable question* of all.

There are four activities in this chapter to help to ground this leadership Practice 5: challenging questions:

- Activity P5.1: Revans' Essential Questions.
- Activity P5.2: Thinking, Feeling, Willing.

■ Activity P5.3: Seven Types of Questions for Leadership.
■ Activity P5.4: After Action Review.

The power of questions

The first meaning of the question is to elicit information. But a question is also a matter of concern, a problem to be solved. To question is to raise doubts that might be the earliest indicators of a fresh challenge. To query or to quest is to enquire into things, to institute a search that may be long and hazardous. But most of all perhaps, the question is the way we navigate around the world, finding our way when lost or unsure.

Take the Danish nightshift.

> ### The Danish nightshift
>
> In recent work with a Danish manufacturing company we noticed that there were always fewer defective products on the night shift. As the shifts rotated, this didn't seem to be due to the particular individuals involved: no matter who was on at night, their quality was better than when they were working during the day. So we asked the employees the simple question: "why is quality higher on night shifts?" "That's easy," they replied. "At night there are no managers to get in our way – so we can get on and do our job properly!"
>
> This simple question – and the response – led to a thorough exploration of the work of the quality assurance department. Among a number of changes was the extent to which the workers were themselves allowed to take responsibility for quality – during the day and at night.
>
> The lesson is: ask – and they might just tell you!

The significance of the power of questions has grown along with our perceptions that the world is more complex and mysterious than we had thought.

A changing world: complexity, knowledge and learning

Some aspects of our world are changing rapidly. This is especially obvious in technological terms. Here are some of the new laws that govern our lives:

■ *Moore's law* – the power of computers doubles every 18 months.
■ *The law of storage* – for a given cost, storage capacity doubles every 12 months.

- *The law of fibre* – the bandwidth capacity of fibre (the backbone of the internet) doubles every nine months.
- *Metcalfe's law* – the power of the network goes up by the square of the people interacting.

These extraordinary developments mask more fundamental shifts in understanding that underlie the importance of questioning to leadership practice. The insights of quantum physics such as Heisenberg's "indeterminacy principle" have gradually undermined the Newtonian predictability that was applied, not only to planetary movements, but also to individual and organisational behaviour. Forty years ago, social scientists were trying to determine the multiple dimensions of organisational structure as if these could be discovered once and for all.

We do not see it like that now. Things have become more mysterious and complex. The study of "complex adaptive systems" (CAS) is the application of complexity science to organisations:

> *What is a complex adaptive system? … "Complex" implies diversity – a great number of connections between a wide variety of elements. "Adaptive" suggests the capacity to alter or change – the ability to learn from experience. A "system" is a set of connected or interdependent things or agents … a person, a molecule, a species or an organisation … that … act based on local knowledge and conditions. Their individual moves are not controlled by a master body … A CAS has a densely connected web of interacting agents, each operating from their own schema or local knowledge.*
>
> (Zimmerman, Lindberg and Plsek, 2001, p. 8)

The questions here are not to do with the mechanical building blocks needed for effective organisation, but with people and how they act and interact: how do relationships develop and how are they sustained? What influences the emergence of particular outcomes in organisational and community settings? CAS thinking suggests that organisational life may often be less orderly and unpredictable than previously thought. CAS undermines previous notions of predictability and rationality in the leadership and management of organisations.

Mobilising knowledge

> *Knowledge does not keep any better than wet fish.*
>
> (A.N. Whitehead, 1932)

Complexity, diversity and unpredictability have particular significance for knowledge and learning. From this perspective, the metaphors of the knowledge store or warehouse employed in "knowledge management" are old thinking. Whitehead's insight indicates that knowledge is not easily pinned down or captured, and a flowing water metaphor might be more appropriate than a storage one. Where once knowledge could be simply acquired, held in libraries and by experts, it is now seen as something that is continually in motion, where the old dates rapidly and is quickly supplanted by the new.

Dixon proposes three fundamental shifts in how we think about it that amount to a revolution:

- *From expert to distributed*. From the idea that useful knowledge is held by small numbers of experts towards the idea that it is distributed throughout the community or organisation.
- *From individual to group*. From the idea that knowledge is an individual possession to knowledge as embedded in a group or community of practice.
- *From stable to dynamic*. From the idea that knowledge is a stable commodity to a view that it is dynamic and ever changing (Dixon, 2000, pp. 148–160).

The revolutionary implications of these shifts can be illustrated by the power of a simple question:

> *In an undergraduate physics class at Oxford University, a student asked the professor: "How can an induction motor work as a generator?" Unable to respond to his own satisfaction, the professor took three years to come up with an answer. In doing so however, he worked out a novel and very cheap way of using an induction motor to increase the yield from a wind turbine. A spinoff company, Renewox, is now being established.*
>
> (*Guardian*, 20 August 2009)

As ever there is more to this story than meets the eye. For example, the professor happened to have both an expertise in spin electronics and a mother who lived in rural Ireland. He had been previously experimenting with wind turbines as a means to help her to reduce her energy costs. This unique combination of factors, personal and professional, would be unknown to the student, who could have had no idea what impact this simple question might have. The questioner was just seeking information, but for the receiver, this question facilitated something that had been brewing for some time. This is how knowledge is created.

It also shows why this sort of knowledge cannot be captured, collected or stored. This was something literally not known before the encounter; it did not exist until the elements were brought together. It will also not last long in its present state because it will quickly become something else: the emerging project now engaging the professor. Yet, though knowledge can't be captured for long, the processes for creating and sharing knowledge can be encouraged and developed.

… and learning

Reg Revans' ecological formula:

$$L \geq C$$

holds that any organism will fail unless its learning is greater than the rate of change in its environment (1998, p. 24). Learning in both individuals and organisations is increasingly essential for survival and prosperity in a complex, rapidly changing world. In the "knowledge era", the abilities to learn, to absorb new knowledge and acquire new skills and capacities are assets for both the person and the business for which they work.

The increasing currency of *learning* rather than training signifies another shift in practice that supports more flexible ways of working. Many of the challenges faced by people and organisations are not technical *puzzles* with programmed solutions but *problems* or *opportunities* for which there is no right answer and no single course of action (Revans 1998, p. 6). Learning is not a compulsory process but a voluntary one involving cycles of action, reflection on the basis of experience, and integration of insights into existing ways of understanding and doing things. Learning cannot be prescribed, but it can be facilitated.

Questioning insight

Revans' great insight was that traditional management and leadership training emphasises the accumulated knowledge of the past (or P) rather than Q – the acquisition of what he called *questioning insight*. Existing knowledge is only a small part of what is needed for action and learning in challenging situations. Here where information is limited, and where no obvious solution exists, it is far more important to find the right question. You only know what knowledge might be useful once you have the right question.

Three questions are at the core of Revans' action learning philosophy:

■ Who *knows* (about the problem, issue or opportunity)?
■ Who *cares* (about this issue)?
■ Who *can* (do anything about this matter)?

These foundational questions deal, in turn, with the problem of finding new knowledge, with the search for and recruitment of friends and allies to help deal with the challenge, and with gaining access to the power and resources needed for achieving your purpose.

These questions are so simple that it is easy to miss their profundity. Try their power for yourself:

> *Turn to Activity P5.1: Revans' Essential Questions*
> *at the end of this chapter and try out these questions*
> *with a current challenge or opportunity that is*
> *facing you.*

However tough the challenge, these questions can be used to develop a way forward. Posing them, and then attempting to answer them, creates a positive frame of mind.

Thinking, feeling and willing

Being listened to is one of the best things that can happen to us. When asked about those who they saw as good managers, a group of staff said that such people:

- were sympathetic and understanding
- showed interest in what I was saying
- respected me and my feelings
- still liked me even when I made mistakes or did stupid things
- sometimes challenged me and made me think
- told me how they saw me, but in a way that helped me to listen to them.

Listening is often quoted as *the* most important characteristic of the good manager or leader. However, most good leaders are not just listening, which, on its own, is a rather passive process, but also questioning. Questioning is much less often noticed than listening, but it is the vital other half of being supportive and responsive. It is the questions, based on the listening, that build the basis for constructive action on the challenges being faced.

Revans' essential questions – Who knows? Who cares? Who can? – are fundamental because they connect with the three basic human processes of thinking, feeling and willing as shown in Figure P5.1.

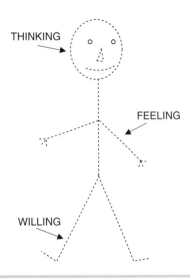

Figure P5.1 Thinking, feeling and willing

The processes of thinking, feeling and willing are all involved in taking action on any challenge. While normally all mingled together, it can be useful to look at them separately to work out the location of the critical question that might lead to the important insight: is it Who knows? Who cares? or Who can?

- *Thinking* is about ideas, concepts, images, metaphors, theories and so on. It is also about reflections, assumptions, mental models and frames of reference that cause us to see situations in particular lights. Thinking may be said, literally and symbolically, to take place in the head.
- *Feeling*, located here symbolically in the gut or the body, is about emotions, sensations and energies, and also about atmosphere, ambience and vibrations.
- *Willing* is about wishes, purposes, intentions and also about power and energy. As noted in Chapter 3, it is will that provides the drive, determination and effort to make things happen. It is the force that translates impulses and directions into practice and is located metaphorically in the legs and feet.

There are many ways in which the idea of thinking, feeling and willing can be used. The concern here is with the asking of good questions to induce insights for forward direction and action. Before the questions comes the listening; try the following activity:

Activity P5.2: Thinking, Feeling, Willing is an opportunity to learn to listen to these fundamental aspects of human action.

Listening in this way may seem a bit unusual at first – because it is. But if you persevere and overcome the awkwardness of silences, you will find this is an attainable skill, and a very valuable one. Good questioning usually comes with supportive listening because it is this that opens up the road to insight.

Questioning insight

Another reason for the importance of asking challenging questions from a leadership position is that this is a practice that is catching. If the senior people question themselves and each other, it encourages everyone else. When visiting any organisation for the first time, it is always easy to tell whether this is a place where people are encouraged to be curious and ask questions. The vitality of such organisations is not just down to the habit of asking questions but about developing deeper practices of inquiry and reflection. The contrast with those other places where people have learned to "know their place" and not raise doubts and inquiries is remarkable. In questioning cultures everyone is more lively and more likely to approach you rather than waiting for you to ask. Asking questions is a sign of confidence: "Can I help you?" goes with "Yes, I can".

Changing the air

Rob is the owner–manager of a small engineering company that makes and services air-conditioning systems. "We've managed to stay profitable but never hit the jackpot because we are more growth than results oriented. If we just stabilised, the results would improve dramatically because we wouldn't be putting time, effort and money into growth projects – like the export one which is absorbing a lot at the moment. But if we don't make the effort now, in five years' time we'll be the poorer for it.

"We have plans and we know where each department is going in quite a lot of detail, but about every three years we ask ourselves some fundamental questions: Are we where we said we would be? Do we want to be here? What should we be doing? We're doing it now. We don't plan this, it just happens; three years into a five-year plan you find that things have changed. What's important is that we've done our thinking about where we want to go. So every three years we do something different to look at what we're doing.

"All these initiatives that we get involved in ... quality, Investors in People, strategic analysis, leadership training and so on ... only replicate what we did as a matter of common sense when we were a very small company. We didn't think about it then, we were small, close-knit and communication was 100%. You never needed prompting then. During the middle years, when the business issues began to take over, we lost that. It's taken conscious effort and thought to bring that back into what is now a larger business. It's ironic that so much effort has to go into doing something that we once found easy!"

The example of the air-conditioning company illustrates the close connection between questions and new knowledge and thinking. Rob is aware of the importance of everyone asking questions, and clearly understands how this keeps the company thinking and learning.

Seven types of questions for leadership

After listening to problems or challenges to which there is no obvious answer, asking good questions is the most constructive response you can make. There is no need to bother with this process if the solution is straightforward or an answer is to hand. The importance of questions and questioning insight for leadership is because of the need to act and intervene in complex and difficult situations where there are no simple solutions.

In such a situation there are some important and helpful questioning responses. Figure P5.2 shows seven types of questions that have different purposes. We have a choice of questions for …

- finding or making meaning
- helping others to reflect and learn from the past
- seeking examples or practical illustrations
- initiating action
- caring and supporting

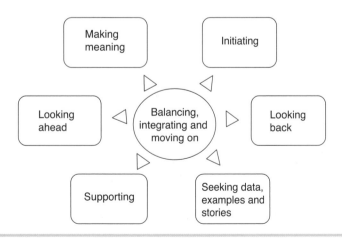

Figure P5.2 Seven types of questions for leadership

■ looking ahead to the future and the consequences of action
■ balancing, integrating, summarising and moving on.

In this "planetary" model of useful questions, those that integrate, summarise and move us on are the sun around which the others circulate. In meetings, these are the traditional questions from the chair to summarise and keep the business moving. In the broader context, leadership stands at this point of movement, balancing past, present and future, summarising progress and maintaining momentum.

These seven sets of questions form part of the toolkit for this leadership practice. Using these different questions, you can help people to make sense of situations, elicit examples, contrast them with past conditions, initiate action and support each other in moving forward to a better future.

Next time you are in a meeting or at a
project group, try out some of the questions suggested
in Activity P5.3: Seven Types of Questions
for Leadership.

Generating challenging questions

Questions are one of the best ways of challenging people. We can observe this power in the negative form when a person in authority asks "Any questions?" and is greeted by silence. Does this mean that none of those present has any questions in their minds? Probably not. Does it mean that they fear the response to a question that might be perceived as a challenge to existing thinking or practice? Quite possibly.

Action learning is a special sort of forum for the posing of challenging questions.

Isobella's challenge

Isobella is the leader of a group of family lawyers in a large city practice. In a first action learning session with colleagues from her professional institute, she was asked what it was about her work that most concerned her and occupied her thoughts at the moment. After giving this some thought, she came up with: I want to improve the relationships with a particular group of colleagues in order to work better with them.

After discussing this in the group, the other members came up with a long list of questions, including:

- How would you describe the relationship at present?
- What is your picture of a good relationship?
- What makes you think that you have a problem?
- What have you tried to do so far?
- Why do you want to do this?
- Do these colleagues want a better relationship with you?
- Who have you talked to about this issue?
- What would working better look like?
- Which colleagues are you thinking about?
- What feedback do you get from your colleagues?
- How do you think you can go about improving these relationships?
- How does this affect your work?
- What skills do you think you haven't got?
- How skilful are your colleagues?
- How might things be if you had better relationships?
- What would your best friend say to you about your working situation?

Isobella was then asked to choose the three questions that most interested her. Especially, which were the most challenging, and had most impact as she heard them? After some thought she picked:

- Do these colleagues want a better relationship with you?
- What would working better look like?
- What would your best friend say to you about your working situation?

The three questions which she picked out as most interesting were those which had either not occurred to her before or had suddenly made her think. Each question led to a new train of thought. As she said about the first question: "When this was said, I thought it was outrageous, a stupid idea. Then I thought – this has never occurred to me! I had been preoccupied with my view of what I thought was the problem ... maybe there is no problem from their perspective?"

A really good challenging question is one that leads the other person to question themselves. Once this self-questioning starts, then new avenues for action and discovery often follow. This means that a good challenge is not just determined by the questioner, but also by the receiver, and that it is the quality of this relationship that matters. In the example that opens this section, the people present did not offer their questions because they were afraid that they might be seen as challenging or disrespectful by a more powerful person. In the action learning set, where people come together as peers to support and challenge each other, the questions are openly offered and it is up to Isobella to decide. She is free to choose. Some people seem to find it hard to grasp this point: but learning of this sort is always a voluntary activity. If Isobella does not trust the questioner, and feel able to be open with her colleagues, then however skilfully put, she will not allow herself to be challenged by the question.

However, given a good quality "give and take" relationship, any group of four or more people can use this activity to generate challenging questions around any situation. Some groups may already do this sort of thing naturally as part of what they are doing – as in the case of the air-conditioning engineers in their early days. Where this has been lost or is not normal, you may need some simple rules and facilitation to develop the process. The main thing is to follow the steps implied in Isobella's story in a rather deliberate and disciplined way, rather than jumping into a free-for-all of talk and advice. Get people to write down their questions once they have heard about the significant issue and then to read them out in turn, ensuring that the person with the issue listens to them and jots them down for future prompting, rather than trying to answer them on the spot.

Leadership as a reflective practice

As noted earlier, an important aspect of this leadership practice of challenging questions is the encouragement of questions and self-questioning in other people. The capacity to question yourself and your own actions, while at the same time being resolute and committed in what you are doing, tends to spread self-confidence and enquiry among all concerned.

The learning organisation idea is a response to the limitations of the classical hierarchical organisation to deliver on the "wicked problems". As we have become more aware of complexity and of the need for learning, various methods and approaches have been developed to encourage self-aware and responsive organising, where people can adapt their offer quickly to meet changing needs and circumstances. Like action learning, many of these approaches set out to encourage people to reflect about their work and then to continuously improve their practice on the basis of their learning.

Reflection is a critical part of the learning cycle. When we reflect – or question ourselves – about the meaning of our experiences, we are on the way to coming up with new ideas, new ways of doing things, new practice.

Reflective practice

Reflective practice is a way of challenging yourself through asking questions. It originates with Donald Schon who argues, like Revans, that professionals encounter many problems, uncertainties and "swampy lowlands" in their work, for which there are no technical solutions. The aim of reflective practice is to cultivate the capacity to reflect both *in* action (while doing something) as well as *on* action (after you have done it).

This has become an important feature of professional training programmes in many disciplines such as medicine, nursing, teaching and social work. The idea is that professional practice can be developed through a spiral of action and reflection, where a person first acts, and then consciously reflects on that action before planning new action, based on what has been learned from the reflection. This has been encoded as DATA – Describe, Analyse, Theorise and Act:

- *Describe* the area of your practice that you think needs improvement.
- *Analyse* the factors contributing to your dissatisfaction. Dig deep to consider the assumptions and underlying beliefs involved here.
- *Theorise* possible ways to improve your practice; how could you do it differently?
- *Act* on your theory, try out the new idea to see how it works in practice.

Reflective practice requires self-awareness and the willingness to inquire critically into your work. This sounds demanding, and so it is, but this is a habit that can be acquired by everyone. For all those people who want to do a good job and to improve as they go along, reflective practice can easily become a normal part of working life. Take the lunchtime supervisors at Burrsbridge School for example.

The lunchtime supervisors

The lunchtime supervisors look after the children during the lunch break. In some schools this is a minding role, but at Burrsbridge School, the supervisors along with all other members of staff, teaching and non-teaching, are encouraged to be partners in the education of the children. As part of this they are represented on the school evaluation team and have elected to have their appraisals in groups.

The appraisals were carried out with the three lunchtime supervisors for each year group by the headteacher and the Key Stage leader for that year. The supervisors were asked to think about the ideal lunchtime experience for the children and to identify three aspects of the sessions that work well and identify why this is so. Then they were asked to think of one thing that could be done differently, and what training or resources they might need for this.

One outcome of this process was that the supervisors asked for extra play equipment for the children and were gratified to find that the head responded immediately to this request. Some lunchtime supervisors are also part-time teaching assistants and therefore involved in more than one way. Two other supervisors found the process so interesting that they started to stay on after lunch as voluntary helpers. They wanted to understand better what was happening to the children in class and how they could further support their learning.

By recruiting the lunchtime supervisors into the teaching and learning process, Burrsbridge School had effectively increased its teaching resources, at no cost to the school, and to the considerable development of some of its staff. And that represents good leadership by the head, the deputy and the Key Stage leaders.

There are many ways of encouraging reflection. Appraisal is a structured way of building it into the normal processes of managing and organising. Coaching, counselling and other development processes rely on the capacity of the learner to reflect in response to questions. A very good way to encourage reflection in a group of people is the review meeting. This works best when it comes hard on the heels of a particular event – a conference, sales launch or perhaps where something went badly wrong. To review patrols and operations, the US Army encourages the practice of *After Action Review*:

Next time you have the opportunity with a group or team, use Activity P5.4: After Action Review immediately after the completion of any task.

Like the other approaches to learning in leadership *After Action Review* will encourage the habit of review and reflection. Gradually people will start to reflect *in* action as well as afterwards.

Another approach to collective self-evaluation is appreciative inquiry or AI. This also works via questions and shares many other characteristics with reflective practice and action learning also. However, AI is distinguished by the stress it places on emphasising the positive and in not using language that can be seen as part of negative thinking such as "problems" or deficits. The next chapter on the fifth leadership practice of facilitation contains an illustration of appreciative inquiry as applied to the development of a new organisational structure. References to AI can also be found in the further resources at the end of that chapter.

The most valuable question?

There is a shadow side to questions and questioning. Questions are powerful tools that can be abused. The possibility of seduction means that the unwary can be lured by the power of questioning into cleverness, pursuit, interrogation and other traps. The question is: are you enquiring to learn ... or what?

Some of the principle traps around the leadership practice of challenging questions are:

- *Giving advice disguised as questions.* Questions of the "Have you thought of using a big hammer on it?" variety, may be genuinely helpful in certain circumstances where a person may be ignorant of available resources, but are more often attempts to give advice or push suggestions rather than a genuine enquiry. If you want to give advice, it is far better to offer it openly: this makes it easier to accept or reject.
- *Influence disguised as questions.* "Are you going to answer the telephone?" type questions are attempts to get other people to do what you want. Such questions are not open ones and do not offer the freedom of movement that they appear to imply. Better to just ask for what you want.
- *Cross-examination.* When one question leads to another and you seem to be "on to something", this can lead to the courtroom situation with the other person in the dock. Questions that start with "How do you explain ... ?" may be along this road, if still a little short of "I put it to you that ... ?"! It can be very helpful to lead someone down an avenue or enquiry, but is the purpose to promote learning? Again, if you want to air a theory, then do so openly.
- *Generating defensiveness.* This is very easy to do. When pursued or cross-examined, a natural reaction is to close up and become defensive: which is generally death to any learning. Pressing people to answer often shuts them down. Even apparently polite or innocent questions can have this effect sometimes. A challenging question depends for its quality on both questioner and receiver, and the relationship between them. So, a challenging question repeated, produces useful outcomes in the right circumstances, but only if the receiver is "up for it". The main rule is to invite people to respond to questions – and always give them the space to decline the invitation.

The traps abound because of the power of the question to get to the heart of things and people. To deepen a discussion of events via reflection or questioning is to arrive sooner or later at values and beliefs. To get clear about this means being honest with yourself: as Douglas Stone and his colleagues at the Harvard Negotiation Project put it:

inquire to learn. And only to learn. You can tell whether a question will help the conversation or hurt it by thinking about why you asked it. The only good answer is "To learn".

(Stone, Patton and Heen, 2000, p. 172)

References

Dixon, N. (2000) *Common Knowledge: How Companies Thrive by Sharing What They Know.* Boston: Harvard Business School Press.

Stone, D. Patton, B. and Heen, S. (2000) *Difficult Conversations: How to Discuss What Matters Most.* Harmondsworth: Penguin.

Revans, R.W. (1998) *ABC of Action Learning.* London: Lemos & Crane.

Zimmerman, B. Lindberg, C. and Plsek, P. (2001) *Edgeware, Insights from Complexity Science.* Texas: VHA.

Follow-up and further resources

Dorothy Strachan's *Making Questions Work: A Guide to How and What to Ask for Facilitators, Consultants, Managers, Coaches, and Educators* (San Francisco: Jossey Bass, 2007) is a very thorough and practical resource on how to ask questions. For leaders as facilitators, this book takes you through the right questions for the five stages of opening a session, enabling action, thinking critically, addressing issues and closing the session. *Leading with Questions: How Leaders Find the Right Solutions By Knowing What to Ask* by Michael Marquardt (San Francisco: Jossey Bass, 2005) draws on action learning ideas and uses a wide range of practical material and organisational examples to make the case for using questions to improve individual, team and organisational performance.

Mike Pedler's *Action Learning for Managers* (Aldershot: Gower, 2008) is a good short guide to action learning and to the practice of questions that are at the core of this approach. Challenging questions are also a feature of reflective practice as applied to professional work and Gillie Bolton's *Reflective Practice: Writing and Professional Development* (London: Sage, 2005) is a useful resource in this area.

Another useful guide to questioning in a tricky context is Douglas Stone, Bruce Patton and Sheila Heen's (2004) *Difficult Conversations: How to Discuss What Matters Most* from the Harvard Negotiation Project. This is a clear and friendly treatment of all aspects of difficult conversations, and has useful comments on the role of questions. Their picture of the three essential conversations ("what happened?", feelings and identity) has some overlap with our thinking, feeling, willing model. This book will give you a great deal of clear guidance and advice for recognising and negotiating these conversations.

Activities

■ Activity P5.1: Revans' Essential Questions.
■ Activity P5.2: Thinking, Feeling, Willing.
■ Activity P5.3: Seven Types of Questions for Leadership.
■ Activity P5.4: After Action Review.

Activity P5.1: Revans' Essential Questions

Revans' essential questions can be applied to any situation of challenge to which you have no obvious way forward.

1 Think of a current issue, concern or challenge that you have and which you would like to act on. This might be to do with a current work task, or about your career, from your family life or to do with your friends. Perhaps it has been on your mind for some time or something that you have been meaning to do and been putting off. It need not be a big thing, but it must be something that concerns you and which you would like to do something about.

2 Now consider the following questions. They are phrased for a shared issue in a team or group, but you can personalise them by changing "we" to "I", etc. You could tackle these questions in small sub-groups or, if you are doing this alone, make a few notes under each question before moving on to the next:

The first three questions are to do with what you want to do:

- *What are we trying to do?* What is your purpose, your goal? What will success look like?
- *What is stopping us from doing it?* What are the barriers? In me, us and other people?
- *What can we do about this?* What is possible? What small first steps?

The second three questions are to do with who can help you and where you can find resources:

- *Who else knows what we are trying to do?*
- *Who else cares about what we are trying to do?*
- *Who else can do anything to help?*

These six questions can be applied to any challenging and problematic situation. They may lead to "questioning insight" the first time you try them, or it may take repeated efforts to find some steps forward. For this reason they are best pursued in a small group dedicated to sustaining the action learning effort over time.

The really difficult and intractable challenges do not have "solutions" as such, but there is always something in the situation that can be changed – either in the problem or in yourself and your situation.

Source: Revans, R.W. (1998) *ABC of Action Learning*. London: Lemos & Crane, pp. 33–41.

Activity P5.2: Thinking, Feeling, Willing

Try this activity for listening silently and with attention – a surprisingly rare occurrence between people but an easy skill to learn.

You can practise this in any meeting where someone is speaking about anything for a certain length of time, but it is probably better done on a one-to-one basis where you can discuss the outcome of your listening with a partner. An ideal situation is where someone wants to talk to you in private about something that is important to them – a coaching session or a conversation about a difficult decision. If this is not immediately available, you could simply ask a trusted colleague to tell you about an aspect of their work that they have been thinking about recently.

1 Listen to your colleague for a decent length of time – say 10 or 15 minutes.

Show your interest and attention by looking at your colleague; pay attention, but don't speak except perhaps the odd word "Yes" or "An … ?": you are there to listen, so sit out the pauses and keep the focus on the speaker.

This gives any speaker an unusual opportunity for an uninterrupted pursuit of a topic; a chance to explore a problem. In a surprisingly short piece of uninterrupted time a person can explore their thoughts and feelings and desire for action. Through the agency of a silent listener, who is there and restraining her or his own desire to talk, a vessel is created in which the speaker can sort out ideas, clarify feelings and recognise wishes.

2 If you listen carefully you may be able to pick out your partner's:
   - *Thinking*. What is being said, the pattern of thoughts; is it logical? Detailed or general? In the past, present or future? Who is being talked about and who is not? What images and metaphors are being used? What assumptions are being made?
   - *Feeling*. What is the speaker feeling? Notice the gestures, posture, tone of voice, way of breathing and the expression of the face, eye movement.
   - *Willing*. What does the person want to do? What is just a wish and what is a definite intention to act?

   You might want to take some brief notes to help your recall after your colleague has finished speaking.

3 When your colleague has finished speaking, and if it is appropriate, play back your observations under the three headings of "thinking", "feeling" and "willing". What did you hear? And what did you not hear? How do these fit with the speaker's own views?

   A variation on this one-to-one session is to try this activity in a small group where everyone is listening to one person. In this format, the listeners can choose their focus and concentrate on just *willing*, *thinking* or *feeling* and take it in turns to feed back their perceptions at the end.

Activity P5.3: Seven Types of Questions for Leadership

The leadership toolkit has questions for all these purposes:

- finding or making meaning
- helping others to reflect and learn from the past
- seeking examples or practical illustrations
- initiating action
- caring and supporting
- looking ahead to the future and the consequences of action
- balancing, integrating, summarising and moving on.

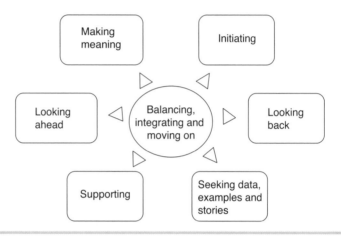

Figure P5.2 Seven types of questions for leadership

Examples of helpful questions under these seven headings are:

- *Questions to help find or make meaning:*
  - What does this mean to you?
  - What is this saying to you?'
  - Can you see a pattern or a theme in all this?

- *Questions that cause others to reflect and learn from the past:*
  - Has this happened before?
  - Can you give some examples of incidents like this in the past?
  - What have you learned from tackling similar situations?

■ *Questions seeking examples or practical illustrations*:
- What sort of things are you talking about?
- Can you give examples of other situations in which you feel this way?
- Who else do you know who has had this issue?
- What is generally seen to be good practice in this area?

■ *Questions about initiating action*:
- You seem to have several ideas for action, how do they fit together?
- What alternatives and options do you have?
- Of the various options, what is the best next step?
- What do you want to do about this?

■ *Caring and supporting questions*:
- I know you are good at … because I've seen you do it before, what is different about this situation?
- How do you feel?
- What would help you right now?

■ *Questions that cause people to think about the future and the consequences of action*:
- What will be the consequences for yourself and all the others involved?'
- What blocks and obstacles are there?'
- What resources will this require?
- Where do you want to be with regard to this in six months' time?

■ *Balancing, integrating, summarising and moving on questions*:
- How is that point consistent with what you said earlier?
- Can you see a clear trend linking the past, the present and the future?
- So, what you seem to be saying is …?
- Can you summarise the actions you are going to take?

You can use this list for ideas to work with in a meeting or project, or to review your efforts afterwards. More important than "getting it right" is the intention to help the other people through your questions. Once you have this then just get started and try some of these ideas, improving as you go.

Activity P5.4: After Action Review

People in organisations are often very focused on the task, but are less good at pausing to take stock and learn from what has happened once the job is completed. Taking just 20 minutes or so to review can result in good ideas to improve practice next time. If the vital opportunity to learn from experience is missed, this results in a "learning loss" – not just for the person and their work group, but also for the whole organisation.

Use the *After Action Review* immediately after the completion of any task. It is done in the group of colleagues who have been involved in the task or project concerned. During the completion of this task each person will have made some observations from their experience; for example, they will have noticed:

- What actions they themselves took (what they did and *didn't* do, what they said, and so on).
- How these actions impacted on the outcome.
- What actions other team members took and how these actions impacted on the outcome.
- The effect of the environment or local circumstances – expected and unexpected.

If these individual observations and personal learning are made available, then everyone has a chance to learn from experience and do better next time.

Step 1: Fix a time for the *After Action Review* – say for 20 or 30 minutes.

Step 2: At the start of the meeting, propose some *ground rules*, e.g.

- Everyone's experience is valid – irrespective of rank, etc.
- Don't hold back – say what you saw and heard.
- "No thin skins" – don't take anything personally, focus on the impact on team performance.
- Propose changes – how could we do it differently and better?

Ask people if they want to suggest others and add these as appropriate, but then move on quickly.

Step 3: Now work through the three basic questions of the *After Action Review*. Ask each person to make brief notes on:

- *What was supposed to happen?*
- *What actually happened?*
- *What accounts for the difference?*

Step 4: Taking the three questions in turn, ask each person to comment and note down on a flip chart a summary of the points on which most people agree.

Step 5: When all three questions have been dealt with in this way, ask:

■ *What could we do differently next time?*

Note any ideas or responses that people think might improve practice.

Step 6: Close the meeting and provide everyone with a copy to take into their next task or project.

10

Practice 6: Facilitation

Facilitation is a process through which a person helps others complete their work and improve the way they work together.
Weaver and Farrell

Facilitation is the right hand of leadership. The leadership practice of facilitation is about helping people get their work done more effectively, as individuals, groups, networks and whole organisations. With the intensification of the pace of work, curiously sometimes, less seems to get done. As the limitations of "command" have become more obvious, the possibilities for facilitative leadership have become more apparent. This means encouraging people to share their opinions of what needs to be done, to engage with decisions and to work collaboratively rather than in isolation.

The idea of facilitation is familiar in the context of managing meetings, but in leadership terms it has the strategic aim of enabling the collective performance of people working together:

> *The strategic challenge is to give the work back to people without abandoning them. Overload them and they will avoid learning. Underload them and they will grow too dependent, or complacent.*

(Heifetz, 1994)

Giving the work back to the people may be easier said than done. The best people to resolve a situation are usually the locals; yet these people may be hesitant, lacking confidence; they may lack the skills or resources or they may be divided, split in their views and opinions. Leadership is frequently surrounded by different views and conflict about what should be done and not done. The practice of facilitation provides the means for surfacing these differences and not avoiding them; and also for providing a structure or framework within which people can progress their work in a productive way.

This chapter offers advice and practical guidance on how to develop the leadership practice of facilitation. It addresses the questions:

- What is facilitation?
- What are the skills involved?
- What is facilitative leadership?
- What is the process of facilitation?
- How can engagement and participation be facilitated in the organisation as a whole?
- Is help helpful?

The four activities in this chapter create a basic toolkit for this leadership practice:

- Activity P6.1: Facilitating the Aims and Objectives for a Team.
- Activity P6.2: Creating a Facilitation Process Map for a conflict situation.
- Activity P6.3: Appreciative Inquiry: generating a collaborative structure.
- Activity P6.4: Guidelines for a Design Team.

What is facilitation?

A dictionary definition: "to make easier, promote and help move forward".

Facilitation is a practical necessity; it is about putting the fine words of leadership into action. This is an everyday leadership practice; opportunities to use the skills of facilitation can be found wherever people are trying to get things done together in unfamiliar situations. The leadership practice of facilitation is a good working habit to develop, but like all practices it is more than just a habit, because it is always being revised and developed.

Why has facilitation become core to leadership work? Generally, for the following sorts of reasons:

- *Learning*: the need to learn new skills, new knowledge and new perspectives on jobs, roles, careers and lives is increasingly inseparable from working.
- *Change*: rapid changes in work and workplaces mean that people can often use help to respond positively to challenges and to see and seize opportunities.
- *Organising*: making the most of people and their potentials, individually and in groups and communities of practice, can be facilitated but not commanded.

As applied specifically to leadership development, "context-sensitive" approaches such as coaching, team development, appreciative inquiry and action learning, all place a premium on facilitation skills. Yet, although it may be the right hand of leadership, facilitation requires very different skills:

Wasim, the owner–manager of a successful and growing chain of retail chemist shops, decided to involve the 16 branch managers in a business planning process. The last business plan had been prepared by external consultants, and the managers did not seem to understand its importance and had shown little interest in it. This time Wasim resolved to engage them from the start in creating the plan and setting the targets. However, when he asked his managers to come up with some ideas for new business developments, he was very disappointed with the response; only a few, rather insignificant proposals came forward.

What happened to Wasim and his ambitious plans to involve his managers? Don't his managers have any ideas? Are they afraid to make suggestions? Or are they simply used to him having all the good ideas in this business?

It is hard to know the answers to these questions when you are the boss. Sometimes it is difficult both to lead and to facilitate, and appointing an external facilitator to help in this rather important process might have been advisable. However, had Wasim had more skills as a facilitator, he might have thought more about how he would get the managers to participate. How could he get them talking and putting forward their ideas?

Table P6.1 shows some characteristic activities of leadership and some corresponding activities of facilitation:

Table P6.1 Leadership and facilitation

Leadership is ...	Facilitation is ...
Taking a long-term view	Helping people to find their own views of the future
Concerned with values and moral purposes	Concerned with clarifying different values and creating common purpose
Pointing out the adaptive challenge to be faced	Asking people what sense they make of their situations and how this challenge affects them
Articulating vision	Encouraging people to understand their own hopes and dreams and enabling self-expression
Focused on the future, on innovation and change	Helping people to make sense of the new, to understand the implications of alternative futures and to ask "what does this mean for me?"
Seeking collaboration and commitment	Exploring opinions, positions and commitment; clarifying the options and seeking common ground
Giving the work back	Helping people get their work done together
Listening to the hard questions	Protecting the "critical friends" who raise hard questions and challenge common assumptions
Moving towards, and not against, conflict and difference	Reassuring people that conflict is normal in challenging situations and helping people get things in perspective and to resolve internal conflicts
Seeking to serve and to improve service to others	Focusing people on the practical issues and tasks and on what they can do to improve the service they offer

Leadership is more concerned with a sense of direction and about what is right and wrong, and not necessarily what is practical or convenient. Skilful facilitation can help here. Where leadership raises a difficult question or challenge to which there is no obvious solution, this can cause self-doubt and confusion. In the face of this, facilitation is irredeemably cheerful, always optimistic, always looking for a practical way to move forwards.

What are the skills of facilitation?

Facilitation is about using the skills and knowledge of how groups work to help people to agree on their aims and achieve them. It includes formal activities such as chairing a meeting, where there is a set agenda and the facilitator has formal authority to control the meeting and to ensure decisions; and much more informal processes where the facilitator attends events, meetings or project teams and intervenes in various ways to help the group work more effectively.

The skills of facilitation are particularly about listening to people and helping them to move forward; they include:

- attending
- listening
- questioning
- empathising
- responding
- reflecting
- summarising
- intervening
- offering models and structures
- confronting
- problem-solving.

Skills are learned principally by practice and feedback from colleagues. It can also be very useful to observe other people facilitating groups and to learn from their example. But how do facilitators deploy these skills? A simple model (Weaver and Farrell, 1997) suggests four main elements for the facilitator to focus on in any situation: the task, the process of working on the task, the group of people involved and their own self-awareness (see Figure P6.1).

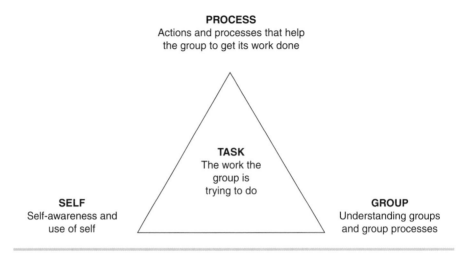

Figure P6.1 The four foci of facilitation

As in leadership itself, the first focus of facilitation is on the task: what are people trying to do? This question alone might be enough to free up a team. But often, someone acting as a facilitator also needs to dig into the process which the team or group of people is using to achieve their ends: How are they going about doing their work? In understanding working processes, it is very helpful to have some knowledge of how people typically function in groups – or what is known as group processes or group dynamics. The fourth focus of self-awareness is important because the facilitator seeks impartiality and must monitor their own actions against certain touchstones or values.

These particular values are what distinguish facilitation from leadership, and explain why it is sometimes hard to combine the two. For example, facilitators will try to uphold values such as:

- Everyone's views and ideas are important.
- Each person should be entitled to have their say and to be heard by the others.
- Disagreement is normal and healthy when it is about direction, goals and the content of discussions. On the other hand we should try to avoid personalising disagreements, as this does not help with decisions.
- If possible, decisions should be made after full discussion and on the basis of consensus.
- People can solve their own problems – but they sometimes need a bit of help.

The values of leadership are sometimes different. In leadership it may sometimes be important just to get on with the task, to push through resistance, and make decisions that do not take everyone's views into account. This does not mean that it is impossible to be a "facilitative leader" – far from it; for much of the time, leadership and facilitation are synonymous. Yet awareness of these differences is important, part of self-awareness and leading yourself (Chapter 5). Occasionally, on big projects or with difficult decisions, it is advisable to split the roles of facilitator and leader in order to use both to their full advantage.

The facilitative leader

In challenging circumstances, leaders able to act as facilitators can help a great deal. In the face of uncertainties, with the ground shifting under their feet, it is hard for people to feel secure and confident in their work. Facilitation can bring a settling and calming influence by helping groups of people clarify their goals and choose practical ways forward:

The new team

In the aftermath of a major shake-up following a merger, with widespread restructuring and redundancies, Sue, the regional director of a large utility, found that she had an almost completely new team. Instead of just managing engineers, she now had a cross-functional group of engineers, customer service people, information managers and administrators. This was a major change for everyone, including the regional director herself. Although she knew from personal experience how unsettling it was, she had little idea of how best to proceed in setting up the new team.

Still in this state of mind Sue convened a first meeting of the dozen or so most senior and experienced people. "Much of this meeting was taken up with people meeting each other and then with discussing the recent changes. Some people were angry and frustrated about what had happened without consultation, others were wary and uncertain about what might be coming next. It was hardly a good situation for being positive." Despite this, she went along with the tone and shared some of her own feelings. After a couple of hours the best she could think of was to suggest that they called it a day for now and fix another meeting for next week. As part of this, Sue asked everyone to come back with some proposals for reorganising the service configurations in the region.

Most of the second meeting was taken up with people familiarising themselves and learning from each other about the different aspects of the new business. Despite this slow pace, Sue was beginning to get a sense of progress. In the last half hour of the meeting she posed the questions "What are we trying to accomplish in this region?" and "How will we know when we are getting there?" She had not really planned these questions, although they were in her mind and this seemed to be the right time. "Of course it would take more meetings to agree the common ground and create a plan that could then be taken out to the wider workforce, but people were listening to each other, they were interested in each other – that felt like a good start."

Had she read a good book on facilitation skills, Sue might have felt that she should have helped the group to:

- agree its purpose and direction
- clarify its objectives
- defined the roles of members
- plan tasks
- map processes
- make decisions and agreements
- air and resolve conflicts
- … and so on.

Yet while these are all the important aspects of facilitating people to get their work done together, they did not seem to be the most important things to do at this time. In the face of disruption, anxiety and novelty, what she actually allowed or helped to happen was more useful. What Sue did as a facilitator in this situation was to:

- bring everyone together
- create space for people to meet and get to know each other
- encourage everyone to share their views of the situation
- allow time for people to listen to each other
- show acceptance of different opinions and feelings
- pose useful questions for progress at the right time.

At the same time, as the leader in this situation, she was also making clear the purpose of the meetings and the goals she had in mind. Facilitation requires an openness and an attention to things other than just the task in hand. This is where it adds a particular dimension to leadership which might otherwise be more singularly focused on the task. Although we tend to maintain that work is a rational activity, the people who do it are not always so; and especially not at any time of shake-up or disturbance. Helping this group of people get on with the job meant helping them move from confusion, apprehension and tension to a more positive frame of mind.

The process of facilitation

Facilitation isn't rocket science, and the process is often quite straightforward. The fundamental human processes of meeting, greeting and expressing feelings and opinions need to be given time and space, after which the logical sequence of the tasks in the first list above can be followed.

But, before sketching out this generic process, what is your basic approach to running a meeting? Here are the three key activities for any meeting; look at this list and, given a two-hour meeting, what would you say was the right order and about the right amount of time to spend on each of them?

1. Tackling the business agenda.
2. Meeting and greeting.
3. Exchanging information.

A common error in facilitating meetings is to try and get to the business too early. Under time pressure it is very easy to underestimate the importance of the human needs displayed in the utilities case. By contrast, one colleague generally adopts this pattern:

1. Meeting and greeting — 50 minutes.
2. Exchanging information — 40 minutes.
3. Tackling the business agenda — 30 minutes.

Her meetings can feel a bit frustrating for those not used to them; they seem to ramble about and go off on all sorts of tangents. But they do seem to come to good decisions, and quickly; right at the end. Her rationale is something like this:

> *People come to meetings glad to see each other and interested to meet any new people. They naturally want to exchange news and gossip before becoming more disciplined about what information they need. By the time we get round to the actual agenda and the decisions, people have been giving thought, consciously or unconsciously, to these issues, and have already worked out their positions. The decision process is usually quick because it is mainly about checking exactly the details of the mandate – what is wanted, and by when. It is all so much easier when people volunteer to take on bits of the agenda – and so much more enjoyable.*

Compare this with some "businesslike" meetings that follow a more predictable pattern, but can result in a lack of commitment to decisions. We got through the business, we were strongly chaired, but there was no opportunity to exchange news and information or express doubts and questions. Consequently, people had to warm up, find their voices, work out all the various agendas, published and unpublished, all under the guise of progressing the business decisions. It looked good but it was actually, in the end, very inefficient and unsatisfying.

Focus on the task

Whatever their approach, the facilitative leader always has the task in mind. It is a matter of judgement how best to run the meeting. Is it best to allow lots of time for exploration or to get quickly down to the job in hand? If the group is facing a new and unfamiliar situation, then they might need time and space to make sense of it; if on the other hand, a group is in turmoil or split over which way to go, then the businesslike route may often be the best way to go because following an orderly process can be healing in itself. Too long spent on sharing of grief or anxieties can makes things worse; better to get on and do something. Here is the basic process for facilitating a group on a task.

> *Activity P6.1: Facilitating the Aims and Objectives for a Team is a generic process for facilitation that keeps the task centre stage and can be used in many situations.*

The framework in Activity P6.1 is a process map to follow to complete any task. The particular example is about agreeing goals in a group, but the process can be applied to any task facing any group such as generating ideas, planning change, mapping pathways and work processes, resolving conflicts, making decisions and agreements, and so on. Using the template, as in Figure P6.2 below, you can create a facilitation process map for any situation. While a map does not guarantee the success of the journey, at least it gives an indication of where to go.

Step	Action	Key questions

Figure P6.2 A facilitation process map

Activity P6.2 shows how you can develop this map of the facilitation process for the much more difficult task of resolving a conflict.

Try Activity P6.2: Creating a Facilitation Process Map for
a conflict situation at the end of the chapter.

Facilitating wider engagement and participation

While much facilitation takes place in small groups of people tackling particular tasks, a key aspect of this leadership practice is the promotion of engagement and participation in organisational life. This may take place via events such as conferences or special "big group" meetings that bring large numbers together to confer or consult. It can also inform everyday leadership actions and more generally the way things are done around here. Is this an organisation where every person's opinion is important? Is this a place where new ideas are valued – wherever they come from?

A facilitative leadership has a different mindset on how an organisation should work. The awareness of the goals and purposes of the facilitator – to give everyone a voice, make consensus decisions and "give the work back to the people" – means that, while you could make the decision yourself, it might well be a much better one if others are involved. The source of this potential superiority is first, because a participative decision process might actually generate a better solution, and secondly because those who have been engaged in finding a solution will be much more committed to implementing it.

Not every decision benefits from wider engagement and participation, but developing these processes around some decisions will generate a wider involvement and commitment in the business. Two examples are offered here for working with wider circles of engagement, starting with appreciative inquiry (AI), which was introduced in the last chapter.

Appreciative inquiry

AI is a useful facilitation tool that can be used to innovate around a stuck situation or to generate ideas for any new venture. It is usually an uplifting experience for those who take part because it always emphasises the positive. It is a good first outing for the facilitative leader who wants to spread their wings beyond the confines of a team or work group.

Activity P6.3 at the end of this chapter, demonstrates the process of carrying out an appreciative inquiry. The example given is of setting out to generate a new structure to encourage more collaborative working among the various departments and sections in an organisation.

*Try Activity P6.3: Appreciative Inquiry: generating a
collaborative structure.*

As with many of the activities in this book, the principles of AI can be much
more widely applied as part of a "can do" leadership philosophy. One difficult
aspect of leadership is the question of how to sustain momentum over the long
term. Once you have created this goodwill and enthusiasm in an AI session or
other event, how can you keep it going?

Working with a design team to facilitate organisational development and change

Some organisations, such as the air-conditioning engineers in the last chapter,
are small and compact enough to involve almost everyone at "town meetings"
or other engagement events. For larger or more dispersed organisations a more
representative process of participation is needed. This is the stuff of
organisational development and major change programmes, which would
normally involve specialist facilitation at various points. However, an
ambitious facilitative leadership can engage people through a process akin to
representative democracy.

A design team represents all the principal groups and stakeholders in an
enterprise and is a microcosm of the whole organisation The aim is to reflect
the diversity of views in a system by including all those people who should
have a say in a particular issue. The importance of local voices and local
knowledge is one of the threads running through many of the leadership
challenges in this book. Many change efforts are imposed top-down without
the understanding and ideas that might come from local voices. Yet action and
implementation are always local, and local commitment is central to
sustaining change in any setting. The design team is a micro- or parallel
organisation structure used to plan and oversee a change effort on behalf of
the whole.

A design team is a good first step in tackling a situation in which it has been
decided that there should be change in the way the organisation works as a
whole. Activity P6.4: Guidelines for a Design Team offers some outline
guidance on how to create and facilitate such a team. More detailed guides can
be found in the further resources at the end of the chapter.

Go to Activity P6.4: Guidelines for a Design Team.

Design teams often have consultancy support to help them both to achieve
their potential as a team and to handle relationships with others in the system,
especially where this includes the leadership team. However a design team will
approach its work and operate in a very different way from a consultancy, and

it is important that they have the autonomy and mandate to do this. A design team might ask the same questions as a consultant, but they will be doing so from a different perspective and for different purposes; the questions will also be put and received differently, and will lead to different discoveries and dialogues.

Is help helpful? (Attributed to Jack Gibb)

Most of the time being facilitative is straightforward and obvious. All of us need practical help and encouragement to do the right and the difficult things. However, the leader as facilitator should always remember that the person or group being helped is the best judge of what is helpful. As a humorous postcard has it: "If things don't improve soon, I shall have to ask you to stop helping me!"

Being helpful is not as easy as it looks because human beings and their relationships are complicated. We can look as though we want help when we don't. Someone who badly wants to help can easily get in the way. And so on. Help may indeed not actually be helpful. The best help sometimes appears in disguise. The critical friend dares to challenge us, and may be right:

Mike was trying to make up his mind whether to leave secure, if no longer challenging, employment and was eventually helped by a friend who made what appeared to be unkind remarks. After more than 20 years with the same employer and with his children leaving home, Mike pondered at length on whether it was time to make a move. His friend David, somewhat exasperated by the dithering, remarked that if he – Mike – were to be cut through the middle, then the legend "Hallam City Council" would be seen on the cross-section, running all through as on a stick of rock. On another occasion, listening to Mike rehearsing his plans for the umpteenth time, he said, "You have more safety nets than Billy Smart's Circus!" Although he hated them at the time, both these remarks were eventually helpful to Mike. He didn't like the thought of being branded for life and resented the suggestion that he could not take a risk. It took another year to make the move, but like grit in a shoe, these comments eventually did their work.

The main thing about acting as a critical friend is to be sure that you *are* actually being a friend and not satisfying a personal need to feel helpful, or indulging in a power trip.

Being helpful in this way is about more than being skilful, it also requires good heart and good intentions. Mistakes made in good heart at least are easier to forgive.

References

Heifetz, R. (1994) *Leadership Without Easy Answers.* Cambridge, Mass: Belknap Press.

Weaver, R. and Farrell, J. (1999) *Managers as Facilitators.* San Francisco: Berrett Koehler.

Further resources

There are perhaps more resources on facilitation than for any of the other six leadership practices. The website of the International Association of Facilitators (IAF) www.iaf-world.org lists many relevant books and other resources.

One of our favourite books on facilitation is the excellent *Managers as Facilitators: A Practical Guide to Getting Work Done in a Changing Workplace* by Richard Weaver and John Farrell's (1999) (San Francisco: Berrett Koehler). This remains one of the best guides to everyday facilitation for the leader or manager. If you aspire to be a professional facilitator then Roger Schwarz and his colleagues have produced impressive and encyclopaedic volumes that must be on the bookshelves of serious practitioners. Roger Schwartz's *The Skilled Facilitator: A Comprehensive Resource for Consultants, Facilitators, Managers, Trainers and Coaches* (2002) is almost all it claims to be. This and the companion *The Skilled Facilitator Fieldbook: Tips, Tools, and Tested Methods for Consultants, Facilitators, Managers, Trainers, and Coaches* (2005) are both from Jossey-Bass in San Francisco.

A much shorter book is Christine Hogan's *Practical Facilitation: A Toolkit of Techniques* (London: Kogan Page, 2003), which is good, practical and appropriately theoretical. Also from Kogan Page is a very simple guide: Cameron (2005) *Facilitation made easy: Practical Tips to Improve Meetings and Workshops.* Bee and Bee's *Facilitation Skills* (London: Chartered Institute of Personnel & Development, 1998) is another good basic guide.

For promoting and facilitating change in large groups and whole systems, Margaret Attwood, Mike Pedler, Sue Pritchard and David Wilkinson provide ideas and illustrations in their *Leading Change: A Guide to Whole Systems Working* (Bristol: Policy Press, 2003). Marvin Weisbord's *Future Search: An Action Guide to Finding Common Ground in Organizations and Communities* (Sydney: Readhowyouwant, 2009) is a second edition and large print version of a very helpful book for facilitating large group meetings, while *The World Cafe: Shaping Our Futures Through Conversations That Matter* by Juanita Brown and David Isaacs (San Francisco: Berrett Koehler, 2005) is a guide to this currently popular approach to encouraging conversation and storytelling as a way of making sense and moving forward in organisations. Finally, David

Cooperrider and Diana Whitney's *Appreciative Inquiry* (San Francisco: Berrett Koehler, 1999) is a simple guide to AI which also gives many further sources and references.

Activities

■   Activity P6.1: Facilitating the Aims and Objectives for a Team.
■   Activity P6.2: Creating a Facilitation Process Map for a conflict situation.
■   Activity P6.3: Appreciative Inquiry: generating a collaborative structure.
■   Activity P6.4: Guidelines for a Design Team.

Activity P6.1: Facilitating the Aims and Objectives for a Team

Here is a standard process using Post-its to generate and agree the aims and objectives for any team. This process map works in almost all situations and can be facilitated without difficulty by most people. It assumes that the team wants to do the task.

Steps	Actions	Key questions
1 Generate aims	Ask each person to write their aims on Post-its, then post up and brainstorm in whole group for any which have been missed	What needs doing in this situation? What do we need to do to fulfil our function and purpose? What could we do that would be useful? Have we missed any important aims?
2 Sort aims	Ask a few volunteers to cluster the Post-its. Then check the meaning of the clusters with the group	Have we got all the possible objectives? What are the main clusters and what are they about?
3 Agree priorities	Ask pairs to agree the top three or four priorities and then compare lists in the whole group	What are the top priority aims for us? Are we agreed among ourselves? Are our priorities the same as those of our key stakeholder, client or customer?
4 Action plan	Ask the group to form into sub-groups – one for each aim – and draft action plans	If we are not agreed on our key priorities, how will we resolve this? How will these aims be accomplished? What needs to be done, by when, etc.?
5 Mandate actions	For each of the action plans, ask the group to allocate roles and responsibilities	Who will do what, by when, etc.? How will we know when an aim is accomplished? How and when will we review progress?

Activity P6.2: Creating a Facilitation Process Map for a conflict situation

Use the template from Activity P6.1 to create a facilitation process map for resolving a conflict with any group or groups:

Steps	Actions	Key questions

1 Start in *the left-hand column* by listing the steps: what are the logical stages you have to go through to get to the desired end point?

  To resolve a conflict, the list of steps might be:

- Acknowledging the conflict: getting agreement on the problem.
- Expressing differences: getting all the opinions and positions on the table.
- Clarifying differences: what are the dimensions of difference?
- Establishing common ground: what do we agree on?
- Negotiation on areas of non-agreement.
- Agreement or decision.

If you're happy with this list, write it into your own process map. If not, customise it to represent the situation you are facing.

2 Next complete *the right-hand column* by listing the key questions that must be answered at each of the stages in the left-hand column. For example, the questions for the first step in the list above might be:

- What is the nature of this conflict?
- Does everyone know about it?
- How important is it?
- Are we agreed that we should try to sort it out?

Continue down the list of steps until you have listed all the critical questions to be answered, before moving on. These questions are as vital as the steps because they tell you exactly what work is needed at each step and when it is time to move on.

3 Finally fill in *the middle column* of the actions you will take as facilitator. The middle column is about involving everyone and bringing about good collective agreements and decisions. Here are some general principles to aid thinking about this column:

- Ask people to write down their initial thoughts on paper or Post-its before discussion. *This ensures that (i) everybody gets a chance to think and (ii) that everyone has something to say.*
- Use pairs, threes or small groups to generate diversity of views or ideas. *People warm up better in small groupings, tend to generate more ideas quickly and are less likely to take up strong public stands that are difficult to retreat from.*
- Use the whole group to make decisions and agreements. *Ideally, democracy generates commitment and a fair allocation of responsibilities.*
- As facilitator, try to limit your contributions to the content of the discussion especially when it comes to making decisions. *You should be focusing (i) on the process and (ii) on getting decisions agreed by the group.*

The middle column might be the hardest to complete. This is the time when the experience of a professional facilitator comes in handy, because it involves understanding the best ways to involve people and to work with the group to accomplish the task. You might find it helpful to talk this column over with someone else.

Obviously actually resolving a conflict is not quite as simple as this might imply – but at least it gives you an idea of where you are heading, and crucially, it might encourage you to tackle a conflict rather than avoid it. With a facilitation plan you now have a road map of where you want to go. So now you can get on with it; practice makes perfect.

Activity P6.3: Appreciative Inquiry: generating a collaborative structure

Appreciative inquiry accentuates the positive and aims to help groups and communities to bring about change through generating new thoughts, images and possibilities.

In the example given below, an AI conference works with one of its members or sub-groups who agree to "hold" or host the change issue. The aim is to help this person or sub-group realise a more positive future; grounded first in what is good about their experience, then powered by images of what would be ideal for them.

Three ground rules

1 The main rule for working in this way is to be determinedly positive. (There are plenty of other forums to talk about problems and negativities.)

2 The redesign issue affects and involves everyone. You will need to recruit enough of these other people to help you with this appreciative inquiry. Choose positive people, including supportive colleagues and friendly clients or business partners.

3 Don't use a facilitator but do it yourself. You might feel silly around the rule of only being positive at first, but it requires everyone to put themselves in that frame of mind for a short time. Try it: it might even work!

The rules of the game are for everyone to *be positive*! All questions, all responses must emphasise the positive.

1 *Brief*. Start with a brief from those who are hosting the object of this inquiry. What are they looking for in this new structure? Perhaps they want to see an architecture that enables the people and groups within and around the business to work together better? Perhaps, as markets shift and businesses change, they are looking for something that can also be changed, easily adapted to future needs? Have them say something about their desired future to get the ball rolling.

2 *Good stories*. Now ask people to tell stories about ways in which their current organisation works really well. Give them a chance to think first and then go round the room and hear stories from everyone.

To help people tell their stories, prompt them with such appreciative questions as:

■ When do you feel most positive and engaged about the way things work around here?

■ Please describe a high spot in your experience of the organisation – when did you feel good about working here?

■ What aspects of organising do we do really well?

■ What have we got right in terms of organisational design?

… and so on.

3 *Positive futures*. After hearing all the good stories and positive images of the current organisation, the next step is to develop some ideas about possible futures.

Now go round the group for a second time, perhaps reversing the order to do so. Now get each person to say how things could be even better. Ask each person:

- What would help you to achieve even more?
- If we re-designed the organisation, what would really delight and benefit your customers and clients?
- How could we improve on the way performance is managed?
- Who would you like to link up with and have a connection with?
- How could you learn more from people in the organisation?
- What would your work look like if it was designed around the things you truly value?

… and so on.

4 *Constructive next steps*. When all the stories and ideas about possible futures have been aired, the whole group then summarises and records the ideas – in this case for organisational redesign. This might take the form of some redesign proposals or some next steps for further research, e.g.:

- What might be done next which does not involve any redesign?
- What further work or research do we need to do to clarify our ideas?
- What redesign proposals shall we put to the board?

You must end by agreeing at least one positive next step towards a more desirable future and also by agreeing how this will be done.

5 *Follow through and momentum*. As maintaining momentum and follow through can be a problem with AI, you could anticipate this by agreeing some ways to help with this. What arrangements can you agree now that will make implementation more likely?

One possibility is to establish an action learning process with several planned meetings over the next few weeks or months (see Chapter 9, P5 *Challenging Questions* for a description of action learning).

Activity P6.4: Guidelines for a Design Team

Design teams add considerable expertise and also credibility in organisational development efforts. If the membership is well thought through, because of who they are they can represent "us"– rather than "them". No survey or questionnaire exercise can match this sort of know-how and feel for the organisation. They can bring to bear local knowledge in deciding what might work, what makes sense and how ideas might be implemented. They offer possibilities for representation of views and consultation on proposals with and from a wide range of people and interest groups.

It requires courage and confidence on the part of leadership to work in this way. By becoming an alternative and authoritative source of opinion, a design team also opens up the possibilities of dialogue and "public learning" with the senior team.

These 11 guidelines cover the main design issues and principles for setting up and working with a design team:

1 *Size.* Up to about 20; whatever is needed to reflect the diversity and harness the energy while remaining manageable as a face-to-face group.

2 *Composition.* Reflect the diversity of the system to ensure that all the relevant organisations, professional groupings, occupational categories, interest groups, age, gender and ethnic mixes and so on, are represented.

3 *Membership.* Design teams may have core members and less regular attenders. A continuous core group is essential and it may work well to have other levels of membership according to circumstances and tasks.

4 *Mandate from leadership.* To work well the design team must have a mandate from a leadership team. They need this brief and the trust to allow them to do their own data gathering and diagnosis of how things are in the organisation. In accepting the mandate, the design team may have many questions, e.g.:
- Why have we taken this on?
- What is this task anyway?
- Where are the resources to do it?
- What does the leadership want us to do?
- What are they trying to achieve anyway?
- How will other people see our role?
- Who is part of this situation and who needs to be involved in resolving it?
- How willing are others going to be to get involved? (Attwood *et al.,* p. 121)

5 *Getting to know each other.* A crucial task at the first meeting of a design team is to give lot of time to people meeting each other and understanding their differences and similarities in relation to the task. This meeting each other needs time to lay a good foundation. It is also likely to surface some differences which may be difficult to handle.

6 *Exploring differences.* These differences need to be explored constructively within the design team. This may not happen at the early meetings and may be better surfaced during discussions on the task. However, exploring these differences is part of the task, and learning from this work in this group is vital for understanding how to react when they appear in the wider organisation.

7 *Collecting data.* Going out, collecting data and information and bringing it back for analysis and understanding is a good way for a design team to find its feet. Members already bring data and understanding with them, but deciding what to collect and from whom, together with the collaborative experience of bringing it back home and making sense of it, is a useful team-building activity.

8 *Designing events.* A common feature of whole systems designs is the "big event", bringing together 50, 100 or even 300 people to give their views, seek common ground and agree next steps. These events can be very dramatic and energising and the design team can play many roles here. With experience, teams can run the entire event themselves, handling the up-front facilitation as well as all the logistics work. A lot of design work goes into such events, from deciding who will be invited to detailed scripting of the activities and timetable of the event.

9 *Relationships with the leadership team.* Although this work may be assisted by consultants, a strong design team can usefully engage in dialogue with the senior leadership, to link action on the ground with overall strategic direction. In this way a design team can find itself coaching or advising the leadership team on the management of any change effort.

10 *Action learning groups.* These are one means for sustaining and carrying through the agreed actions from "big events" and conferences. The design team may have already experienced this process in their own working together and they are well placed to encourage and monitor action and learning within the wider system.

11 *Organisational learning*. The design team acts as a conduit for learning throughout the organisation. It does this through its everyday work of consulting its constituents and feeding back information and decisions. Public exchanges in events may also generate considerable learning within and across stakeholder groups. This can be further orchestrated via mechanisms such as action learning groups which can be brought together from time to time to exchange views and pool their findings.

11

Practice 7: Networking

Introduction

Leaders live in networks. Networks are the lifeblood and primary energy sources in all organisations, because they are the key to *connection power* – getting things done through the people you know. Connection power is about the influence, informal authority and inspiration that is generated and transmitted through personal relationships. This source of power has been well understood by diplomats and political analysts from time immemorial, but it is often underrated by managers and leaders. The leadership practice of networking has grown in importance with the advent of the "information age", the significance of "knowledge work" and the needs and expectations of those who do this work.

Networks are webs rather than hierarchies of relationships. They make it easy to contact and access relevant people when we need help to accomplish tasks. Compared with traditional structures, they are usually described as flat, flexible and fast to adapt. They also tend to be less stable and often invisible or ephemeral because they appear only when activated by individuals. Networks connect people whose status depends more on their knowledge and access to resources than on position. This means that such relationships may be the most valuable source of information about what is happening in any situation. Peers, if they are willing, can offer advice or counsel, give feedback on behaviour and help you think through the options for action – all without fear of grace and favour.

This leadership practice involves building personal networks but also helping other people to enhance their connection power through developing organisational networks. Networks provide the wherewithal to cross departmental boundaries and other disputed territories, including hierarchies, to get things done. Through connecting as peers we can access people in authority structures, both more and less powerful than ourselves. If you know your boss only as a boss, and not also as a fellow member of a project or the local branch of your professional association, your "bandwidth" with that person remains much narrower than it might. And the same is true of people who work for you. The narrower the bandwidth, the fewer the sources of information, power and influence.

Some people are sceptical of the value of the networking phenomenon. If you are not a natural networker yourself, you might be dubious about the activity and those who practise it so assiduously. You might even disparage it as "Notworking"! But there are many practical reasons why you should question this attitude. "Knot-working" for example, is a critical part of making sense and solving problems in complex environments. As we shall see in the second part of this chapter, to tackle the really difficult challenges, leaders are turning to network ideas and trying to marry up the qualities of these forms with the traditional "command and control" organisation. Networks are also central to learning and innovation; better-connected doctors, for example, are more likely to adopt practice innovations than those who are relatively isolated (Rogers, 2003). In knowledge-based work, a person's effectiveness rests increasingly on the richness of their personal networks (Cross, 2000). In his study of general managers, Kotter (1995) found that those most likely to be successful in their careers, are those who develop the most effective lateral relationships.

The leadership practice of networking has twin aspects; it is both a personal practice and an organisational one:

- *Personal networking.* In the first part of the chapter some of the key properties of networks are introduced. The importance of *strong and weak ties and bridging and bonding* are illustrated through stories and activities. This part concludes with ideas for developing the effectiveness and reach of your personal leadership network.

- *Leadership and the network organisation* is the application of network ideas to the organisation of people and resources. What does it mean to organise on the basis of network principles? How can the benefits and properties of personal networking be harnessed in groups, projects and organisations? This second part of the chapter looks at different types of networks for policy, learning and service delivery and considers *organisations as structured networks* with examples from the worlds of big companies and public services. It concludes with advice on *developing networks* including *nine principles for network organising.*

This chapter also contains three activities for mapping and extending your personal networks and *The Network Due Diligence Checklist* for organisational networks.

Personal networks

Personal networks vary greatly in shape and extent. As individuals, we have personal characteristics that make some of us more natural networkers from the nursery onwards. A first step is becoming aware of your own preferences and how these affect your actions and those around you. A second step is, from whatever base, to build your networks and connection power as an essential element in your leadership.

> Recently I attended the inaugural lecture of a friend and colleague of some 30 years. The hall was filled with an excited community, many of whom had never met before. They were family and friends, academic colleagues, clients and business acquaintants; they were old students, some now retired, and new postgraduates. Also present were some local dignitaries from the university and the city.
>
> I reflected on the diverse nature of this network. Previously invisible, it would soon disappear again and forever. Though virtual and transient, it was over 30 years old, enduring and continuing. How much effort David must have put in to creating and maintaining it – but then he was always a network wizard, enjoying the company of many kinds of people and delighting in moving in different worlds.
>
> On leaving, I met another old colleague, also due to deliver his inaugural. I commented on the size and liveliness of the congregation; "Yes," he said, "isn't it terrifying, I only want half a dozen at mine."

Personal networks are unique, available only to or through the person who composes and maintains them. They come in all sizes and express personal preferences and ways of working. They can be seen as a personal extension of the person who animates them. Carole Stone is one of the queens of network wizardary (2001) and is said to have 30,000 entries in her electronic address book. Such is the attraction of this practice that she has turned networking into both a job and a business, along with the founders of Facebook, MySpace and the many other social networking sites. This does not mean that everyone has to become a network wizard, but anyone who wants to contribute to leadership and influence events can't afford to ignore this practice and this source of power.

Networks also serve as personal safety nets. Chloe, a marketing manager, was apparently unfazed by the imminent disappearance of her organisation: "I'm not too worried" she said, "I'm sure I will find a berth because my main value to any organisation are my contacts and networks." In all these contexts, as extensions of people, personal networks are vital to organisations.

Take time out now to think about your personal network. Networks are like string bags, any one knot is only connected to, say, four others, but those four are connected to four more, so that the original knot or node or person is only one step away from 12 new people and only two steps removed from a further 36. Faced with a problem to which we don't know the answer, we call the person most likely to know, if she doesn't know, she probably knows someone who does …

What do you notice about your contact network? Are you a person who has lots of contacts, or someone who prefers a small, enduring network?

Go to Activity P7.1: My Personal Network.

A brief scan of your personal network will tell you about how you work and who you rely on for advice or help. The bigger the network, the more potential sources of information, help and encouragement you have to hand. There is a cost to this because networks have to be maintained through various forms of social contact, electronic, telephonic and face-to-face.

Strong and weak ties

A further step in understanding your network is to look at the strength of your relationships within it. The American sociologist Mark Granovetter produced one of the most influential insights of social network theory with his distinction between strong and weak ties. We have strong ties with those people that are regular and frequent contacts, family members, friends and workmates. We spend a lot of our time in and on these relationships.

However, from a networking perspective it turns out that the weak ties are critical for new learning and knowledge. These are people with whom we have infrequent and irregular contact, but can nevertheless reach when we want to. Granovetter's original research was based on how people went about finding jobs; and his observation was that it was the weak ties which were crucial in enabling people to reach contacts and resources that were not accessible via strong ties. Robert Cross (2000) has also demonstrated the power of weak ties in showing how far people reach outside the firm in search of useful knowledge. In his research on management consultants, his respondents relied more heavily on weak ties with people outside their own units to find the actual ideas to resolve work problems, while using their strong internal ties to help test and gain approval for possible solutions.

To think about your strong and weak ties, look back at your personal network from Activity P7.1: My Personal Network and map your contacts as in Figure P7.1.

Go to Activity P7.2: My Strong and Weak Ties.

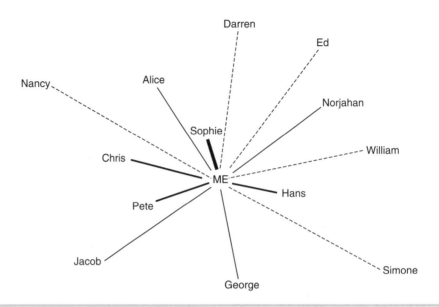

Figure P7.1 Strong and weak ties

In Figure P7.1 the central person has strong ties with Chris, Pete, Hans and especially Sophie. They may work closely with these people, perhaps in the same work group, and consult them often, probably relying on them for personal support. The people joined by thin or broken lines are the weak ties; these are people met less often and perhaps consulted on specialist issues. The weak ties are to those people with whom you share particular interests or concerns, from whom you can occasionally get valuable information or help on a one-off basis. If you rely on a small tight network, you may find that you are short on weak ties. Weak ties are usually links made through other people; these are the ties of which we can say: "I don't know but I know someone who does …":

During a national rail strike, I had to get to Dover to catch a train to Milan. I had to drive but what would I do with the car for two weeks? After consulting the directory of my professional association, I was able to call a person who worked for the Harbour Board. We had never met but we shared professional interests and identities. He very kindly agreed to find me a parking space for two weeks, even sending a key through the post. Apart from saying thanks and me sending the key back, we have never been in contact since.

The "strength of weak ties" depends on a most remarkable aspect of human beings: the willingness to help strangers. It is surprising sometimes what we are willing to do for someone who asks for help. And this extends much farther than helping the friend of a friend. For example, membership of professional societies often brings with it an obligation to engage in "diffuse reciprocity" with other members. This means being willing to give something to someone without expecting a direct return from that person. Network theorists point out that there is a rational calculus at work here: as a member of the same group, I am willing to help you without expecting you to pay me back, because I assume that when I need help in future, some other group member will be willing to give it.

Whether your actions are down to simple altruism or enlightened self-interest – as you never know when you will need a parking place in future – this quality of trust that underpins networks is a very useful and attractive aspect of human behaviour. It has to be noted here of course, that networks *exclude* as well as include people: this trust and willingness to give is extended to some but not to others. This aspect results in the frequently heard allegations about "old boys networks" and "it's not what you know but who you know". These rueful accusations attest to the negative consequences of networks for non-members.

Bridging and bonding

Bridging and bonding are two more useful ideas from social network analysis that extend the discussion of strong and weak ties. Bridging refers to the "reach" of a network: how far does it extend socially, occupationally and geographically? What interest groups or knowledge areas does it cover? Bonding measures the quality of strong ties that provide the cohesion and resilience of a network. We bond with those with whom we have personal relationships renewed on a regular basis. How strong are these bonds? What weight will they take?

Bonding or bridging are not just technical terms but also matters for personal preference. The costs of network maintenance also figure here. Are you a person who likes to bond with a few close colleagues or friends, or do you prefer a wider network of acquaintances? Or can you do both?

Look at Figure P7.2: Bridging and Bonding: put yourself in one of the four squares.

The "local hero" box can be a popular place for many people, and not a few professionals are "loners" by formation and preference. "Butterflies" have many, many contacts but don't linger for long and may sometimes lack the strong ties to deliver on tasks. Then, there are the network wizards, who are

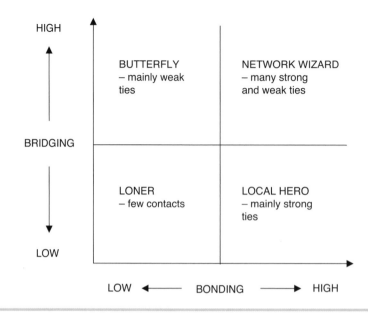

Figure P7.2 Bridging and bonding (adapted from the original by John MackMersh)

both proficient and committed to networking as a key part of their leadership style. These people have a strong awareness of the importance and power of networking and consequently spend a lot of time building and maintaining their networks.

As someone interested and committed to leadership, what are the implications for your networking preference? What are your strengths in bonding and bridging?

Those who are ambitious and seek out leadership roles may well have acquired some of these habits and preferences on the way. On the other hand, for those on whom leadership is thrust, you may be challenged to overcome long-held habits and actively seek to widen your networks. You don't have to become a network wizard, but you do probably need to get out and around more in leadership work.

Extending your reach

Depending on your situation, you and your colleagues will almost certainly benefit from extended networks, both through building up strong ties around particular tasks or projects and by increasing your reach in search of new knowledge.

Tetracycline adoption among doctors

In a classic experiment among doctors, Coleman and his colleagues found that innovativeness in adopting the drug tetracycline was associated with seven measures of network interconnectedness:

■ Affiliation with the hospital as a regular staff member.
■ More frequent attendance at hospital staff meetings.
■ Sharing an office with one or more doctors.
■ Being named as a source of information and advice by other doctors.
■ Being named by other doctors as someone with whom they discussed their patients.
■ Being named as a friend by other doctors.
■ Reciprocating the same links reported by other doctors who chose the respondent as a discussion partner.

These seven factors of interconnectedness were a better predictor of innovativeness than any personal characteristics; in other words, what happens between people is more important for innovation than what is within individuals. (Source: Rogers, 2003, pp. 299–303.)

Coleman's seven measures of interconnectedness provide a handy prescription for extending your network. Can you translate these into your own context to see what might be involved? The way to extend your reach to bridge beyond your immediate situation and your organisation, is simply to get out more.

Common purpose

A friend, who had spent most of her life in a particular industry, joined a local *common purpose* programme with people from different working environments – commercial companies, local government, charities, voluntary associations and the professions. She found the programme "eye-opening" and, despite her senior position, managed to participate in all the monthly sessions for a year. She hit it off with a fellow member from a charitable organisation and, a year or so later, this changed the course of her career.

Getting out creates the chance for chance to happen. There are many, many ways of doing this of course. It is important not to overlook the obvious opportunities such as conferences and courses. Such events legitimate networking. Whatever the quality of their formal presentations, it is typical for them to be rated in evaluations for the value of meeting new people and the informal conversations. The formal programme gives you an excuse to go and meet people.

Encouraging others

The benefits of reaching out are not just personally important, they are also vital for your colleagues and for your organisation. If personal networking is one of the first responsible practices of leadership, then thinking about how to organise in order to encourage your colleagues to increase their reach and connectedness, comes a close second. This can be approached at several different levels.

On a one-to-one basis

You can encourage your colleagues to read this chapter and do the activities for themselves and become aware of their own personal networking practice and preferences. Ask them to think about the opportunities they have for increasing their reach through:

- working parties
- special project groups
- professional associations
- communities of interest and practice
- alumni groupings
- internet communities.

Or even by setting up their own special interest groups. One striking aspect of the history of science is the number of times when two or more researchers were approaching the same idea at the same time but were in different locations and unaware of each other. This is less likely to happen in big science these days, but it is very likely to be happening more locally. Who else is interested in what you are doing? How can you get in touch with them? What could happen if you started talking about it?

In groups and meetings

Any regular and routine business meeting can be transformed by very simple changes to promote discussion and exchange.

Under pressure from agendas, many of these meetings begin too abruptly with Business Item 1. Instead of doing this, start with a "round robin" (going round the group to hear from each person in turn without interruption), on, for example, "What's new in widget design this month?" This creates possibilities for people to contact each other later and talk one to one, but it may also help with the business in hand. In many meetings, this sort of listening and communicating time at the outset will do wonders for later business-focused discussions, because everyone has been involved and refreshed by the ideas.

Redesigning working space

Some workplaces are actually designed to promote meeting and networking. While communicating and talking to other people is a major part of work, many offices and workplaces are built apparently to isolate people as much as possible. Narrow corridors maximise personal space while reducing conversation space. Some visionary architects have tried to do different things.

The Ark

Close to the Hammersmith flyover in London, the Ark resembles an ocean liner. It was designed by Ralph Erskine to make it easy for people to meet, to relax, to discuss, to exchange ideas ... more like "a village under a roof" than a conventional office. The entrance floor has a large meeting point with large "world information" screens, a multipurpose auditorium for lectures, conferences, sales meetings and artistic performances, and a square with atrium and bar. The designer's brochure saw it as "An escape from the traditional, centrally governed business into a network-oriented one .... An open concept, designed for people to communicate, to help ideas flow, to make information come alive". You might even say, to give chance a chance. In 2006, having been occupied by single clients, the building underwent a radical refit to increase the letting space for multiple tenants. This has resulted in the stripping out of the central village and connecting walkways that spanned the atrium in favour of two smaller atriums turning "the doughnut into a pretzel".

Failing your own Ark, you can think about meeting and conversation space and how to use it. You have choices about where to hold meetings: have this one at your house? Whatever the room, how can you maximise the space for "corridor conversations" to give chance a chance? For example, round tables are better for sharing views than rectangular ones; dispensing with the table is another mood-changing intervention. Even making small physical changes to your usual room can have a major effect on conversation.

Leadership and the network organisation

*The internet is profoundly disrespectful of tradition, established order
and hierarchy.*

(Fareek Zakaria)

If you are starting to think about the possibilities for encouraging networking among your colleagues, you are beginning to think of networks not just as personal webs of information and influence, but as ways of organising. Although we may tend to think of networking as something that an individual does, when we look at the big picture we can see that it is of course, something that lots of people do. When we look at it this way, networking is a collective practice that we do together. It is a way of organising together, and not only that, but for many purposes it may be a better way.

The idea of industrial clusters – firms in the same trade or industry that gather together in the same geographical area – has been around for centuries. Karl Marx noted them and, much later, Michael Porter (2004) commended them. In these clusters, firms do not go in for vertical integration with every function in house, but become very specialised, taking on just a small sliver of a product or service according to their core competence. This is only possible because of the dense network of suppliers and business partners to add in the other parts and complete the service to the customer.

For business organisation, the seminal notion is the value chain, which does not respect the boundaries of formal organisations. The contemporary language of sub-contracting, supply chains, alliances, partnerships, inter-locking ownership and so on attests to a growth in inter-organisational collaboration and connectedness. The rise of the network is also fuelled by the rapid advances of information technology: the internet and World Wide Web provide both the conceptual model and the practical enablers of networking.

For all these reasons, networks have been described as the organisational form for the twenty-first century, and although organisational networks differ in various ways from personal networks, the two are closely linked. Organisational networks need much more than alliance agreements and electronic connectedness to make them work. Organising the value chain across departments, businesses and agencies requires managers and leaders to change the way they interact. The practice of personal networking supports the efforts to organise in networks.

What is a network organisation?

A simple definition of an organisational network is:

> *a grouping of individuals, organisations and agencies organised on a non-hierarchical basis around common issues or concerns, which are pursued proactively and systematically, based on commitment and trust.*
>
> (WHO, 1998)

In principle, in network organisations, people are connected not so much through command and control structures but on the basis of:

- *common goals*
- *operating through personal relationships* of mutual interest, sharing, reciprocity, trust
- *status and authority* based on knowledge, usefulness, sharing and innovativeness and not on formal position or qualifications
- *organising through nodes* – individuals, teams or organisations; *ties or links* – relationships, connections, working partnerships and associations; and *spaces* for learning, innovation and emergence.

For organisations seeking greater flexibility, adaptability and improved service delivery, the network form is an attractive prospect. Yet, like previous ventures such as matrix organisations, there are delicate balances of power to be achieved, and the self-organising potential of networks can easily be restricted by attempts at central control. Getting it right is a formidable challenge for any leadership, especially if they are used to commanding and controlling.

To facilitate leadership via influence and without formal powers, a network organisation needs a set of strong and agreed values and principles. The makers of Goretex set out to create an internal network based on some key principles.

W.L. Gore

W.L. Gore, founded in 1958, is famous for its "Goretex" fabric, known for its breathability and waterproof qualities. The company is made up of small units of no more than 150 people who work together and know each other well. Each unit is organised on "lattice organisation" principles and contains multiple and overlapping lattices of people (similar to communities of practice). The linkages and connections between the lattices and the units are given special emphasis.

To make the lattice work, four simple rules act as guiding principles for everyone:

- Try to be fair in all transactions inside and outside the organisation.
- Encourage the growth and development of all associates.

- ■ Make commitments and stick to them.
- ■ Consult with others before taking actions that might threaten the business.

Networks rely more on responsible self-organisation than on tidy role structures, and making this work rests heavily on good relationships between people. Each staff member, or "associate", chooses their own work tasks, subject to peer feedback and discipline. Each chooses a sponsor who takes a personal interest in that person's progress and development. Sponsors thus acquire what Bill Gore called "natural leadership": leadership by being chosen by others. In 2009, for the twelfth consecutive year, the company appeared in *Fortune*'s annual list of the "100 Best Companies to Work For".

Organisations as living systems

For Capra (2003), networks are the basic principle of organisation for all forms of life – cellular, animal and human. Castells (2000) argues that we live in a networked world society, in which global financial markets, networked via computers, have facilitated the rise of global capitalism focused on shareholder value. As Glenny (2008) shows, this interconnected world economy now challenges governments through the power it confers on markets, large corporations and even on sophisticated criminal and terrorist networks.

Pioneer organisations like W.L. Gore lead away from the old, but lingering, ideas of organisations as machines that can be managed and controlled from a fixed point. How we organise ourselves is evolving in response to changing conditions and human desires. Interest in network organising is underpinned by a metaphor of organisations as living systems, modelled on life itself, complex but adaptive. A living system is:

> *a system of independent agents that can act in parallel, develop models as to how things work in their environment, and, most importantly, refine those models through learning and adaptation.*
>
> (Pascale, Millemann and Goija, p. 5)

The principle that self-organisation deals better with complexity than central control is found in many natural systems such as flocks of birds and shoals of fish. Here change and turbulence are a normal part of life; as is the "resistance to change" bemoaned by so many so-called "change agents". But these moaners are working with the wrong metaphor: machines may be controlled, but living systems respond to impulses, not instructions, and actively choose what they notice. They can be disturbed or influenced, but not changed according to some external plan.

Leadership for self-organisation

To adopt a living systems perspective on organising, the patterns of communication, relationships, networks and alliances become the focus for organising efforts. These shifting and adaptable aspects of the company hold the key to greater flexibility, learning and innovation. However, most work organisations are not just living systems, but have many machine-like aspects. When we are in them, we often behave in remarkably orderly ways, conforming to rules, processes, procedures and control systems. At the same time, these aspects of life are not what motivates us, energises or "turns us on". The dual, "cyborg" nature of human organising, both living system and machine, means that network organisations need both to be designed and allowed to emerge. The challenge for leadership is how to maintain some central control over work that requires a great deal of local autonomy and freedom? The question is:

How can we maximise the advantages of self-organisation by putting in place only the minimum requirements for overall alignment and control?

The minimum "machine" requirements that allow for emergence and self-organisation will vary with the type of network under study. There are a huge variety of network forms to be found under this currently fashionable label, ranging from the transport and facilities firms that simply use the word to describe their geographical and route systems to the rich variety of the 60,000 "global civic society networks" listed in the *Yearbook of International Organisations* (Union of International Associations, 2007–2008).

Three types of network

How a network may be configured, facilitated and developed depends on its purpose: what is the network for? (Figure P7.3).

■ Policy networks are a mainstay of governments and international communities. They produce ideas and models and rehearse potential agreements. They are *convened* and chaired.

■ The service delivery network is *managed* with a clear hierarchy of decisions, tighter rules and more demanding bottom lines in terms of productivity, cost reductions or other synergies.

■ Learning networks attract members around common training and development needs. The network ideal lends itself well to the purpose of disseminating ideas, sharing practice and resolving problems. Learning networks need relatively few resources or rules and have a bottom line of

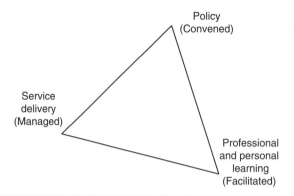

Figure P7.3 **Three types of network**

member satisfaction. They are *facilitated* or convened rather than managed.

Many networked organisations are hybrids of one or more types. Learning aims can sit quite happily with either policy or service delivery purposes, yet combinations of ends can create tensions and result in rapid change as members' energies and interests shift. For example, learning and service delivery can work well together, but if the degree of managing increases, the amount and quality of learning may go down.

Connecting with others in a learning relationship is a good way to start any network. Starting here is lower risk than committing to joint service delivery, and is a good way to open up new areas of work. As the CRINE network shows, joint working and service delivery can grow out of successfully learning together:

CRINE

CRINE (Cost Reduction Initiative for the New Era) is a network of contractors, suppliers, consultants and trade associations in the UK oil and gas industry. It began as a learning network in response to the 1992 oil crisis with the aim of sharing ideas and best practice to achieve cost reductions of 30% for offshore developments by sector-wide efforts rather than individual actions. By 1997, costs had fallen by 40% and attracted so much international attention that the initiative spread to Mexico, Venezuela, India and Australia.

After reaching their initial goals, the members felt that the relationship was worth maintaining and set up the CRINE network in 1997 to increase their share of the non-UK market. Steered by a representative body and managed by a small coordinating group, CRINE seeks to establish a learning and continuous improvement culture, encouraging collaboration rather than confrontation between suppliers and customers. It works through "supported networking", with financial, technical and other support from government, major operators, trade, research and academic bodies to the network of actors in the supply chain. Activities include newsletters, websites, workshops and conferences, technical projects and other initiatives such as the *first point assessment programme* that uses seconded engineers from major subscribers to assess and improve supply chain capability in companies. (Source: Bessant, Kaplinsky and Lamming, 1999.)

Service delivery networks require careful preparation, negotiation and development but, as Toyota, Benetton and others have demonstrated, they can carry wide-ranging responsibilities on impressively light infrastructures. Such organisations utilise and also limit self-organisation to tightly specified ends and in this way, along with the transport networks, are perhaps the most distant from the peer ideal of the network organisation described earlier.

Organisations as structured networks

In their ideal form, networks are flat, freeform, self-animating structures. In seeking to harness some of these qualities, the challenge is to add some degree of structure and management in order to control and direct them. Networks excel in sharing know-how and delivering locally at low cost, but they are notoriously difficult to steer or to hold accountable. Goold and Campbell (2002) offer a complex but well thought-through template for designing organisations as "structured networks". Their framework comprises four "drivers" of organisational fit that set the constraints for the designer:

- Product/market strategies – how will the organisation succeed in its various chosen fields of operation?
- Corporate strategy – what are the priorities for the organisation as a whole?
- People – what are the skills and preferences of the available people?
- Constraints – what are the external, environmental and other internal factors that limit the design possibilities?

These straightforward drivers are complemented by five design principles for the configuration of sub-units and their interrelationships:

- Specialisation – are the unit boundaries defined so as to maximise the benefits of specialisation?
- Coordination – are all the activities that need to be most coordinated included within single units?

- Knowledge and competence – does responsibility devolve to those with the best available knowledge and competence?
- Commitment and control – does the design facilitate low-cost coordination with high commitment?
- Innovation and adaptation – will the structure promote innovation and adaptation as circumstances change?

These design principles will inevitably pose a variety of dilemmas and difficulties in being implemented in any organisation. Nonetheless the drivers and principles provide a useful checklist against which to weigh any organisational design proposals. Measuring against the drivers should indicate whether form will indeed follow function. It will also highlight two critical tests for any proposal which seeks to harness the desirable qualities of the network within a corporate control structure:

- What are proposals for "corporate parenting" in the network? And will these add value to the operating units, or merely add redundant hierarchy?
- Do we have the people and the skills to operate the proposed structure?

The advantages claimed for the network organisation are flexibility and freedom of action at local level together with speedy learning and knowledge sharing. This depends a great deal on the sophistication of the design being proposed. Of particular interest here are the questions:

- Do creative people and specialist units have enough autonomy, freedom and protection from the parent organisation?
- Have we specified clearly enough the coordinating links between units: both the strong links of accountability and the weak links of knowledge sharing and learning?

All these questions point to the limitations of organisational design: we should do the best possible in terms of design, but so much depends on how this design is interpreted and enacted by the people who inhabit it. To meet the leadership challenge, networks have to be carefully designed, but even more skilfully led. Semler (2003) asserts that *not* controlling is so difficult for people in senior positions, that this is the very factor that gives Semco its competitive advantage. In this well-publicised Brazilian manufacturing company:

> *No-one is in control. If you don't even know where people are, you can't possibly keep an eye on them. All that's left to judge on is performance.*

The aim of a network structure should be to enable the people and units to work well together, a new architectural folly is in the making. One large multinational company has adopted a structure for knowledge networking based around four overlapping sets of global communities.

Big company plc

This global business employs 40,000 people in more than 40 countries and has created a set of structured networks based on four types of "knowledge communities". This classification provides the basis for corporate support in terms of specialist help and resources. The four types of community with their corporate support priorities are:

- Functional communities – hierarchically organised and part of the main organisational structure, e.g. HR, Finance. *Support priority: essential.*
- Initiative networks – project-based or problem-focused groups of people collaborating worldwide on specific tasks in short hierarchies with a project manager, e.g. Procurement; Business Strategy. *Support priority: high. Key to added value.*
- Communities of practice (COPs) – practice-based groups of people worldwide with some hierarchy and corporate responsibility, for example, for producing "best practice" guidelines, e.g. maintenance engineers; supply chains; HR remuneration and benefits. *Support priority: medium.*
- Interest or knowledge communities – interest-based groups of people worldwide, including professional, academic and leisure interests; no hierarchy. *Support priority: low.*

This knowledge structure overlaps with the normal business functions, but for certain purposes, this acts as an alternative structure for organising. These networks of communication, friendships and alliances are a potential source of much flexibility, learning capability and creativity. In fact, they may often be where the actual organising is happening. This new lexicon of communities is an alternative map of the organisation, giving a different basis for the distribution and allocation of resources.

Organising for health

In the complex arena of public services, a key goal is to achieve "joined up working" between agencies to achieve coverage, equity of access and value for money. In such fields as planning, education, social services and health, many partnership and network relationships include public, private and "third sector" agencies to achieve their aims. The effectiveness of these inter-agency relationships is crucial to the quality of the service delivered, which results in a wide variation in standards. The quality of elderly care, for example, varies markedly between one town and another, depending on the relationships between the agencies with a statutory responsibility for providing the care and the public, private and not-for-profit contractors who deliver it. Where the relationships are poor and neglected, so, usually, are the clients.

In the UK's health services, clinical networks are increasingly used to develop and improve these relationships. Under the NHS 10-year plan, cancer care has been a top priority over the last decade, and the cancer network has been the organisational instrument chosen to effect this. The 30 cancer networks in the UK have the big responsibility of ensuring the equitable provision of services and the efficient use of resources across regions of up to two million people. The leadership of these networks is a vital and challenging task, for they are not statutorily accountable organisations like NHS Trusts and have relatively few resources. Network leadership means persuading and influencing the separately managed and accountable hospitals and health organisations to work on the "value stream" across their organisational and professional boundaries to promote consistently high quality and to remove inequities of access or treatment.

An experienced NHS manager contrasts this sort of leadership with his professional development as a hospital manager:

> *You learn how to be a manager in the NHS by working within a hierarchical structure ... leadership is about how well you can manage in this very clear environment ... in the clear columns of hospital specialisms and departments. In a network there is no command and control, we have a huge range of organisations but they are not accountable to us – if anything we are accountable to them. Leadership is the ability to influence people over whom you have no direct authority ... but that's not what people have learned.*

A formidable effort at collaborative leadership and organising is required to bring about such ideally seamless services as cancer care. Rather like some formal colonial states, the geographical and professional boundaries of the network and its constituent organisations have often been drawn up without the participation of those who are supposed to make them work. Nevertheless, valuable learning has come from the attempts to develop these networks to date. One account of the systems, structures and rules needed to bring about this collaboration, gives the following list of essentials.

Essential features of an effective NHS clinical network

- Clear objectives in terms of improvements in service outcomes.
- Clear management structure and accountability arrangements.
- A lead clinician.
- A network project manager.
- Shared evidence bases and document protocols.
- Active involvement of all disciplines in the relevant care pathways.
- Effective systems for dissemination of information for patients and staff.
- Regular meetings of network staff.

■ Active patient involvement.

■ Joint clinical audit across the network.

■ Shared commitment for regular review of network objectives, achievements and development.

■ Shared approach to the development of best practice and staff training.

■ Regular performance management by an outside body.

■ Sound financial management with equitable contributions from constituent organisations.

■ Committed ownership by contributing organisations. (Source: Davies, 2001.)

No work could be more important than that of the NHS's clinical networks. Upon them rest the great expectations of patients, carers, managers, leaders and politicians. Whilst they are not easy to lead and manage, they have been chosen because of the previous failures of both market mechanisms and hierarchical organisation. Developing the network alternative demands a lot of the leadership; it takes great commitment, persistence and many hours of effort to build the number and quality of relationships that can eventually deliver the vision.

Developing networks

The *essential features of an effective NHS clinical network* can be adapted to make a useful starting point for anyone thinking about developing a more formal network organisation. A network will only work if the members want it to; so the development process for any network involves working through all the planned arrangements with those who will be required to operate them.

Developing and facilitating networked organisations is a new challenge for leadership. Networks may need legitimacy and recognition as much as resources, and a good way to start is to look and see what exists already. Though they will need some local interpretation to suit your circumstances, here are some general development principles that apply to all types of network, from learning to service delivery.

Nine principles for network organising

■ *Connect what exists:* as networks are normal forms for many trade, professional, voluntary and community associations, the first question is: what exists and how can we work with this? Linking up existing networks might be much easier than bringing together unconnected people.

■ *Preparation:* do "due diligence" on the network (see below). Start-ups are crucial. What are the common goals, simple rules and governance arrangements?

■ *A central figure:* the best networks often have a person or small group as a central hub, a source of information, connection and the "face behind the web". It helps if these people are good brokers and diplomats.

■ *A directory of members and contact details:* with a sentence or two about each person's know-how and interests to encourage self-organisation and "weak link" connections.

■ *A newsletter:* a simple, but regular news-sheet that can be distributed electronically and on paper.

■ *Meetings:* have some regular opportunities for people to meet each other spontaneously and energetically to share ideas and experiences.

■ *Teach networking skills:* encourage people to learn about connecting, brokering and trading. One set of simple rules for network meetings is:
  – listen
  – ask questions
  – give as well as take.

■ *Encourage self-organisation:* self-interest is a powerful motivator. Having too few rules or too many rules inhibits activity. What are the few simple rules on which the network will operate?

■ *Facilitate leadership, governance and accountability:* where multiple organisations sponsor the network, some unity at the top is necessary. A partnership board or convening group can represent the whole.

For service delivery networks, more formal processes such as those of the clinical network example above are needed. To carry heavy responsibilities on light infrastructures needs careful preparation, negotiation and development. Activity P7.3: The Network Due Diligence Checklist will help with the first of these at least.

Go to Activity P7.3: The Network Due Diligence Checklist.

The *network due diligence checklist* is a checklist of questions to be addressed in appraising, establishing or developing any network organisation. Before embarking on any network development, it is a good idea to work such a checklist as preparation and rehearsal with a steering or initiative group. This will help you avoid the more obvious pitfalls and prepare you for the development work that follows.

Conclusion

Networks are associated with all kinds of innovations in commercial and social life, from transportation and food distribution, to health care and community development and including the collaborations of nation states. The network idea seems to fit with the current era of globalisation, electronic connectedness and ecological concerns. The adoption of a systemic networked perspective will require changes in values, political will and operational rules to support life in a more sustainable way.

Networks are very attractive to organisations seeking improved service delivery, learning and innovation. Yet their self-organising nature constitutes a formidable challenge to leadership skills. Networks also have a dark side. As mutual benefit associations they can operate as cliques or gangs with negative consequences for others. Balancing the desirable but selfish qualities of self-organisation with the broader concerns for inclusivity, alignment and accountability is a central challenge in leading with networks.

References

Bessant, J. Kaplinsky, R. and Lamming, R. (1999) *Using Supply Chains to Transfer Learning About 'Best Practice'*. A report to the Department of Trade and Industry, London, January.

Capra, F. (2003) *The Hidden Connections: A Science for Sustainable Living*. London: HarperCollins.

Castells, M. (2000) *End of the Millennium*. Oxford: Blackwell Publishers.

Cross, R. (2000) "More than an Answer: How seeking information through people facilitates knowledge creation and use." Paper presented to the Academy of Management Conference, Toronto.

Davies, L. (2001) *Clinical Networking in Trent: Principles & Practice*. NHS Trent.

Glenny, M. (2008) *McMafia: Crime Without Frontiers*. London: Bodley Head, Random House.

Goold, M. and Campbell, A. (2002) *Designing Effective Organisations: How to Create Structured Networks*. San Francisco: Jossey Bass.

Granovetter, M. (1973) The strength of weak-ties. *American Journal of Sociology*. **78**(6): 1360–1380.

Kotter, J.P. (1982) *The General Managers*. New York: Free Press.

Porter, M. (2004) *Competitive Advantage; Creating and Sustaining Superior Performance*. New York: Free Press.

Rogers, E.M. (2003) *Diffusion of Innovations*, 5th edition. New York: Free Press.

Semler, R. (2003) *The Seven Day Weekend*. New York: Century.

Stone, C. (2001) *Networking: The Art of Making Friends*. London: Vermillion.

Union of International Associations. *Yearbook of International Organisations: Guide to Global Civic Society Networks (2007–2008).* Munich: K.G. Saur.

WHO (1998) *Health Promotion Glossary.* Geneva: WHO/HPR/HEP/98.1.

Further resources

Personal networking is one of the oldest secrets of success since at least Dale Carnegie's *How to Make Friends and Influence People* (London: Vermillion, 2007), first published in 1936, and which has sold 15 million copies. There are many more recent competitors, most of which say very similar things. Carole Stone's *Networking: The Art of making Friends* (London: Vermillion, 2001) is one of these.

More relevant here is Curt Grayson and David Baldwin's *Leadership Networking: Connect, Collaborate, Create* (Greensboro, NC: CCL Press, 2007). This is a very slim (32 pages) but valuable introduction to networking and how to build a network to enhance your leadership. In a different class to the usual "how to" books, the advice is based on six principles for how to conduct yourself as a networking leader, including being authentic, using your power responsibly, trading resources, negotiating and dealing with conflicts. It comes from the *Centre for Creative Leadership*, which is a generally good source on many other aspects of leadership: http://www.ccl.org/leadership/about/index.aspx.

One of the best general sources on network ideas is Fritjof Capra's *The Hidden Connections: A Science for Sustainable Living* (London: HarperCollins, 2003). This readable account shows how network principles underlie all forms of life from the most primitive cells to human societies, corporations, nation-states and the global economy. A good chapter deals with *Life and Leadership in Organisations*. Reading this book reveals how networking is not just an increasingly widespread social phenomenon but also a critical source of power in the world.

From an organisational perspective, Michael Goold and Andrew Campbell's *Designing Effective Organisations: How to Create Structured Networks* (San Francisco: Jossey Bass, 2002) is a design primer which attempts to marry the decentralised network with hierarchical organisational structures. While not a simple book, it is practical with a firm focus on implementation. For a broad take from a knowledge perspective, Etienne Wenger, Richard McDermott and William Snyder's *Cultivating Communities of Practice: A Guide to Managing Knowledge* (Boston, Mass: Harvard Business School Press, 2002) is a readable and practical guide.

More specifically focused on public service, but with a serious application of network ideas to organisational change, is Mark Considine, Jenny Lewis and Damon Alexander's *Networks, Innovation and Public Policy: Politicians,*

Bureaucrats and the Pathways to Change Inside Government (Basingstoke: Palgrave Macmillan, 2009). This brings many of the network concepts to life and is well illustrated with case examples. Finally and from an academic perspective, Wikipedia has a good page on social networks and social network analysis, which includes a useful glossary of key concepts such as centrality, betweenness and structural holes: http://en.wikipedia.org/wiki/Social_network.

Activities

- Activity P7.1: My Personal Network.
- Activity P7.2: My Strong and Weak Ties.
- Activity P7.3: The Network Due Diligence Checklist.

Activity P7.1: My Personal Network

My contacts: write down the names of the people you consult and talk to on each of the questions in the table below.

"Who can I ...	Inside work	Outside work
... go to for general sharing and catching up?		
... ask about specialist information in my field of work?		
... ask about solutions to business issues and problems?		
... get help from with thinking through a particularly difficult work issue or question?		
... get approval and validation for a course of action I am thinking of taking?		
... ask for advice about a tricky moral or political issue?		
... tell good news to?		
... tell bad news to?		
... share a secret with?		
... take a risk with?		
... just say "hello" to and keep in touch from time to time?		

What do you notice about your collection of names? For example:

- Are you a person who has lots of contacts, say 20 plus, or a person who prefers a small, enduring network, say six or so?
- Are you relying on the same person or persons for many different types of advice or help?
- Are you better connected at work or outside work?

Activity P7.2: My Strong and Weak Ties

Look at your personal network from Activity P7.1: my personal network.

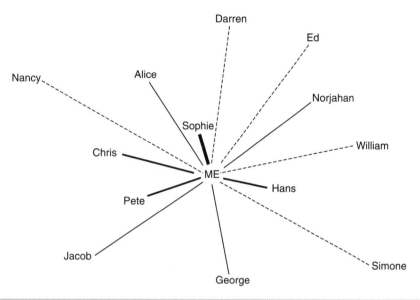

Figure P7.1 Strong and weak ties

Now map your contacts as in Figure P7.1 putting yourself at the middle of the web and connecting yourself to all the other people by lines of different thicknesses or strengths:

- Use thick lines to join yourself with your frequent contacts and for people with whom you are close – these are your strong ties.
- Use thin or dotted lines to connect yourself with less frequent contacts and people you are less close to – your weaker ties.

In Figure P7.1 the thick lines show the strong ties that provide the bonding and resilience in a network. The thin or broken lines are the weak ties; these provide the reach and diversity of a network.

What do you notice about your strong and weak ties? For example:

- Are you a person who works out of a small group of close contacts, or do you maintain a wide range of contacts? Or both?
- Are you happy with your strong ties? Are they as strong as they could be?
- Are you as well connected outside your work group and workplace as you should be? Should you be making more contacts or getting out and about more?

Activity P7.3: The Network Due Diligence Checklist

Due diligence is a term borrowed from merger and acquisition situations, where it means taking appropriate responsibility and spotting likely pitfalls, especially in legal and financial terms. Here due diligence serves as a way of thinking through and creating sound foundations for network organising. This is a checklist of questions to be addressed in appraising, establishing or developing any network organisation.

Before embarking on any network development, work through the following checklist with a steering or initiative group.

1 Domain and purpose:
- What is the focus or specific area for the network?
- What is the basis for interaction and networking?
- Where is the energy? What is the passion?

2 Community
- Who are the people concerned?
- What is the "whole system"? Where are the boundaries?
- Who is in? Who is out?

3 Animation and mobilisation:
- What exists already?
- How do we get the ball rolling? (NB: in contrast to "rolling out".)
- What is the sequence of activities? What is the first step?
- How will this be an inclusive or exclusive process?

4 Exploring and building common ground:
- What is the diversity of different interests?
- Where is the common ground?
- What is the process for defining common ground *and* special interests?

5 Organisation and governance:
- How will the network be maintained and supported?
- How will decisions be made?
- How will the network be managed?
- What sort of leadership is encouraged?
- What is the structure?
- What are the simple rules?

6 Behaviour:
- What are the norms for good behaviour?
- What are members' responsibilities for sharing, spreading and linking with others?
- How is good behaviour rewarded?
- What is bad behaviour?

7 Learning:
- How will practice and knowledge be shared and developed?
- What will be the learning activities?
- What knowledge, practices, techniques, tools and resources are available?

8 Performance and accountability:
- How will performance be measured? By whom?
- To whom are we accountable? For what?
- What is the evidence for learning, innovation, change?

9 Lifecycle development:
- What are the stages of development in the network?
- Where are we now?
- What is our next step?

10 Network learning
- How has the network as a whole learned?
- What are we learning about organising in networks?
- What is the value of the network? To whom?

Part 3

Developing Leadership

12

Developing leadership in individuals and organisations

Introduction

In this chapter we will deal with both leadership in the individual sense (what leaders do) and collective (organisational leadership) sense. Using a model of individual and collective leadership, we develop four perspectives that can be used as a basis for a leadership development strategy in any organisation.

We also consider the long-standing question of whether leaders are born or made, discuss the "onion skin" model of personality and its implications, and review the arguments for how leadership can be learned. Following this we suggest a way of thinking about learning strategies, and in particular the relationship between learners and those from whom they might learn. We think that this is a more active, more collective and more flexible alternative to the learning cycle associated with David Kolb (Kolb, 1975; Kolb, 1984) which tends to be the learning model in use on leadership development programmes (Figure 12.1).

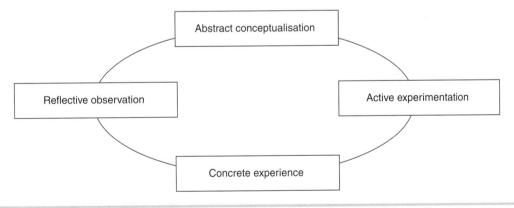

Figure 12.1 The Kolb learning cycle

The later parts of the chapter focus on the contribution you can make to collective leadership, and with how the development of leaders can be linked to leadership in this wider sense. This culminates in a group leadership development activity that you can use with your colleagues, perhaps with the support of an action learning set.

This chapter builds on the first leadership practice of *Leading yourself* (Chapter 5) and in offering ideas, models and activities for further developing your own leadership capabilities and those of the people around you. Before moving on to the discussion of the important aspects of leadership development in organisations, you might want to summarise your learning from the book so far in your own personal leadership development plan.

Go to Activity 12.1: My Leadership Development Plan.

Leaders and leadership

This chapter is about the *development* of leaders and leadership.

The distinction between leaders and leadership is important and we want to talk about both. Leaders are individual people, like you, the reader of this book, and leadership is about the quality by which direction is chosen and pursued in a group, team, organisation or whole society, industry sector, nation state. Think of the organisations you work for, or on, or in, and whether you think they have, over the years, been well led. Leadership in this sense is something that transcends the comings and goings of individuals. Leadership is in the culture and traditions that you absorb as a leader when you join an organisation, and of course, leaders, you and others, can make a difference by changing that culture over time. It's a two-way process.

In dealing with both leaders and leadership, we recognise that books are read by individuals and not by organisations, but a book can also act as a core text for a development programme, and its ideas can be used to define an organisation's concept of leadership. It can also be read and discussed by groups of people who work together, and used to experiment with new approaches to their leadership practices, using the challenge checks in Chapter 2 and the DIY 360° feedback tool from Chapter 5.

Activity 12.2 will help you to pursue your leadership development in the company of some colleagues and allies.

Go to Activity 12.2: A Leadership Reading and Action Group.

Creating a support system for leadership development is a good first step to thinking about it not just as an individual matter but as one which concerns the whole enterprise.

Where is the leadership that matters?

As this book points out, leading/leadership is no one thing; it varies with the challenge, the context and with many other things. This creates a challenge for leadership development in organisations; where should you focus your effort and expenditure?

The best starting point is not: What is leadership? Or how is leadership developed? But, *where is the leadership that matters?*

Figure 12.2 is a useful way of looking at this question:

	Individual leadership: (human capital)	Collective leadership: (social capital)
Leadership by the few	Heroic leadership	Top teams: leadership by top or other teams
Leadership by the many	Leadership at all levels: leadership distributed among people in the network, or delegated to people in the hierarchy	Shared leadership: a shared culture of leadership, in the traditions and DNA of the organisation

Figure 12.2 **Where is the leadership that matters?**

At the top-left is the heroic leader with whom we are most familiar and which is most talked and written about. Many people equate the word leadership with this position, are not aware of the alternatives and think that this is what they need to aspire to. This is the Richard Branson position and his equivalents in the political, military, Church and other worlds. (However as noted below, Richard Branson may also be an emblem or an icon of the collective Virgin leadership culture and style.)

At the top-right is the senior leadership team, but it could also be teams at any level, or in an organisation's network arrangements. For example, Andrew Kakabadse (2002) promotes top team development as key to organisational success, and Garratt (2010) also sees top teams as key to organisational success, emphasising this with the thought provoking sound-bite: "the fish rots from the head".

The bottom-left position is leadership at all levels or leadership by the many, but as individuals. Tesco say that "one of the most important forms of leadership is the leadership behind the people that serve our customers". In the NHS about 150,000 people at ward level have gone through a programme called "leadership at the point of care" with a theme of empowerment, over three days with a one-day follow-up. One of the authors did an evaluation of this programme, and this showed that it was quite successful. Although such people are heavily constrained by job descriptions, health and safety regulations and performance targets there are still many things they can do. One person introduced a policy of giving patients' visitors cups of tea as well as the patient. Small stuff perhaps, but it persisted, which is not always the case with the effects of leadership development programmes. If 150,000 people start doing some small new things then it can add up to quite a lot.

According to Burgoyne *et al.* (2005) most organisations spend about 80% of their leadership development budget on top "heroic" leaders and their "high potential", "leadership pipeline" (Charan *et al.*, 2001) successors. An exception to this was Barnardo's, which provides a wide range of child welfare projects and now has only one children's home of the sort traditionally associated with them. A main "pinch point" in its business model is fundraising, particularly with the large number of charity shops that it relies on. So Barnardo's spends a large proportion of its leadership development budget on these people. Leadership in this context is particularly challenging, since the shops are largely staffed by volunteers.

At the bottom-right position leadership is shared widely throughout the organisation. The term "distributed leadership" has been popular in recent years (Pedler and Burgoyne, 2006), particularly in the educational sector, perhaps because education professionals value their professional autonomy, a feature shared by a number of other sectors. Distributed leadership is often taken to be bottom-left, that is, leadership at all levels in a hierarchy, but a more careful reading of the literature suggests it is at least as much bottom-right, where leadership is in the culture and traditions of the organisation. Organisations that enjoy success over many years despite the comings and goings of individuals rely heavily on this. The élite "ancient" universities like Oxford, Cambridge, Durham and St Andrews and possibly the company Unilever provide examples. A telltale sign is when we know the organisations but can't name the managing director, CEO or vice-chancellor: the institutional branding is much stronger than that of the leader. The opposite is true of Richard Branson and Virgin, or Alan Sugar and Amstrad.

Blended leadership development

Yet, taking Virgin as an example, Branson is clearly a heroic leader, but he is also something else: a symbol and icon of the Virgin cultural brand. So top-left and bottom-right work together. Branson also has a small, stable top team with people who have been with him from the early days and who spend a lot of time together at his West Indies retreat. They are also probably quite good at empowering local, operational leaders in the broad ranging Virgin empire, that is the bottom-left position.

This illustrates how the parts of the matrix in Figure 12.2 work together. A large organisation may need a balanced mix of the types, perhaps mainly driven from one sector. On the basis of research in the further education sector, Collinson (2005) has used the phrase "blended leadership" to describe the staff's liking for the autonomy of distributed leadership, but also wanting someone to tell them where the goal posts are (and perhaps resisting them being moved around too much), and with whom they can discuss the resources they need.

From Figure 12.2 there are two basic development approaches for the leadership that matters. In the two left-hand side boxes, education, training and individual developmental approaches set out to develop human capital, whilst in the two right-hand side boxes, the aim is to develop social capital through more collective and organisational development (OD) approaches. The hybrid form mixes the two. For example, the Advanced Management Programme (AMP) (Mintzberg and Gosling, 2002) recruits six people from each of six organisations (who then have six modules in six different business schools around the world). Company groups sit together around cocktail tables and work on joint problems in action learning style, sharing learning with the other groups and applying ideas from the rest of the programme.

	Individual leadership: (human capital)	Collective leadership: (social capital)
Leadership by the few	Heroic leadership	Top teams: leadership by top or other teams
Leadership by the many	Leadership at all levels: leadership distributed among people in the network, or delegated to people in the hierarchy	Shared leadership: a shared culture of leadership, in the traditions and DNA of the organisation
Leadership development approaches	Education, training and personal development	Soft organisation development

Hybrid approaches

Figure 12.3 Development approaches for the leadership that matters

Learning leadership

Possibly the oldest debate about leader development is whether leaders are born or made. Nature is inherited, possibly carried by genes, while nurture is learnt, formally or informally, with or without our awareness. We have to be careful with nature: I may be like my mother or father, but I cannot assume this is genetic. As it happens I (John Burgoyne, writing the final version of this chapter) am an academic, and so was my father. I think this is because I grew up with this kind of role model, in a world where this was seen as a good thing to do, and where the rules of the game of this culture were all around. This kind of inheritance is called "memetic" rather than "genetic": the inheritance of ideas. There is the saying that, physically "you are what you eat", for which the psychological and social equivalent is that "we are who we meet"; and this goes right back to parents, siblings, those we grew up with from birth.

The argument between born or made continues. There is a kind of middle ground between born and made: some characteristics may be learnt early in life, and after that are very unlikely to change; in other words they appear to be things we are born with. Some attempts to help people change, particularly those based on psychodynamic or psychotherapeutic methods, take this approach (Harrison, 1995). Another idea from evolutionary psychology is that the *will* to lead may be largely inherited, but the *ability* to lead may be largely learned (Nicholson, 1997, 1998, 2000, 2005). As in the American Airlines slogan: "recruit for attitude, train for skill". The argument is also complicated by the fact that leadership is many things, so you or I may be born to be a leader in one sense but not another.

A great deal of leadership learning is natural and uncontrived. Many leadership development practices recognise this, for example mentoring (Clutterbuck, 1985), and have their origins in informal processes which are then established more formally to ensure that they happen more reliably and for everyone, and not just the lucky few. Although leadership learning is largely experiential, formal programmes do make a contribution via inputs about process of leadership, concepts for strategic and critical thinking and the encouragement to learn to think big. This contribution seems to be especially in terms of confidence and in providing the time to stand back and reflect, through the different "spectacles" provided by the programme, and through the opportunity to network and share experiences with other participants, whether this is designed in or not.

In terms of "thinking big", an educational economist, Derek Bosworth (Bosworth and Jobome, 2001; Bosworth, 2005, 2006), has shown that firms with more managers educated to degree level do better. This is because, he argues, they are more willing to make bold moves and redesign whole systems, in the style of business process re-engineering, rather than tinker and make small incremental changes. This is good news for universities and bad news for business schools, as it does not matter what subject the degree is in, it is the high-level critical reasoning rather than the content that makes the difference. Good news for you too if you have a degree but not an MBA or the like.

Born, made and the "onion skin model"

This way of thinking suggests an "onion skin" model of personality: on the surface the things that immediately affect the world through our behaviour, or skills, or current ideas, aims and objectives, change and can be changed relatively easily. In the middle are attitudes and underlying conceptual mindsets, for example a scientific or engineering view of the world, which can change or be changed but with much greater difficulty, and thirdly, at the centre, core beliefs, values, sense of purpose, identity, which either cannot change or be changed at all, or only with extreme difficulty. This results in the centre of the onion being the "self", which in the case of the literal onion is the seed containing the genetic code. Self is again the subject of born or made arguments, although it seems clear that much is learned: if you had been born into a very different culture (Christian, Muslim, etc.) you would probably be a very different person.

In terms of leadership development , Roger Harrison (1995) argues that we should only go as deep into the "onion" of other people as we need to achieve our purposes. This can be argued for on both moral/ethical and instrumental efficiency grounds.

Learning strategies

The DYSCO (Developing Yourself, your Career and your Organisation) model (Burgoyne, 1999) offers a map of learning approaches linked to relationships with experts and expertise.

Figure 12.4 shows the first part of this model. This proposes that learning is what changes our "inner" knowledge, skills, attitudes, values and bank of experience, through the three processes of input, experimentation and reflection.

Input is when we listen to, see or read prestructured material, as in listening to a lecture or reading a book. Experimentation is when we take action on the world and observe and interpret the consequences. The third process is reflection in which, for example, we look for patterns in our experience.

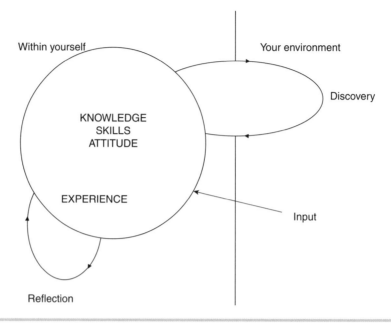

Figure 12.4 The DYSCO learning model: part 1

Unlike in the earlier Kolb learning cycle model, you can do these processes in any order that you like. You can also do your reflection with other people: whereas Kolb seems to imply that this is a purely internal process, in fact reflection can be a collective activity and is often enhanced by working in a group or team.

A second part to the model is seen in Figure 12.5. This is about your attitude to expertise and your relationship to its source, be it person, book and so on. You can see experts or expertise as truth, or just a source of ideas to consider and try out, or somewhere in between, where you share experience and test the idea together. These positions on expertise are called dependence, independence and interdependence:

Dependent	Interdependent	Independent
"There is some truth or tried and tested solution to this problem – finding it is the approach to learning in this situation"	"This situation is special, however, there may be ideas, experiences, practices that have been tried out in similar situations that may help me understand and deal with this one"	"This problem and situation I am facing here is unique and I will have to work out for myself what is going on and invent a special way of dealing with it"

Figure 12.5 The DYSCO learning model: part 2

Again, you can take different attitudes to experts and expertise in different situations, depending on the nature of the issue or challenge addressed, the credibility of the source, and what you feel you already know.

The third and final part of the model is shown in Figure 12.6, which puts the previous two parts together to give you a map on which you can make a learning journey. The text in the nine boxes sets out the stances that you, the learner, would take if you operated out of this particular position:

	Input	Discovery	Reflection
Independent	I will hear about this and see ideas, applications and values, and decide for myself what to adopt	I expect to have the opportunity to try out different ways of acting, have new experiences and draw new conclusions for myself	I will work out for myself what is true, workable and valuable, using the suggestions of others
Interdependent	I will hear about new ideas, procedures and beliefs and work out, with teachers and colleagues, which to follow	I will try things out with others and work out with them what the conclusions are	I will use the insights of others to make sense of my experiences
Dependent	I will be told or shown what is true as a theory, what will work as a skill or procedure, and what is right morally and ethically	I expect to be able to demonstrate their effectiveness, and have experiences that show how things work	I will be guided to an understanding of the truths and patterns behind my experience

Figure 12.6 **The DYSCO learning model: part 3**

Instead of a fixed learning style, you now have a range of learning strategies to choose from. There is nothing to stop you using all or most of these in different settings.

Try this activity together with some people who have been through the same or similar learning programme. Taking the DYSCO model: part 3 diagram, see if you can map on it your learning experiences throughout the programme.

Go to Activity 12.3: Programme Learning Review.

Collective leadership: linking leaders and leadership

This section is about you as a leader, the leadership context that you operate in and are part of, and how the two are integrated, and how you can work on this from your end. How does your leadership environment, current and past, shape you as a leader, and how do you shape it?

We have made the distinction between leaders, individuals like you, and leadership, the collective practice of leadership in an organisational setting. The collective practice of leadership is not just the sum total of the work by a group of individuals, but their shared mindset, culture, traditions, the very language and concepts that they jointly use to make sense of the world and decide how to act in it.

From the individual point of view, leadership development is usually just one of the opportunities on offer to you, but from an organisational perspective, it is about the means and mechanisms to acquire, develop and utilise the leadership capability that is available. There is some evidence that leadership development works better when it is integrated as part of a bundle (Fox *et al.*, 1990), with three strands:

- The first strand is *acquisition*, which is to do with obtaining the services of talented people in the first place, then with internal recruitment into new roles.
- The second is *development* and includes both formal and informal learning, education training and development, placements for development purposes in part at least and organisation development in the soft sense described earlier.
- The third is about *utilisation*, and includes performance management, career development, pay and reward systems and hard organisation development in the sense of restructuring (Burgoyne, 2006).

These strands can play together, as for example performance management and reward, and performance management and the identification of development needs. Career development systems tend to be of two kinds. One moves you around like pieces on a chess board; this includes succession planning in its conventional form. The second is the "internal (and external) market" model, where jobs are advertised and you apply for them, if you want, with or without encouragement.

Taking these three strands of the bundle raises a number of interesting and strategic questions. Thinking of yourself at the receiving end of all this:

- How do you present yourself for internal and external recruitment?
- How does the team you are in offer itself for internal use, or to move as a whole elsewhere?
- How do you play your hand in a merger/takeover situation or restructuring situation?

And in terms of development:

- How do you mix your use of the range of things on offer to balance your developmental diet, and what are you positioning yourself to be "utilised" for?

Finally, under utilisation:

■ How can you use these various systems proactively: performance management, career management, pay and reward systems, and restructuring (which are often all going on at the same time)?

How you can do this depends greatly on the particular context and the perceived needs of your organisation at this time. There are some sectors, like the health sector for instance, where people largely move within the "industry" but between, for example, NHS Trusts. These tend to work on the "free market" system, but are strongly influenced by personal networks and reputation. To some extent this applies to all sectors, but there are preferences for "fresh blood" or "growing your own timber" which are stronger at some times than others, and in some places more than others.

We hope this gives you some food for thought on how you as an individual can relate to your leadership context, and that it suggests some ideas on how you might want to work with or change this. Perhaps this is also something that you could introduce as a discussion with your team or group of colleagues, to see if there are any changes that you want to try out together?

A group leadership development activity

You may see the organisation of leadership development in your organisation as someone else's job. Think again: if you want to contribute to leadership in your situation, then you can do a lot to involve others in tackling the challenges that you see around you. Just noticing these issues and opportunities, and bringing them to the attention of others, is a leadership act in itself, which if done unwisely or unskilfully, can draw the wrong sort of attention.

Here's another idea for recruiting your friends and colleagues and involving them in thinking about the leadership practices in your organisation. Earlier in this chapter we offered you a personal leadership development plan (Activity 12.1: My Leadership Development Plan); here is another version that invites you to look at you and your context in parallel.

Go to Activity 12.4: A Group Leadership Plan.

The role of action learning

If you are able to find a group of people with whom to work on developing leadership, then you have the basis for an action learning set. Action learning is perhaps the most significant approach to leadership development to have emerged over the past 30 years (Pedler, 2008, p. 1) As pioneered by Reg Revans, action learning is based on the idea of development through taking considered action on organisational challenges and learning from this experience.

Action learning can help with all sorts of organisational challenges. We have noticed, for example, that organisational projects and networks can easily fail from two principle causes. Failing comes from implosion or explosion, where either the internal bonds between people are stronger than those to external clients so that the project loses its focus, or where the external connections are stronger than internal ones and the network gets pulled apart. Action learning can help to deal with situations like these and maintain balance and focus by facilitating bonding within the group while at the same time developing the strength of links to the external challenge and the stakeholders.

Like mentoring, action learning has its roots in a natural process, but one that is not usually done systematically or in such depth. It can usefully be thought of as going round the Kolb learning cycle in the company of others.

References

Bosworth, D. (2005) *Management, Strategy and Performance*, PowerPoint presentation.

Bosworth, D. (2006) Management skills, strategy and performance. In *Skills and Economic Performance*, Porter S. and Campbell, M. (eds.) London: Caspian, pp. 225–236.

Bosworth, D. and Jobome, G. (2001) Management skills and enterprise performance: a review of the literature. Liverpool Business School: Liverpool University, pp. 1–173.

Burgoyne, J.G. (2006) What is the role of management capability in improving company performance? In *Skills and Economic Performance*, Porter, S. and Campbell, M. (eds). London: Caspian, pp. 210–223.

Burgoyne, J.G., Boydell, T. and Pedler, M. (2005) *Leadership Development: Current Practices, Future Perspectives*. London: Corporate Research Forum, p. 65.

Charan, R. Drotter, S. and Noel, J. (2001) *The Leadership Pipeline: How to Build the Leadership Powered Company*. San Francisco: Jossey Bass.

Clutterbuck, D. (1985) *Everyone Needs a Mentor*. London: Institute of Personnel Management.

Collinson, D. (2005) Dialectics of leadership. *Human Relations* **58**(11): 1419–1442.

Fox, S. McLeay, S. Tanton, M. Burgoyne, J. and Easterby-Smith, M. (1990) Managerial Labour Markets: Human Resource Management and Corporate Performance. *ESRC Project*.

Harrison, R. (1995) *The Collected Papers of Roger Harrison*. Maidenhead: McGraw-Hill.

Kakabadse, A. Jackson, S. and Fandale, E. (2002) *Meeting the Development Needs of Top Teams and Boards*. London: CRF.

Kolb, D. (1984) *Experiential Learning*. Englewood Cliffs, NJ: Prentice Hall.

Kolb, D.A. and Fry, R. (1975) Towards an applied theory of experiential learning. In *Theories of Group Processes*, C.L. Cooper (ed.). Chichester: Wiley, pp. 33–58.

Mintzberg, H. and Gosling, J. (2002) Educating managers beyond borders. *Academy of Management Learning & Education* **1**(1): 64–76.

Nicholson, N. (1997) Evolutionary psychology: toward a new view of human nature and organizational society. *Human Relations* **50**(9): 1053–1078.

Nicholson, N. (1998) How hardwired is human behaviour? *Harvard Business Review* **76**: 134–147.

Nicholson, N. (2000) *Managing the Human Animal*. London: Texere Books.

Nicholson, N. (2005) Objections to evolutionary psychology: reflections, implications and the leadership exemplar. *Human Relations* **58**(3): 393–409.

Pedler, M. and Burgoyne, J. (2006) Distributed leadership. *View* (11):2.

Activities

- Activity 12.1: My Leadership Development Plan.
- Activity 12.2: A Leadership Reading and Action Group.
- Activity 12.3: Programme Learning Review.
- Activity 12.4: A Group Leadership Plan.

Activity 12.1: My Leadership Development Plan

The model of leadership described in this book is based on what you can *do* about leadership rather than just thinking about it. Any leadership act is framed by the three dimensions of:

- *Challenges.* These are the leadership challenges that face us – personal and collective. They come in all shapes and sizes and may be problems, opportunities for growth, people issues or conflict situations. It is the way we approach these challenges that determines leadership ability and will.
- *Context.* Everything takes place within a context. Context is about the on-site conditions for action, including history and influences from the wider world. What is the situation of the challenge you face? What are the background conditions that apply at this point in time? These set the context for leadership.
- *Characteristics.* These are the qualities, attributes, sets of behaviours and competencies that each of us has. These are the gifts, qualities and skills that we (and all those colleagues around us) can bring to bear on any *challenge* within any particular *context*.

Leadership Practices

The *7 Leadership Practices* that make a critical difference to success are:

1 Leading Yourself.
2 Being on Purpose.
3 Power.
4 Risk.
5 Challenging Questions.
6 Facilitation.
7 Networking.

This *leadership development plan* invites you to carry out a self-analysis against these *7 leadership Practices*.

Have a go, give it some thought and get some feedback from other people to develop your learning about yourself as a leader.

P1 – Leading Yourself

Leading yourself is about harnessing the transferable skills developed from working with any leadership challenge: it is about learning to fish for yourself, and not just accepting the gift of fish from others.

As you develop your practice in contributing to current challenges, so you increase your abilities to face any new ones in the future.

It means adopting a learning attitude to everything. For every action you take, for everything you see happening, for every person you encounter, for every problem or opportunity you meet – you ask what lessons can be learned.

What does leading yourself mean to you – what is it and why does it matter?

| |
| |
| |
| |
| |
| |

What evidence would you give, for example in a job application or interview, of your ability to lead yourself?

| |
| |
| |
| |
| |
| |

How good do you think you are at Leading Yourself?

Not at all   ⟶   Very good

     4   3   2   1

P2 – Being on Purpose

Being "on purpose" is about making things happen. It involves both the will and determination to make it happen, and knowing what to do to achieve this. Purpose is about specific goals or aims and also about a deeper and more enduring sense of purpose rooted in values. It is this deeper sense of purpose that makes the risk of leadership worthwhile. Leaders do things "on purpose".

Like all other practices, the ability to find direction and purpose can be developed and refined. It is important to find and understand your own purpose, and to develop your own practice of being on purpose. It is also important to be able to achieve common purpose with others – which can be a very different matter.

What does purpose mean to you – what is it and why does it matter?

What evidence would you give, for example in a job application or interview, of your ability to be on purpose?

How good do you think you are at being purposeful?

Not at all   ⟶   Very good

        4   3   2   1

P3 – Power

Nothing happens without the use of some power, and power comes in many forms. Power is the ability to act, to get work done, to make things happen. Power can be both damaging and constructive, and using it for its beneficial effects while avoiding it for its destructive potential is a subtle practice.

In the context of leadership, power is social and relational; it is power with, from, over and through other people. The unequal distribution of formal power in work organisations gives rise to the development of many alternative sources of power, which are often mobilised in more or less hidden political processes.

Wise leadership requires a knowledge of power, its sources and forms and how they may be used. Studied throughout human history, power remains a subject of endless fascination. Although highly desirable, it is a dangerous thing, associated with high risk. Yet lack of power is a problem too; powerlessness is also corrupting and makes of us victims and slaves.

What does power mean to you – what is it and why does it matter?

| |
| |
| |
| |
| |
| |

What evidence would you give, for example in a job application or interview, of your ability to be powerful?

| |
| |
| |
| |
| |
| |

How good do you think you are at being powerful?

Not at all   ⟶   Very good

4   3   2   1

P4 – Risk

Risk is the possibility or probability of undesirable or even catastrophic happenings. Some forms of risk are relatively objective, such as mechanical or system breakdown or failure; others are more subjective, such as risk to reputation or self-esteem. The cost, damage or pain involved in taking risk is sometimes for you and sometimes for other people. The consequences of risks may be either long term or short term, and can limit the future possibilities for action.

Leadership involves risk, because leaders must sometimes take difficult decisions on the basis of inadequate information. In this territory, it is important to become familiar with risk, its nature and its effects. The fear may never be fully overcome, but the practice of living with risk can be developed. This involves the ability to estimate and plan for risk, but also the cultivation of personal habits and approaches to taking and living with risk.

What does risk mean to you – what is it and why does it matter?

What evidence would you give, for example in a job application or interview, of your ability to live with risk?

How good do you think you are at living with risk?

Not at all   ⟶   Very good

     4   3   2   1

P5 – Challenging Questions

Questioning is the key to creativity, action and learning – it is where fresh ideas come from. Through questioning, other people's opinions and views can be drawn out, tested and brought into the decision process. Developing this practice is a critical aspect of leadership capability, because it is through challenging questions that purpose and direction are found.

The practice of asking challenging questions involves querying existing beliefs and practices in a more profound way than is usual. Astute questioning can bring out hidden assumptions and surface values and beliefs that would otherwise remain hidden. Critical questioning needs to be constructive in addition to challenging, and if this is achieved it can lead on to powerful action and learning.

What does "asking challenging questions" mean to you – what is it and why does it matter?

What evidence would you give, for example in a job application or interview, of your ability to ask challenging questions?

How good do you think you are at asking Challenging Questions?

Not at all   ⟶   Very good

     4   3   2   1

P6 – Facilitation

Leadership is often about getting groups or teams to work together effectively, and is usually best done by helping people to do it for themselves. Facilitation literally means making something easier, and is a subtle form of influence.

The word "facilitator" often means someone who manages meetings, but in the context of leadership facilitation it is an essential operational practice to enable people to share perceptions of what needs to be done, to co-operate on tasks and to work collaboratively rather than in isolation. Effective facilitation is measured both by enabling or empowering individuals to act and to learn and also by collective performance – by how well people work together.

What does facilitation mean to you – what is it and why does it matter?

| |
| |
| |
| |
| |
| |

What evidence would you give, for example in a job application or interview, of your ability to facilitate?

| |
| |
| |
| |
| |
| |

How good do you think you are at Facilitation?

Not at all   ⟶   Very good

4   3   2   1

P7 – Networking

Networking is the key to connection power, one of the most underrated forms of power. Influence, inspiration and informal authority are exercised through networks of informal relationships inside and outside organisations and professions. These "invisible" informal networks are a vital source of knowledge, information and energy into any organisation.

Building personal networks makes it easier to contact and access relevant people when we need help to assess situations and accomplish tasks. A wide network gives the ability to cross departmental, professional and organisational boundaries to get things done. Such networks also help to create power for the others in these relationships. Getting out more and networking is a crucial leadership practice.

What does networking mean to you – what is it and why does it matter?

What evidence would you give, for example in a job application or interview, of your ability to network?

How good do you think you are at Networking?

Not at all ⟶ Very good

    4   3   2   1

Prioritising your leadership practices

What are the leadership practices that matter most for you – now and in the future?

Imagine the kind of work that you will be doing in the future. This is likely to be a combination of what you would like to be doing and what you will have the opportunity to do if you can convince others of your capability. Imagine writing a description of the abilities and capabilities required for this work, using the leadership practices that you have just considered. What are the most important practices for you?

Now give each of these leadership practices a ranking for importance in column 1, from 1 (low) to 4 (high). In column 2, copy in the ratings you have given yourself for capability at each practice – this time from 4 (low) to 1 (high). Multiply your column 1 and 2 scores to give a priority score for each practice in column 3. These scores give you a measure of priority, from 1 (very low) to 16 (very high). See Table 12.1.

Table 12.1 Your priority leadership practices

Leadership practice	Importance for my future work: From 1 (low) to 4 (high)	How good I think I am now at this: NB from 4 (low) to 1 (high)	My priority for development: NB multiply columns 1 and 2
1. Leading Myself			
2. Purpose			
3. Power			
4. Risk			
5. Challenging Questions			
6. Facilitation			
7. Networking			

The way this scoring system works is that numbers for the *importance* of the practice and your current level of *capability* run in opposite directions. The logic is that the higher the importance and the lower the capability the bigger the score. The higher the combined score, the more likely you are to benefit from focusing on this.

Obviously this is just one indicator. Use your judgement in considering your priorities, consult valued colleagues and friends and change them if you see a reason for so doing.

Now that you have completed your analysis, this will help you to direct your action and learning for the future. As an aid to your leadership development plan why not keep a leadership learning diary to help you measure your progress and to reflect on what you are learning:

Leadership learning diary

Learning leadership involves adapting to new roles, tackling demanding tasks and using power in organisations, and it also means learning a lot about yourself.

No-one ever becomes a leadership expert, except in books, but everyone can improve their practice. The idea of practice means that learning and improving are an integral part of working. People have an unlimited capacity to learn from experience, but a limited capacity to learn from being taught. This can only happen if you reflect on your practice through ongoing self assessment and feedback from helpful colleagues.

Completing the personal learning diary

Complete a personal learning diary at least three times. A useful time to do this is following any event when you observed or learned something about leadership.

You might include your thoughts about:

- New approaches you have attempted – what worked well and not so well, and what you will do differently as a result.
- New insights about yourself and how these link to your strengths and weaknesses.
- How you make sense of any personal feedback you have received.
- Things you have noticed about your behavioural traits in action.
- What you have learned about the leadership practice of your colleagues.
- Your progress in developing the seven core leadership practices.

Try to write around 200 words for each of the three diary entries – you will then find it an invaluable reflection tool for your ongoing self-development.

Activity 12.2: A Leadership Reading and Action Group

1 Invite some people who are interested and fix a first meeting of a leadership reading group.

2 Agree to read this book or part of it.

3 Then meet again and discuss:
   ■ What you like (and don't like) about this approach to leadership.
   ■ What you agree with (and don't agree with).
   ■ What is useful here that can be applied to your own situation.
   ■ What new ideas are coming out of this discussion so far.

4 Now consider what actions you could take – individually and collectively:
   ■ How you might try these ideas in action, in an experimental and responsible way (i.e. trying something genuinely new, but without taking undue risks, especially for other people).
   ■ How can you implement these ideas? (It may be something you can do on your own, but if not, you may need to develop a project to get the influence to do it.) The action learning process (see Chapter 2) will help with this:
      – Who knows about the problem/challenge/issue?
      – Who cares about it?
      – Who can do something about it?
      – Who has the resources to do something about it?
      – Are these combined in one person?
      – If not can we do something to bring them together?
      – How can we influence these people?

5 Action and support: now go ahead and do whatever actions you have agreed. Also agree any help that you can give each other in achieving these aims. Also fix a date when you will all meet again.

6 Continue to meet regularly to review progress, re-plan if necessary, and especially to reflect on what you are learning from these experiments, how you might spread and share this with others, what else you can do.

Activity 12.3: Programme Learning Review

1 Think of a development programme that you have participated in.

2 Using the DYSCO Model Part 3 diagram, map your learning experiences throughout the programme. Remember that the beginning is not necessarily the first day, but the first engagement, a pre-course selection or briefing process, pre-work or a joining pack. Think about these carefully because they tend to set up the "psychological contract" about how you will learn and the attitude to expertise that you are expected to take.

3 Consider also whether there are other stakeholders involved beyond yourself and the programme provider, for example your line manager or HR person. Think about the multi-way contracting that went on between all these parties leading to your participation in the programme.

4 Finally, look at the journey you have plotted on the map and consider these propositions:
- It is good to have quite a lot of variety on the horizontal dimension, preferably many small blocks in each rather than a few big ones.
- On the vertical dimension the programme should "start where you are".
- The programme should end with you exiting through the top of the map – after all you are on your own after that.

Do these propositions ring true for you? How did what happened compare with these principles? Does this give you any insight into what worked and what did not?

Activity 12.4: A Group Leadership Plan

Leadership practice	For me as a leader	For this team or group	Implications?
P1: Leading Yourself What does it mean and why does it matter to me/us?			
What evidence would I/we give, e.g. in a job application, of the ability to lead?			
How good am I/are we at leading?			
Rate this between 4 (poor) and 1 (good)			
P2: Being on Purpose What does it mean and why does it matter to me/us?			
What evidence would I/we give, e.g. in a job application, of the ability to be "on purpose"?			
How good am I/are we at being purposeful?			
Rate this between 4 (poor) and 1 (good)			
P3: Power What does it mean and why does it matter to me/us?			
What evidence would I/we give, e.g. in a job application, of using power well?			
How good am I/are we at using power?			
Rate this between 4 (poor) and 1 (good)			

Leadership practice	For me as a leader	For this team or group	Implications?
P4: Risk What does it mean and why does it matter to me/us?			
What evidence would I/we give, e.g. in a job application, of the ability to be work with risk?			
How good am I/are we at working with risk?			
Rate this between 4 (poor) and 1 (good)			
P5: Challenging Questions What does it mean and why does it matter to me/us?			
What evidence would I/we give, e.g. in a job application, of the ability to ask challenging questions?			
How good am I/are we at asking challenging questions?			
Rate this between 4 (poor) and 1 (good)			
P6: Facilitation What does it mean and why does it matter to me/us?			
What evidence would I/we give, e.g. in a job application, of the ability to facilitate?			
How good am I/are we at facilitation?			
Rate this between 4 (poor) and 1 (good)			

Leadership practice	For me as a leader	For this team or group	Implications?
P7: Networking What does it mean and why does it matter to me/us?			
What evidence would I/we give, e.g. in a job application, of the ability to network?			
How good am I/are we at networking?			
Rate this between 4 (poor) and 1 (good)			

Index

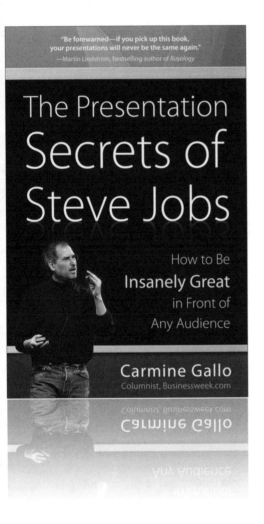

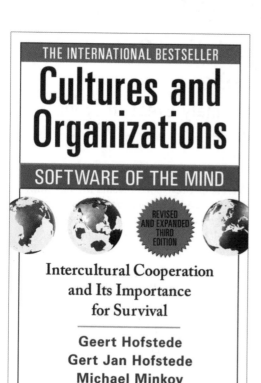